"Tu confiden[...] heritage in [...] and stories play out in his recipes. *The Memory of Taste* is a great book for readers who want to learn about the context of traditional Vietnamese food through Californian influences that makes Tu's food unique, but can also help make sense of your own cherished food memories."

—BRANDON JEW, JAMES BEARD AWARD-WINNING AUTHOR AND CHEF OF MISTER JIU'S

"Bold and unapologetic in its words and flavors, *The Memory of Taste* is a testament to how powerful diasporic stories are in the language of food. In an intimately familiar story, Tu reminds me that those of us who have survived the generational trauma of war and forced migration are blessed to honor the past and pave a more beautiful way forward with delicious nourishing meals that connect us all to our shared humanity."

—REEM ASSIL, AWARD-WINNING CHEF AND AUTHOR OF *ARABIYYA*

"Chef Tu's *The Memory of Taste* beautifully intertwines culture, cuisine, and personal revelation, offering an enlightening and heartwarming exploration of heritage through food. The engaging narratives and unique recipes provide a fresh perspective on cultural representation. The portrayal of fish sauce embodies the soul of Chef Tu's story and Vietnamese cuisine, making this book a must-read for anyone seeking a deeper connection to food and heritage."

—LEAH COHEN, CHEF AND OWNER OF PIG & KHAO AND PIGGYBACK NYC, AUTHOR OF *LEMONGRASS & LIME*

"*The Memory of Taste* resonated with me deeply as a refugee child with parents who had to flee a war-torn country. Tu's candid storytelling took me on a journey of profound emotions filled with delightful recipes. Most importantly, it shows how cooking and food can help us connect more deeply with our family's history and identity."

—NITE YUN, CHEF AND OWNER OF NYUM BAI AND LUNETTE CAMBODIA

THE MEMORY OF TASTE

This book is a heartfelt offering to those, especially our mothers, who have experienced the pain of feeling overlooked, silenced, or erased. It is a reminder that every individual's story holds immense value and significance. Through these pages, I aspire to ignite a profound sense of understanding and empathy, illuminating the fact that each of our families, despite any hardships endured, possesses beautiful narratives worth sharing.

May this book serve as a guiding light, illuminating the path toward embracing the diverse tapestry of human experience. May it provide solace and empowerment, reminding us that our stories, even in moments of pain, carry a unique beauty that deserves to be acknowledged and celebrated. YOU are loved.

THE MEMORY OF TASTE

Vietnamese American Recipes from Phú Quốc, Oakland, and the Spaces Between

Tu David Phu and Soleil Ho
Photographs by Dylan James Ho and Jeni Afuso
Foreword by Stephen Satterfield

4c

4 COLOR BOOKS
An imprint of TEN SPEED PRESS
California | New York

CONTENTS

vii   Foreword
1   Introduction
7   A Note on Sustainability

1 | ME & BA'S KITCHEN 13

34   Cơm | Rice
34   Cơm Tấm | Broken Rice
34   Gạo Thơm Hoa Nhài | Jasmine Rice
35   Xôi | Sticky Rice
35   Dán Me | Tamarind Paste
35   Nước Sốt Me | Tamarind Sauce
36   Dán Sả | Lemongrass Paste
36   Nước Màu Dừa | Coconut Caramel Sauce
37   Nước Mắm Sánh Kẹo | Fish Sauce Caramel
39   **Fish Sauce Contains Multitudes**
40   Nước Mắm Chấm | Everyday Fish Sauce
40   Nước Chấm Chay | Fishless Dipping Sauce
41   Nước Mắm Dừa | Coconut Fish Sauce
41   Nước Mắm Gừng | Ginger Fish Sauce
42   Nước Mắm Khóm | Pineapple Fish Sauce
42   Nước Mắm Me | Tamarind Fish Sauce
43   Nước Mắm Tỏi Ớt | Chile Fish Sauce
43   Muối Ớt | Chile Salt
44   Muối Tiêu Chanh | Salt, Pepper, and Lime Dipping Sauce
47   Mỡ Hành | Green Onion Sauce
47   Mỡ Hành Gừng | Ginger and Green Onion Sauce
49   Củ Cải Chua Ngọt | Pickled Carrots and Daikon
49   Nước Cốt Dừa Tươi | Fresh Coconut Milk
50   Củ Hẹ Chiên | Fried Shallots
50   Nước Luộc Cá | Fish Stock
51   Nước Luộc Gà | Chicken Stock

2 | WE ARE FROM PHÚ QUỐC ISLAND 55

58   **Where to Eat on Phú Quốc Island**
60   Gỏi Cá Trích | Herring Salad
62   Gỏi Xoài Xanh Khô Mực | Green Mango and Dried Squid Salad
63   Con Sò Ướp Chao | Grilled Scallop with Fermented Tofu
65   Bún Nhâm Hà Tiên | Coconut and Fish Sauce Rice Noodle Salad
67   Bún Kèn | Curry Coconut Noodles
69   Bánh Canh Chả Cá | Fish Cake and Tapioca Noodle Soup
72   Tôm Rang Me Chua Ngọt | Tamarind Black Tiger Prawns
74   Cơm Gà Hải Nam | Hainanese Chicken and Rice
77   Cá Trích Nhúng Giấm | Vietnamese Fish Shabu Shabu

3 | WE ARE OCEAN PEOPLE 81

85   **Total Fish Domination**
89   Canh Chua Đầu Cá Hồi | Hot Pot-Style Salmon Head Sour Soup
92   Xương Cá Hồi Ghiên Giòn | Fried Salmon Frames
93   Lườn Cá Hồi Áp Chảo | Crispy Skin Pan-Roasted Salmon Fillets
94   Cháo Cá | Fish and Seafood Porridge
96   Bụng Cá Hồi Sốt Cà Chua | Tomato-Braised Salmon Belly
98   Trứng Cá Trích Tảo Bẹ | Herring Roe on Kelp
99   Cá Bơn Chiên Muối Sả Ớt | Fried Sand Dabs with Lemongrass and Chile Salt
101   Cá Vược Nướng Giấy Bạc | Foil-Baked Whole Sea Bass

4 | WE LIVED THROUGH WAR 105

109 Cơm Chay Mỡ Hành Gừng | Scorched Rice with Ginger and Green Onion Sauce
110 Rau Muống Xào | Stir-Fried Water Spinach
113 Cá Kho Tộ | Clay Pot Catfish
114 Bánh Tôm | Prawn Fritters
117 Bánh Phở | Phở Noodles
118 Phở Gà Miền Nam | Southern-Style Chicken Phở
122 Phở Bò Miền Nam | Southern-Style Beef Phở
125 Bò Tái | Thinly Sliced Steak
126 Xôi Xoài Thái | Thai-Style Sticky Rice with Mango

5 | WE ARE INAUTHENTIC AS HELL 129

132 Khổ Qua Xào | Stir-Fried Bitter Melon and Eggs
134 Cá Khô | Fish Jerky
135 Huyết Cá Tái Chanh | Tuna Bloodline Tartare
136 Cánh Gà Kho Gừng | Ginger-Braised Chicken
139 Sườn Chiên | Caramelized Pan-Fried Pork Chops
140 Nui Sườn Chiên | Caramelized Pan-Fried Pork Chops and Macaroni
143 Bánh Chuối Nướng | Mom's Banana Bread Pudding

6 | WE ATE WHAT THE GARDEN GAVE US 147

151 Lựu Trộn Muối Ớt | Pomegranate Seeds with Chile Salt
152 Gỏi Cuốn Cá Ngừ | Tuna Summer Rolls
155 Gỏi Gà | Vietnamese Chicken Salad
158 Gỏi Bắp Chuối | Banana Flower Salad
161 Canh Cá Nấu Ngót | Vietnamese Fish Hot Pot
163 Nghêu Xào | Stir-Fried Clams
165 Bún Chả Giò Khoai Môn | Taro Spring Roll and Rice Noodle Salad
166 Bún Bò Sả Ớt | Lemongrass Beef, Chile, and Rice Noodle Salad
169 Sâm Bổ Lượng | Vietnamese Herbal Tonic Drink

7 | I RUN THESE SHORES 171

174 **Where to Eat in Oakland**
177 Gỏi Cuốn Cá Cornets
178 Caviar à la Nước Mắm
181 Âu Cơ Trứng | Crab Beurre Monté Chawanmushi
183 Duck Liver Dumplings
186 Mì Xào Tỏi Nấm Cục | Truffled Garlic Noodles
189 Bánh Canh Tôm Hùm | Lobster Boba
193 Bánh Canh Carbonara
194 Xôi Gà Thập Cẩm | Chicken Fat Sticky Rice

8 | UNFAMILIAR TRADITIONS 197

201 Bánh Ít Trần | Sticky Rice Dumplings, Tu and Jean Style
203 Gỏi Cuốn Hàn Quốc | Pork Bulgogi Summer Rolls
207 Súp Hải Sản Thập Cẩm | Seafood Egg Drop Soup
208 Cơm Cua Hấp | Dungeness Crab Donburi
210 Gà Nướng Kampuchea | Kampuchea-Style BBQ Chicken
212 Vịt Nướng | Roasted Hoisin-Glazed Duck
215 Phở Vịt Nướng | Roasted Duck Phở
217 Bánh Hỏi Heo Quay | Woven Noodles with Crispy Pork Belly
220 Bò Quay Kampuchea | Kampuchea-Style Prime Rib
222 Chè Trôi Nước | Sticky Rice Dumplings in Syrup

224 Acknowledgments
226 About the Contributors
227 Index

FOREWORD

Working in restaurants in the 2010s was a blur. Probably because of where I was—surrounded by activists, chefs, writers, and restaurant openings permeating a dizzying Bay Area food scene. Some of us, like Tu, grew up there, and the rest moved to the Bay for its tradition of culinary arts, progressive politics, or a mix. Having worked in fine dining restaurants in the early aughts, the legacy of the subsequent decade was a cast of more melanated narrators and actors. *Our Stories* became a rallying cry and an entire category. We were understanding our power, interrogating it, and galvanizing our community through food and cooking. I met Tu through a group of these mutuals and in the middle of all of this activity: 18 Reasons, a community cooking school, was hosting a dinner with a rising Vietnamese chef. As Tu speaks through his food, I first heard him through his Cơm Gà Hải Nam (Hainanese Chicken and Rice). And I've been listening since then!

Tu and I are connected through food. We instantly saw in each other a profound respect and reverence for food and the lessons we'd learned from it. We didn't know the details of each other's lives, but in fact, each of our lives had been saved by food, and we could sense that in one another. At the very least, we both saw food as a vehicle to understand ourselves and the world.

It should really come as no surprise that Tu and I both went on to become professional food evangelists, using media to share our own stories and learn about everyone else's. Tu's ministry is the more delicious one between the two of us, so the book will only improve from here! *The Memory of Taste* is a reflection of Tu's deep curiosity and natural proclivity for teaching. It is a patient and personal reflection that brings both the chef and his dish into full context. Tu's work in this book comes from wanting to be understood.

You cannot defend what you don't know, and we have seen—clearly and tragically—the consequences for our Vietnamese kin: that incalculable cost of obfuscation. Food is how we make (and remake) ourselves agents in the telling of our own stories, deemphasizing the stories told about us by others.

The Memory of Taste is an insertion and an assertion. It acknowledges that taste is our most intimate sense, and an intimacy unmatched in our other experiences. The flavors we know tell the story of who we are. That's why Tu can see himself in a jar of fish sauce: Its components have become a throughline that keeps us connected to who we are in a world where identity can be hard to find.

I've watched Tu grow year after year in his craft. I've heard his voice and message coalesce as he has become a forceful champion for his people and their stories. *The Memory of Taste* is the product of years of Tu's work, and the message is clear: The legacy of his people will not be erased. The stories that weave together the recipes are an essential part of the dish. You will leave more inspired and enlightened, in life and in the kitchen.

With *The Memory of Taste*, you've tuned in to the work of a creator with an unquenchable curiosity and a penchant for sharing his gifts and passion with charisma and authenticity. I'll be rooting for you from the rafters— I look forward to meeting you there! Congratulations, Brother Tu.

Stephen Satterfield

INTRODUCTION

It was always hard to talk to my parents about anything but food. For most of my life, I didn't know anything about their past: their childhoods in the Vietnamese island of Phú Quốc or how, as young adults, they escaped from war. Other families might get some warm, chest-deep glow from reminiscing together. That's not the case with mine. For my parents, their memories haunt them. They would brush off any questions about the past as quickly as I could ask them. To me, their time in Vietnam was mostly a giant question mark.

While working in fine dining restaurants at the beginning of my career, I was usually the only Viet guy in the kitchen—but it wasn't necessarily my racial identity that singled me out. I felt it in those casual moments between rushes in the kitchen, when all the cooks would get to talking about memory and family, in that intimate way that develops when you're working elbow-to-elbow and sweating all over each other for twelve hours at a time. Those were the times when we'd talk about what we ate as kids, our first tastes of perfectly ripe tomatoes, and the way our mothers or grandmothers would massage olive oil into lettuce from their gardens. I say "we" here, but I'm lying. It was them, but it wasn't me.

At the time, I saw my family history as this gaping nothingness: a series of silent head shakes, pursed lips, and changed subjects. There was nothing "respectable" for me to be nostalgic about—no mind-blowing food moments that would stand up to some bourgie tomato story. Was I going to tell my fellow cooks about all the vegetable scraps and fish heads that my parents would save to keep me and my sister fed, just so they could make jokes about how I grew up eating literal garbage? Hell no! So, when I heard other chefs talk about their upbringings with all the hazy-eyed romance of a Jane Austen novel, I shut up. All I felt was jealousy and resentment.

I don't remember when it started, but when I was a kid, I tended to project way too much of what I saw on TV onto my own life. Back in the '90s, it was shows like *Family Matters*, *The Fresh Prince of Bel-Air*, and *Step by Step* that showed me what a "normal family" was. When people asked me about my home life, I would stretch the truth a little so we could fit the mold. The way I told it, my dad wasn't a fishmonger who worked under-the-table night shifts; he was a "fish expert": something vague enough so you could plausibly imagine him taming dolphins at the aquarium. And I would say my mom was a "seamstress," a word that sounded harmless on the surface. What I didn't tell them was that she worked in sweatshops, earning a fraction of a penny for each piece of clothing she made. A normal family would work 9-to-5 jobs and eat sloppy joes for dinner. A normal family would be so mentally and physically far away from the nightmare of war that they might as well be on a different planet.

I pieced together the real story of my parents later in life, from sometimes-conflicting snippets that I got from relatives in the United States and Vietnam and from hints that my mom would drop as we cooked together. It goes something like this. In Phú Quốc, a conch-shaped island off the southern shores of Cambodia, my parents met at a fish market. My mom, who came from a wealthy family of fish sauce–makers, suddenly noticed the buff young Viet-Khmer guy selling fish that he and his brothers had caught that morning. In the fight between her family's disapproval and her feelings, the feelings kicked disapproval's ass to the curb. You'd think that just a tug-of-war between feelings and family would be enough strife and drama for a lifetime. But then there was the war.

It was a war that most Americans still barely know anything about, but it's the poison that beats in the heart of my family's trauma, so America owes it to my family—and so many others—to at least hear about it. So here goes. From 1965 to 1973, the United States—led by Lyndon B. Johnson and then Richard Nixon—dropped 2.7 million tons of bombs onto Cambodia in what they called "Operation Menu." Out of that chaos rose the Khmer Rouge, a paranoid and genocidal military regime that ruled over Cambodia, waging war on Vietnam as well as on its own people. In the early 1970s, when my parents were still just two teenagers in love, my dad was drafted by the People's Army of Vietnam to fight against the Khmer Rouge. I don't know what my dad saw back then; I only know what came after. When my dad returned, it was to a home scarred by war. He and my mom were certain that if they had stayed, they would have starved. So they left.

Both barely into their twenties, my parents escaped Vietnam by boat. Cut off from home, they were stripped of all their possessions when they were robbed by pirates at sea. They ended up in a Thai refugee camp for nine months. It was at the camp where my mom sewed for money and learned how to utilize and stretch every single scrap of food she was able to get her hands on. Years after they left, that fight for survival and that life-or-death frugality stayed with them, reappearing in our lives every day when we sat down to eat a meal.

It took me so many years to see my family's food for what it really was. When you're taught in European-style fine dining to only use the most pristine tips of asparagus for a tasting menu course, you develop this ingrained mental hierarchy of what "good" and "bad" food is. Even if you end up using the not-so-pretty produce for other purposes, you can't help but think of it as undesirable or not worth the money. In this environment, it was easy for me to stumble down the slippery slope of thinking that my family's food was inferior. From there, it wasn't too far of a leap to start feeling ashamed of where I came from. Over the years, I've had to consciously let go of those ideas and drag myself off of my fancy-chef high horse to really appreciate what my parents gave me.

Cooking with my parents led me to a deeper appreciation of our customs and foodways and opened a window to their past. While my mom showed me how to collect strands of corn silk to use in a dish, her fingers working with a master seamstress's precision, I caught glimpses of the skills that allowed her to survive in a refugee camp. When my dad would take me grocery shopping, I would hear stories about the long lineage of fishermen he came from while he scrutinized the seafood counter for the best—and most affordable—specimen to bring home. He told me both of my grandfathers were famous free divers on the island, known for diving into the ocean three hundred feet deep to save people from sinking ships.

Those rare times when my parents let their masks slip just a little, I could see into the memories of conflict, alienation, and food insecurity that built them into the people I've known my whole life. The kitchen was the safest place for me to ask, "I remember this flavor; can you tell me more?"

Everything that I ate growing up was a piece of this huge puzzle that was my family. There were porridges and stir-fries enriched with whatever my dad would bring home after long hours working at Fisherman's Wharf in San Francisco. He filled our fridge with scraps: scallop frills, fish bladders, bloodline, and fish heads. My mom would slowly extract all the flavor she could out of the cheapest cuts of meat and fish, simmering fish bones and chicken carcasses on the stove to break down the collagen into nutritious stocks and soups, and I would dart in and out of the kitchen the whole time, tasting each phase of the broth with her. On good days, we'd have celery, onions, and carrots to add to the stocks. On bad days, we'd only have rice and instant ramen to eat. The kitchen was stocked with repurposed jars and plastic tubs filled with leftover scraps: orange peels for candying, cucumber seeds, and corn silk, which she'd sauté to serve on rice.

Anything my mom couldn't cook—and that was a high bar to clear—she'd stir into the soil of her garden. Under her care, inedible animal organs, crushed oyster shells, and spoiled milk transformed American dirt into the passion fruit, brown sugar cane, Thai bird's eye chiles, kumquats, and guavas of her home island.

Before I ever got to visit our hometown in Vietnam, I could taste it. My parents brought Phú Quốc home when they laid baskets of fresh herbs, rice paper, and marinated fish on our dinner table and taught me and my sister how to roll everything up into the perfect bite. Fish sauce, the pride of the island, was a constant presence and a reminder of our people's resourcefulness and ingenuity. My parents' memories of home hurt, but even that pain—as raw as it still was decades later—couldn't keep them from dropping breadcrumbs for us to follow.

There was always beauty in the food my parents made: I just wasn't ready to see it. Decades ago, if you wanted to cook Vietnamese food in a restaurant setting and have it be respected, you had to cook it in a Frenchified, Jean-Georges Vongerichten-in-sandals kind of way. In order for it to be valid, it had to be fused with a more "respectable" cuisine. But why couldn't Vietnamese food be considered elevated and valuable on its own? Food has a long history of being used to separate people and define who has "good taste" and who doesn't; who belongs and who is the outsider. I saw it in restaurants that celebrated French colonialism in Vietnam outright while making blander versions of our food, and I experienced it in my career, through criticisms that I was cooking food that was "too Asian" for "normal people."

It's hard to communicate the full scope of what it's like to be a Vietnamese chef in America, in this world, without bringing up the impacts of white supremacy. In this era, when American government officials are actively trying to keep people uneducated, I don't think a lot of people truly understand what "white supremacy" means. To me, it's a system that seeps into everything around us, constantly entrenching a society where whiteness is the prizest possession you could have: one whose access no money, no power, not even proximity can buy. When I was a kid, my teachers taught us to look up to the conquistadors who enslaved and massacred indigenous people in North and South America. No history lessons ever mentioned the Vietnam War. In culinary school, I learned that if I wanted to make it as a chef, the easiest way to do it was to cook Western food. For most of my life, I was taught by American culture that the stories of people like me—like my family—didn't matter. Even worse, all the people that I ever hoped to impress were taught the same. It would have been no big thing at all for me to erase my entire story for the rest of my career, and I'd had plenty of practice already.

When I was finally able to see the value in what my parents taught me, I realized that, as a chef, all I wanted to do was to tell my story through food. If I could use my skills to break down other people's walls, to show myself and my family for what we are, everything I'd been through would have all been worth it. Through pop-ups and storytelling events, I've learned how to create space for these very complex identities—not just in Oakland, but throughout Asian America. I found my voice advocating for immigrant and refugee cuisines like mine to gain the respect they deserve.

For me and my family, taste is the connector between past and present. When I think about how nostalgia and food work together to form "the memory of taste," I think of the flavors, cooking methods, and food wisdom that are passed on to us by our families, biological or otherwise. It's the particular way your ancestors twirled their noodles in bowls and the smells that crept into your nostrils every morning before you woke up. These are the food traditions rooted in family, lineage, heritage, and culture, influenced in infinitely complex ways by time and place. It's an idea that I hope can help other people appreciate their individual histories, even if they've been maligned by white supremacy and its agents as inferior, or worse, not worth thinking about at all.

I learned most of the recipes in this book from my parents. Others are threads that I pulled along the way, building the foundation my family laid for me. This book brings together the lessons my parents learned from years of surviving and thriving along their journey from Phú Quốc Island to the San Francisco Bay Area. But if you're expecting a classic set of traditional Vietnamese recipes passed down word-for-word from generation to generation, this ain't it.

If my memories of home are the ground I stand on, then all I learned from the food scene of the Bay Area is the fertilizer. In the middle of such abundant diversity, not to mention an abundance of incredible produce and seafood, countless cooks and chefs—many of them migrants, immigrants, or their descendants, like me—found their voices through a distinct kind of pidgin language specific to our California upbringing. My take on Viet cooking is exactly this extremely Californian combination of nostalgia for what came before as well as a strong sense of pride in the place that raised me.

For starters, I'll begin with a rundown of everything you'll need to cook the recipes in this book. It's basically the same stuff you'll find in Mẹ's (my mom's) pantry, which is full of fish sauce and peppercorns from Phú Quốc, dried and preserved specialties from her garden, and all sorts of random stuff she learned to use while living in the United States. The next few chapters after that will go deep into the seafood-centric culinary stylings of Phú Quốc—and if my family can cook it all in their home kitchen, so can you. I'll also be sharing some of the dishes I grew up eating in Oakland, paired with advice on how to incorporate more food recovery habits into your cooking routine. (I personally don't like to say "food waste," because I don't want to suggest that we ate garbage.) To cap it off, I couldn't resist sprinkling a little bit of cheffy stuntin' into this book, so you'll get some fun and, fine, slightly bourgie recipes at the end for when you really want to ball out. And I've got some ideas for Viet-Californian celebration dishes that you can whip out when all your friends, cousins, aunties, uncles, and everybody else suddenly decide to show up at your place.

Whether you're a Viet food expert yourself or someone who's never even touched a whole fish, I hope these memories of taste spark something in you like they did in me. The recipes and stories in this book are the generational wealth that I received from my family; and now, they're gifts I'm passing onto you. Savor their skins, plant their seeds, suck out their marrow—make the most of them.

A NOTE ON SUSTAINABILITY

> "We are not defending nature;
> we are nature defending itself."
> —**Resistencia Indígena, 2019**

My philosophy on sustainability is deeply woven into this book, and I think it's important to explain where I'm coming from. The word "sustainability" feels kind of cheap these days, especially in the food world. I see a lot of restaurants engaging in a surface-level kind of sustainability, a set of environmentally friendly practices that is mostly exercised by which labels the chefs look for when they go shopping: farm-to-table; pesticide-free; "humanely raised." And at lots of these "sustainable" restaurants, the halo of ethical planetary stewardship is a blessing reserved only for those who can pay a premium for it. You might think you're in this to stop climate change and save the whales, but that can't happen when you're just catering to the rich. Real sustainability extends an ethos of care to the whole community. Get a grip.

Multiple studies have found rampant mislabeling of seafood, meat, and produce as sustainable at restaurants and markets around the world, making it harder for people to know what they're actually eating. Famous fine dining restaurants known for farm-to-table dining, like the Willows Inn and Blue Hill at Stone Barns, have recently come under fire for misleading customers about where their food actually comes from and treating their low-wage workers like shit. In 2022, New York's Michelin-starred Eleven Madison Park pivoted to a vegan menu to demonstrate that a fine dining restaurant could be a leader in environmental sustainability, only for it to come out later that the restaurant was producing a massive amount of food waste in the pursuit of vegetables aesthetically perfect enough for its $335 tasting menu. As we've found out, an aesthetics-only sense of sustainability might be profitable, but it's not the real deal.

In the professional restaurant world, I came across this short-sighted attitude a lot. As a son of working-class refugees who struggled to access even basic, non-artisanal fresh produce like iceberg lettuce, I couldn't understand how being yelled at while putting together high-priced tasting menus featuring fancy-ass heirloom radishes belonged in the same universe as the noble pursuit of saving the world.

7

But there's another take on this idea that I later realized I'd known all along, even if my family never used a $5 word like "sustainability" to describe it. In my parents' world, sustainability was generational wisdom and common-sense frugality. You help the world not out of some high-and-mighty sense of morality or good taste, but because it's just the smart thing to do. You cook the head, eyeballs, and tail of a fish because to waste it would be an affront to the effort it took to get a fish in the first place. To my parents, the ultra-American practice of only eating a small percentage of an animal, or throwing out misshapen fruits and vegetables, is equally diabolical to spitting on your grandma. But I have to admit that there was a time when I too thought those wasteful practices were how you achieved greatness in the food world.

Case in point: When I was in culinary school, I thought I was really doing something when I decided to show off by cooking my mom a meal. She was horrified when I presented her a perfectly pan-fried fish fillet. "What about the rest?" she asked, pointing at what I'd left in the sink. The fish wasn't endangered or anything, but it didn't matter: I had let so much of it go to waste. In that moment, the gap between our perspectives couldn't have felt wider. I could have turned indignant, dismissing her as a plebeian who didn't understand great food. But as her criticism sunk in, I felt ashamed.

Wasting food is also more than just a personal failing—it's a huge factor in environmental destruction. According to the Environmental Protection Agency, Americans have been steadily wasting more and more food since it began tracking data in 1960. That year, the country sent 12.2 million tons of food to landfills. In 2019, Americans generated 66.2 million tons of food waste, with no signs of slowing their roll going forward. Besides the frankly inhumane fact that we're doing this while people within the country go hungry every day, the food that sits in landfills generates an insane amount of methane, a major driver of climate change. After such a long history of representing the worst in food waste, American chefs daring to claim any authority in the field of food sustainability is not just ridiculous, it's a disgrace.

It's that idea that attracted me to ocean conservation and sustainable food organizations like Postelsia that center indigenous expertise in their work. (They work with farmers and ocean stewards around the world to find sustainable solutions that make sense for them; for my part, I help tell those folks' stories through food.) These organizations push back against the idea among mainstream environmental groups and funders in the Global North that only credentialed experts can save the planet by correcting the bad habits of the rest of the world; that these self-proclaimed "elites" have the exclusive knowledge of what's valuable or not in any given place. Sometimes this so-called "expertise" looks like an ocean conservation group stereotyping the fishing practices of entire countries as uniformly bad, flattening the narrative and erasing the efforts of those who are doing good work. Other times, it's dudes like Britain's King Charles or multibillionaire and emerald mine heir Elon Musk arguing that "overpopulation" in African and Asian countries is a main driver of climate change, when in fact, the richest 10 percent of the world's population (themselves included) produce the same amount of greenhouse gas emissions as the remaining ninety.

To give a more local example, the original and rightful guardians of the Bay Area, the Ohlone people, have long known what colonizers only figured out later: If you take good care of it, the Bay Area can be a feast, where you can scoop razor clams by the basketful from its numerous beaches, where morels and porcini mushrooms can carpet the woods after a good rain, where the waters can be a traffic jam of fat salmon and Dungeness crabs. But instead of respecting the Ohlone people's deep understanding of the land, colonizers kicked them out of their homes, overfished the waters, and planted non-native trees and grasses that have made our wildfires worse every year.

One group doing amazing work is the Asian Seafood Improvement Collaborative, which uplifts small-scale sustainable fisheries in places like Cà Mau in Vietnam. I recently had the honor of visiting woman- and family-run fisheries there and in another province, Sóc Trăng, where cooperative models and fair wages empower workers to do everything the right way. In these cooperatives, women and girls learn critical skills that allow them to take charge of their own lives and support their families. They not only produce some truly incredible black tiger prawns; they also restore mangroves that can shelter their coastal communities from typhoons. I even got to cook a few dishes for the workers and their communities—no pressure, right? I took the heads of whiteleg shrimp and cooked them with garlic, ginger and lemongrass, and I used that rich, savory liquor to flavor fried rice. And I made a few in a very Phú Quốc way: skewered, charred on a grill, and flavored with Mỡ Hành Gừng | Ginger and Green Onion Sauce (page 47).

What I've learned through my environmental advocacy work is that the true measure of sustainability is different for everybody. From WildAid, an organization working to fight the global illegal wildlife trade, I realized the importance of mutual respect and knowledge pooling across communities to making changes stick. Through Postelsia, I saw how effective conservation programs could be when they allowed everyone in a community to participate. Fighting climate change might feel like a huge problem, but you can still find hope, and real solutions, in the small act of connecting with other people.

So, that's where my not-so-secret agenda for this cookbook comes in. It's based on an idea of sustainability that is less of an either-or binary and more of a practice that you keep up with. I'm not going to go all colonizer and tell you what to eat and what not to eat, but I'll share the techniques I inherited from my family that are key to making beautiful food while being a responsible steward of the environment. I'm going to trust that you know what's best and most sensible for you, so let's just start from there.

1

ME & BA'S
KITCHEN

For me, the kitchen pantry is one of the most intimate places in the home. And it's more socially acceptable to peep into someone's pantry than their medicine cabinet. Everything—from the spices to the packaged goods to the dried herbs stuffed into ziplock bags—tells a story about what someone values and where they've been. So naturally, to begin the story of my family and our food, you've got to start with our pantry.

If you poked your head into the kitchen cupboards of the tiny Oakland apartment where I grew up, you'd be hit with the piquant, floral scent of black peppercorns. The spices we bought didn't come in fancy jars, but rather plastic pouches that you'd tear the tops off of, so their smells escaped freely, mingling with each other to form a vaguely Southeast Asian bouquet. Your nose would wrestle with the competing aromas of the spice mixes my mom—my Mẹ— kept on-hand to make phở bò (page 122), phở gà (page 118), canh chua (page 89), and other Vietnamese soups. You'd see peeling brick-colored labels on cans of beets, anchovies in tomato sauce, and other mysterious, very American things that Mẹ picked up from the food bank. There'd be sugar dispensers—the kind you see on greasy-spoon diner counters—filled with white granules of MSG and reused SunnyD jugs of ferments, both culinary and medicinal.

Mẹ sourced what she could from the big-box grocery store near our home, but the rest of the goods were harder to get. Whenever we got a chance to visit Vietnam, our lug-gage would be filled with bottles and spices for the return flight. But it's not like you can book a flight to Vietnam every time you run out of pepper. So how do you cook a dish when you can't get the important ingredients, like lemongrass and bitter melon? Save the seeds, otherwise impossible to find in the United States, from an old fruit or rustle some up from your friends with their own gardens, and you can just grow it yourself, just like my mom did. Her garden, grown out of a strip of dirt on the side of our building, had everything the grocery store didn't: Thai pomegranates, passion fruit, brown sugar cane, bird's eye chiles, and so much more. The yield from her garden made its way into ferments, spice pastes, and baggies stuffed into the freezer. When I graduated from high school, they finally bought a house with a backyard where my mom could really expand her operation.

When I was a kid, there were weeks when, if you really looked closely, the only substantial ingredients you'd find in our pantry were rice and packages of Top Ramen. During those times, the pantry told another story. The hard times my family lived through, whether in a Thai refugee camp in the '70s or in our Oakland apartment in the '90s, made their mark on the way we ate and stored food. The jars, the preserves, and even the garden came into being to protect us from the hunger my parents knew all too well. And they didn't rest when we had enough food to go around: Instead, they used the time to prepare for the next time we didn't.

In the summers, when the fishing haul was good and the sun was the closest to Earth it'd be all year, you'd find the roof of our apartment building covered in trays of fish slowly drying in the blazing heat. Nets, made by my mom from bits of scrap fabric, kept the flies off (mostly). My parents would be in the kitchen for hours: my mom, constantly stirring a pan of peppercorn-studded fish sauce caramel; my dad—my Ba—using a sharp knife to butterfly dried fish fillets, then slathering them with the caramel. Left on repurposed fridge racks for 3 to 5 days, this Cá Khô | Fish Jerky (page 134) would become moist and sweet, with a concentrated blast of ocean salt in each bite. It filled our freezer for months. My parents' adherence to this seasonal going-through-the-motions, from my mom's knowledge of just how far to take the caramel to the way my dad inspected each fillet as it dried on our roof, connected them to Phú Quốc, where fishermen have done the exact same thing for generations.

My mom's pantry sprouts multiple roads to Miền Tây, the western region of Vietnam also known as the Mekong Delta. The Delta is the ecological nerve center of that part of the world and runs through the Cambodian border to the west and the coastal community of Vietnamese islands known as Kiên Giang, which includes Phú Quốc. The land in the lower delta floods during the rainy months, making it the ideal place to grow rice—in fact, the Delta is where most of the rice in Vietnam is grown. And its connection to the sea has made Miền Tây a center of regional trade since the first century CE, when it was a key stop for merchant fleets transporting spices, jade, and other goods throughout the Indian Ocean. That history is why we put bird's eye chiles, descended from Mexican peppers, into our fish sauce and how the dosa-like bánh xèo got its iconic turmeric-yellow coloring. With so many cultural influences in our history, the people of Miền Tây have developed a taste for big, explosive flavors and a deep knowledge of how to build them.

All of these components, painstakingly gathered and grown, made up the foundation of our palates at home. They also reflect the fact that, for a long time, my parents couldn't just go to the store and buy whatever ingredients they wanted: They had to rely on their ingenuity to recreate the dishes they grew up eating. The raw materials of a meal, including whatever my parents could scrounge up from the butcher shop or the sea, would become familiar with a dash of Phú Quốc fish sauce or a sprinkle of minced lemongrass from the garden. Doing all of that labor to stock the pantry was, in a potent way, how we maintained and reinforced the memory of taste, and it was with deep gratitude that we ate the food my parents longed for.

So there's the "why" of the pantry: Here's the "what." I've organized these lists to walk you through some of the things you'd find in my parents' kitchen, which of course include most of the ingredients you'll need to cook the recipes in this book. There are also a handful of recipes at the end of the chapter for pantry staples, such as my foolproof techniques for cooking rice (see page 34).

SPICES

I'm not gonna judge you for buying pre-ground spices, but do keep track of their age, as they go rancid faster than whole spices. Buy small amounts at a time and swap them out every six months.

FIVE-SPICE POWDER

A balanced blend of sweet, bitter, sour, salty, and savory spices, Chinese five-spice powder has the something-for-everybody appeal of an iconic boy band. It's perfect for adding depth to meat marinades and rubs, like what you'd use for Bánh Hỏi Heo Quay | Woven Noodles with Crispy Pork Belly (page 217) or Sườn Chiên | Caramelized Pan-Fried Pork Chops (page 139). My mom would always buy five-spice in those 99-cent pouches they have at Asian markets, but I'd nudge you to use my own blend, Chef Tu Phở Seasoning (distributed by Spice Tribe) instead.

GOCHUGARU

I started using these Korean chile flakes a lot when I met my wife, Jean, who made kimchee stew religiously when we first moved in together. With its fire engine-red color, gochugaru is a great addition to chili crisps and seasoning mixes. Gochugaru does change the character of a dish since it's spicy, but I love the visual impact.

KNORR BRAND'S HẠT NÊM

I spent a long time trying to figure out what the "secret ingredient" was in all of my relatives' cooking. Turns out this green bag was what my mom and all of my aunties were stashing deep in their cabinets. Knorr's hạt nêm is pretty much MSG on steroids: It's a concentrated powder made from pork bone marrow and meat. If you'd rather not add anything porky to your recipes, look to mushroom-based equivalents, like Nom Nom Paleo Magic Mushroom Powder.

MONOSODIUM GLUTAMATE (MSG)

I love MSG in all of its beautiful forms, and the kind I always keep in the pantry is the Aji-No-Moto brand. To be honest, my parents actually demonized it, saying it would over-stimulate the tastebuds. But even as they disparaged it, they still used it—a dash of MSG was always in our phở. MSG is key to adding savory depth to dishes, but it's also true that, similar to white sugar, it can be abused as a way to cut corners when it comes to flavor.

ORGANIC CANE SUGAR

When I was in high school, my mom suddenly got really into organic ingredients (thanks to her new Costco membership, I think). Her first step into that world was with cane sugar. So this is what I try to use in any recipe that calls for a basic sugar. Since it's not as refined as white sugar, it leans closer to the caramelly notes you'd find in palm sugar, making it a better fit for Vietnamese recipes when you don't have palm sugar available. If you can find palm sugar where you are, default to that. But otherwise, this is what you should use whenever I mention "sugar" in a recipe.

PALM SUGAR

Like maple syrup, palm sugar comes from the sap of the source tree. The sap is boiled down and reduced until it becomes concentrated and thick. I like that palm sugar imparts a different taste than commercial white sugar: It's not straight-to-your-veins sweetness; rather, it has complex fatty, caramelly, and coconut-like flavor notes as a result of the cooking process. This makes palm sugar a natural fit for recipes that call for a darker caramel flavor, like Gỏi Cá Trích | Herring Salad (page 60) or Nước Mắm Me | Tamarind Fish Sauce (page 42). In wet markets throughout Southeast Asia, you'll find artisanal palm sugars of all shades for sale, heaped in woven baskets or concentrated into bricks. If you're stateside, you might find it for sale crystallized in pyramids or blocks, in a semi-liquid caramel form, or as a paste. Look for either straight-up palm sugar or coconut sugar. Store at room temperature in a sealed container or bag.

SESAME OIL AND SESAME SEEDS

I learned a lot about sesame from my wife: One of her many talents, honed through a lifetime of eating Korean food at home, is sensing when sesame seeds are just about to go rancid. Her family uses toasted sesame oil like southern Italians use olive oil, so you could say they're kind of connoisseurs of the stuff. While high-quality organic toasted sesame oil, like that from the Korean brand Ottogi, might seem pricey, it's so much better to have a small amount of a great oil versus a lot of a not-so-great oil. Check the label before you buy: Sesame should be the only ingredient.

For sesame seeds, I prefer the round, teardrop-shaped ones since they give the final dish a crunchier texture than the flatter kind. Toasted sesame adds nuttiness to a dish, and it's totally worth it to toast the seeds yourself over low heat in a sauté pan. Keep tossing them continuously so that all sides are toasted, and stop once that nutty, roasty perfume hits your nose. It should take about 10 minutes. Pre-toasted seeds are convenient, but they'll go bad more quickly.

STAR ANISE
A key player in Chinese and Indian spice blends, star anise has a warm and licorice-y flavor. In southern Vietnamese cooking, it's essential for phở.

TAMARIND PULP
My favorite dishes that I had in Phú Quốc were basically anything glazed in tamarind—"me" in Vietnamese. The pulp, which comes in brown, beanlike pods from the tamarind tree, adds a pleasant sweet-and-sourness to seafood like shrimp (page 72) and mussels and goes great with salty ingredients like fish sauce. At stores, you'll find the pulp, seeds and all, pressed into dense blocks that you'll have to boil to soften so that you can remove the inedible seeds. After boiling, the pulp becomes a glaze that you can use in any recipe that calls for tamarind. A block of tamarind pulp will generate a lot more tamarind glaze than you'll need for a single recipe, but I suggest processing a whole block in one go and keeping the glaze in a jar. It keeps in the fridge for a very, very, very long time.

TURMERIC
Introduced to Vietnam by way of India, turmeric has found its way into a few iconic Vietnamese recipes, including Bún Kèn | Curry Coconut Noodles (page 67), the stunning soup-salad hybrid in which turmeric-tinted fish tumbles over fresh shredded papaya and rice noodles. The powder lends a sunny yellow color in batters, while whole fresh turmeric root can be steeped with other ingredients for flavor (or pulverized and served as juice "shots" for way too much money). When buying the powder, look for single-origin turmeric from companies like Spice Tribe and Diaspora Co.

VIETNAMESE BLACK PEPPER
In Phú Quốc, black pepper is synonymous with what's called Khmer pepper. (It's Cambodian in origin, but to plants, national borders don't really matter. In fact, Kampot, the city known for growing Cambodia's best pepper, is less than 20 miles from

the island.) The pepper is grown in mineral-rich red clay soil that makes the pepper berries shine bright, and climate-wise, the pepper plants thrive in that region. It's pungent, with citrus notes that make your mouth water. Unlike some pepper varieties that might just taste spicy, with nothing else to them, these Vietnamese peppers have real flavor to them.

VIETNAMESE WHITE PEPPER

I've always resented the French culinary convention of only using white pepper with white fish—so as not to clash with the color, they say. Look: White pepper is about so much more than its color. It's floral and sharp, with hints of pine and enough heat in a single pinch to flavor a whole pot of congee. Much of the world knows commercial white pepper as pepper berries that have had their skins removed, often through soaking.

CONDIMENTS

Putting together a strong collection of condiments is essential to making just about any Asian food, and most people I know take their brand loyalty extremely seriously. This is obvious at any big Asian grocery store, where sauces for stir fries, marinades, and dips can take up multiple aisles.

COMMERCIAL FISH SAUCE

When I say "commercial," I'm talking about the big brands you'll find in American stores: Squid, Three Crabs, and Thai Kitchen. Like olive oil, there are definite grades of fish sauce on the market, with some being great for finishing dishes and others being better suited to background work. Commercial fish sauce is muskier than the artisanal stuff, since it uses an extract made from not-so-fresh ground-up fish, guts and all. A well-stocked Vietnamese kitchen will have a few kinds of fish sauces, so keep a commercial brand on-hand for general seasoning. Toss a couple of dashes into your spaghetti sauce, or use it in a marinade.

FRIED GARLIC AND SHALLOTS

A sprinkle of fried alliums adds an ineffable "oomph" to salads and vegetable dishes, especially Gỏi Gà | Vietnamese Chicken Salad (page 155). Paired with raw herbs like mint and rau răm (also known as Vietnamese coriander), a fried shallot is a nice counterbalance to the natural astringency of greens. If you have the luxury of time and a well-ventilated kitchen, go ahead, Martha Stewart the hell out of your fried garlic and shallots and make them from scratch (page 50). But I'm just gonna tell you now that store-bought will save you a lot of tedium and mess. Buy them in small containers (3.5-ounce jars are typical) so they don't sit too long and get stale.

HOISIN SAUCE

To me, hoisin sauce is the most magical form of soybeans, the embodiment of their peak potential. Like, if *X-Men* psychic Jean Grey were a soybean, hoisin would be her reborn form, Phoenix. Maybe natto is Dark Phoenix. This metaphor is getting away from me. Anyway, hoisin is a fermented bean sauce with origins in Cantonese cuisine, where it's a key ingredient in char siu. It's versatile, with lots of uses in wok cooking and general barbecue, too. There's a bottle of hoisin on every table at southern Vietnamese phở shops, where you can either squirt some into your broth or have some on the side for dipping your meat. (I prefer the latter.)

MAGGI SEASONING SAUCE

I used to think Maggi was straight-up soy sauce until I went to culinary school. And when I learned it was actually Swiss, and not Vietnamese? My mind basically melted. Vietnamese cooks use Maggi as a general seasoning: It can add different salty notes to a dish, and you don't need a lot of it. In my family, we'd have meals with small dipping bowls of Maggi on the side, some crushed chiles steeped within. You'll also find Maggi seasoning in places like Mexico, where it's sold with a higher acid content, making it great for sprinkling onto grilled spring onions served with tacos.

OYSTER SAUCE

I'd compare oyster sauce to miso, another ingredient that's a really important savory building block in marinades and sauces. Its base is oyster extract, and the texture is pretty thick, like hoisin sauce. In lighter dishes, like the steamed greens you always see on dim sum menus, oyster sauce adds more weight to the taste. When I was a kid, I lived for my mom's caramelized pan-fried pork chops (page 139), which she'd marinate with oyster sauce, sugar, and other aromatics. After the chops were done, my dad, wasting nothing, would fry rice or pasta in the leftover pan drippings.

PREMIUM FISH SAUCE

The Cadillac of fish sauce—to me, at least—is the stuff my mom's family has been making since 1895. It smells like dried anchovies—it's not fishy per se, but has a dark, almost wooden whiskey barrel–like aroma. It's comparable to what an aged soy sauce would smell like: deep and dark. My mom's family makes it in the traditional way, using just anchovies, salt, and water, and aging it for 12 to 15 months. (Commercial fish sauces tend to bulk up their product with additional ingredients and flavor and color additives.) Until recently, it's been nearly impossible to find fish sauce of this caliber in stores in the United States. To me, Son brand fish sauce, made on neighboring Son Rai Island, is a dead ringer for my family's.

SA TÉ

Sa té is Vietnamese chile sauce, but it's more than just a blend of spicy peppers. Minced lemongrass adds citrus notes, while shallot gives it body and fragrance. I'm wild about Tiger Saté, which is handcrafted in small batches in Houston, Texas. The creator behind Tiger Saté, An Dao of Pantry by Nature, immigrated to the United States from Vietnam with her family when she was young. Like most Vietnamese in the diaspora, food was a way for her to connect to her memories of home. To capture the flavors of her grandmother's cooking, she created this sa té from her memory of taste—and it's amazing. Use it as a final-step seasoning in soups like phở.

SAMBAL OELEK

Sambal is Sriracha's fruitier, lacto-fermented cousin. It's bright, with a very short list of ingredients: red chiles, vinegar, and salt. It pops with fresh pepper flavor, almost like you crushed them yourself, so it's an easy shortcut for dips and dressings. I'd eat it in just about any context. It's got its own flavor profile, but in most applications, it's still fairly interchangeable with Sriracha: I see the difference between the two as similar to the difference between apple cider vinegar and rice vinegar. Some recipes call for chrouk metae, a similar, Cambodian-style sauce, but you can swap in sambal oelek, which is easier to find at most supermarkets.

SRIRACHA

The sauce we know as Sriracha in the United States was invented in the 1980s by Huy Fong Foods' David Tran, a Chinese-Vietnamese American refugee. It's relatively young, as far as sauces go, but it's now a bona fide institution in Viet restaurants everywhere. In this sauce, the flavors of hot red peppers, fermented garlic, vinegar, and sugar are held in a delicate balance, making it the versatile "little black dress" of cuisine. You'll find it swirled into phở broth (pages 122 and 215), and, yes, mixed with mayonnaise at your local Asian fusion spot. A lot of American food companies have integrated Sriracha into their dishes, and I think it's because every restaurant keeps a giant bottle of the stuff in the back for the line cooks.

VINEGAR

Acid is critically underutilized in the cuisines of the Global North . . . unless you count pickles. You see that human craving for sourness with every squeeze of lime into a bowl of phở. In northern Vietnam, they swap limes for dishes of white vinegar steeped with garlic—a similar effect, but subtler. A hint of vinegar is enough to slash through rich meats, keeping the salt and fat from overwhelming your palate. It's good to diversify your vinegar collection, too, since each kind adds a different character of acid to your dishes. Rice vinegar, made from fermented rice, is less sharp than distilled vinegar. (Anytime I call for rice vinegar in a recipe, it's the unseasoned kind by default.) Coconut vinegar and apple cider vinegar have fruity undertones that are well-suited to balancing out meat dishes.

CANNED AND DRIED GOODS, RICE, AND NOODLES

For some rice products, like short-grain rice and glutinous rice flour, I generally recommend Koda Farms, a small-scale producer based in South Dos Palos, California. But among my mom and aunties, Three Ladies Brand is considered the crème de la crème. Stick with that one for Southeast Asian varieties of rice, including broken jasmine rice. You'll find my basic rice recipes on pages 34–35.

BÁNH TRÁNG (RICE PAPER WRAPPERS)

Rice paper wrappers are made from rice flour batter that's been steamed on top of woven mats, which creates the distinctive basketweave pattern imprinted on the surface of each sheet. It's a must-have for wrapping summer rolls (pages 152 and 203), of course, and a new generation of Vietnamese street food vendors have started to fry them, turning them into crunchy salads and tostada-like snacks. To use as a wrapper, soak in lukewarm water for just a few seconds right before using. Keep it wet for too long and it'll disintegrate.

BROKEN RICE

I think if you asked the international community to define the national dish of Vietnam, they'd say phở, summer rolls, or spring rolls, because those are the things that are most popular outside of the country. But I feel strongly that if you ask anyone in Vietnam, in the cities, they're gonna say cơm tấm—broken rice. There, especially in Saigon, broken rice is often served flanked by fish sauce–marinated grilled meats, egg meatloaf, pickles, and other accompaniments. It's my rice of choice for Sườn Chiên | Caramelized Pan-Fried Pork Chops (page 139). Far from being a simple byproduct of milling, broken rice has taken center stage as something desirable on its own. See, Vietnam is jasmine rice country. And to produce those perfect and slender grains of rice, you need to beat them out of the stalks. Naturally, that process leaves behind a lot of imperfect, broken-off grains that you can't sell at the same high price. (Besides, a mixture of broken and unbroken rice wouldn't cook evenly.) Since it was an affordable alternative, broken rice became a staple food— the stuff people survived on through decades of wartime food rationing. It tastes the same, but the texture is less fluffy and a bit drier.

COCONUT MILK

Miền Tây is rife with coconut trees, so the people of that region really make use of the fruit. Coconut milk has an unmatchable cooling effect that's super necessary for life in a tropical climate. One of the great coconut milk dishes is Bún Nhâm Hà Tiên | Coconut and Fish Sauce Rice Noodle Salad (page 65), a simple dish that's just swimming in the stuff. My family used a lot of canned coconut milk when I was growing up; but once in a while, when she was feeling really ambitious, my mom would make her own from fresh coconuts. If you're feeling ambitious, too, you can find instructions on squeezing your own coconut milk on page 49.

COCONUT SODA

Coco Rico is 100 percent my jam. Carbonated and flavored with coconut extract, it's got a slightly creamy texture with a totally clear color. Even though it's Puerto Rican, you'll find the green cans in a lot of Vietnamese and Cambodian American kitchens, where people use the soda in a lot of interesting ways, such as in the pork belly–braising liquid in thịt kho and even to add sweetness to Nước Mắm Tỏi Ớt | Chile Fish Sauce (page 43).

DRIED SEAWEED

Like beans, seaweed is also a dessert ingredient in Vietnamese cooking. Kombu, a dried kelp, is often reconstituted in water and served with a plethora of ingredients (lotus seeds, plumped basil seeds, kumquats, and more) and flooded with ginger syrup (page 222). In terms of sustainability, seaweed is one of the best ingredients you can eat: It's carbon-hungry, nutrient-dense, and requires very few resources to thrive. You can buy big dried sheets of the stuff at most grocery stores now.

DRIED SHRIMP

The analogy I like to use for dried shrimp is that it's as integral to building flavor in Vietnamese cooking as kombu is in Japanese cooking. Dried shrimp adds an element of oceanic

salinity and amino acids that translate to umami flavor. Really, shrimp can turn a flat-tasting broth into something with real muscle behind it. The main varieties you'll find are going to come from the South China Sea or Louisiana. I recommend the ones from Kho Market, which ships nationwide from New Orleans.

FLOURS

My mom always kept little baggies of different flours in her pantry. They're the foundation of the vast library of "bánh" dishes: cakes, breads, and Bánh Ít Trần | Sticky Rice Dumplings, Tu and Jean Style (page 201). The main ones to keep on hand are bột năng (tapioca starch), bột nếp (glutinous rice flour), bột gạo (rice flour), and bột ngô (cornstarch). Koda Farms sells a great glutinous rice flour, called Mochiko, which democratized mochi-making for home cooks. If you're at an Asian store, look for Erawan brand flours (with the three-headed elephant as its logo). Otherwise, Bob's Red Mill has good organic versions of all of these.

GLUTINOUS RICE

You'll often encounter glutinous rice in desserts like Xôi Xoài Thái | Thai-Style Sticky Rice with Mango (page 126). At Vietnamese parties, there'll more than likely be some platters of steamed sticky rice, dyed in a rainbow of colors and sprinkled with a mixture of toasted sesame seeds, sugar, and salt. It's also an essential ingredient in bánh tét, a Lunar New Year treat where it's steamed in a banana leaf with marinated pork and mung beans.

MUNG BEANS

The bean sprouts that you see piled onto garnish plates at phở joints are all born from mung beans. But in most Vietnamese recipes, split, dried mung beans are what we go for. My mom would steam them in a tray, while I prefer to boil them in a pot. Depending on their texture, the beans have different uses. In the

savory version of Bánh Ít Trần | Sticky Rice Dumplings, Tu and Jean Style (page 201), the springy parcels are stuffed with mixture of mashed potato–soft mung beans and pork.

NOODLES
What is a life without noodles? A well-stocked Vietnamese pantry has a diverse collection of noodles in it, with each fulfilling its own culinary niche. Dried rice noodles are the heavy hitters here, and it takes a bit of finesse to get them right. Boil them just until they get tender, and make sure you're ready to shock them in cold water once they come out. Otherwise, the starch will glue the hot noodles together as they dry. A lot of noodle recipes in this book, like Bún Chả Giò Khoai Môn | Taro Spring Roll and Rice Noodle Salad (page 165), are all about cold noodles, anyway.

Dried bún, otherwise known as rice vermicelli, is a slippery noodle best suited to salads. Somewhat similar in thickness is bánh hỏi, most often presented in dried or fresh rectangular sheets. It's also made from rice flour, but the batter is fermented, giving the noodles a slightly sour taste. Another rice noodle we use a lot is bánh phở, the thin, flat noodles used in soups. These are easiest to find in dried form in the United States, but the fresh ones are worth seeking out: They're springy, supple, and not as chewy. Cryovac-sealed noodles need a quick blanch in boiling water to prep, while the softer ones sold on Styrofoam trays can be served as-is.

Another fresh noodle I like to use is bánh canh, a chewy and soft tapioca flour noodle. Sometimes they're also made with rice flour. Tapioca makes the noodles super elastic and bouncy—think boba. They're easy to make fresh (see page 69) if you can't find them in a store. Otherwise, you can swap in Japanese udon.

The recipe for spring rolls (page 165) also makes use of non-rice noodles, like miến, or bean thread noodles. Made with mung bean or sweet potato starch, miến become transparent when cooked and add a nice chewy texture to meat fillings.

PASTA
I know—you're like, wait, pasta? What kind of Vietnamese book is this? But Vietnamese people use the hell out of some dried pasta, which we call "nui." It's not necessarily fusion, like miso carbonara or something; most of the time, we use short pasta, like macaroni or shells, to bulk up soups. A lot of home cooks prefer tricolor rotini for the texture and appearance. If we didn't have cooked rice on hand at home, my parents would sometimes use pasta to soak up the pan drippings from Sườn Chiên | Caramelized Pan-Fried Pork Chops (page 139).

PINEAPPLE JUICE
My family would always keep those cocktail-size six-packs of Dole pineapple juice on hand to throw into soups like canh chua (page 89), where that acidic flavor is essential. Any brand will do; just make sure there's no sugar added, or else you'll have to adjust the recipe.

PRESERVES

These are ingredients that my family would either buy from the store or process at home for long storage. Some are simple, like the corn silk we'd dry in the oven overnight, while others, like the caramel-glazed fish jerky, are hours-long productions.

DRIED CORN SILK

The shiny fibers that stick out from the tip of a corn cob are usually thrown away in pursuit of the plump yellow kernels, but my mom would no doubt holler at you if she saw you doing that. Corn silk is actually full of antioxidants, and it's been used as a diuretic in folk medicines and teas in Latin America for millennia. The easiest way to keep it is to dry it overnight on a baking sheet in a gas-powered oven—just let the pilot light do all the work. Once it's brittle, you can make a tea out of it or chop it up and add to other things—dumplings, stir fries, soups—to give them more heft. Since it's all dried out, you can keep it at room temperature pretty much indefinitely.

DRIED FISH JERKY

My parents used this recipe to preserve fish when our access to it was plentiful. I've seen my dad make fish jerky with giant skate (similar to sting ray) that he's fished underneath the Bay Bridge. Fish jerky was also a good way to make use of the rockfish and sole that he brought home from his work as a fishmonger. I have to say, the jerky flavored with my parents' special fish sauce caramel, Nước Mắm Sánh Kẹo, is incredibly delicious. It's best kept in the freezer and pulled out as needed. See pages 37 and 134 for recipes.

DRIED SHIITAKES

A plant-based way to build savory flavors in soups, shiitakes are concentrated fungal forest essence. My mom would always buy them from the Chinese medicine store in Oakland's Chinatown, where they spoke both Vietnamese and Cantonese. You need to rehydrate them in cold water, but afterward, you can use the leftover shroomy water to add flavor to broths and sauces. When cooked, shiitakes have a firmer, meatier bite than fresh mushrooms. Sliced shiitakes will rehydrate faster and will be slightly more expensive.

DRIED SQUID

One of my favorite Vietnamese street foods is dried squid, flattened into a long, crispy sheet in a mechanical press, then toasted over hot coals and served with Sriracha. Its briny flavor and jerky-like texture, combined with Sriracha's sweet garlic spice, is 100 percent my shit. At grocery stores, you'll find dried squid sold as a tangle of fibrous meat and as a sheet—grab the latter for my recipe for Gỏi Xoài Xanh Khô Mực | Green Mango and Dried Squid Salad (page 62).

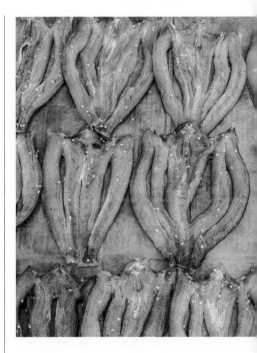

VIETNAMESE MEDICINAL INGREDIENTS

Ginseng, jujubes, and goji berries were always in circulation at home. Sun-dried, then kept preserved in the freezer or above the fridge, these ingredients often went into home remedies. My parents kept a collection of jars filled with medicinal tree bark, rice wines, and these ingredients. Influenced heavily by traditional Chinese medicine, this indigenous herbology lives on in the ointments prepared in my family's kitchen.

GARDEN

My mom's garden has always been her happy place. We were so lucky to live in the East Bay, with its blazing sun and Mediterranean climate. The weather granted her garden abundance; and in so many ways, my family's collective well-being depended on it. It gave us food and medicine, sure, but it was also a pocket of beauty in a world that didn't always have much beauty to spare.

BANANA LEAVES

In the non-tropical climate of Oakland, our banana tree never really thrived—let's just say, it survived, at least. It would drop a flower maybe once a year, and forget about any bananas. But the leaves of a banana tree are just as useful as the fruit. In Vietnamese cooking, they're used for wrapping ingredients, like sticky rice (page 35) and fish, before steaming. The leaves impart a subtly sweet, comforting aroma into the finished product. You can find them at Latin American and Asian markets, most often in the freezer section.

GINGER

What can't ginger do? One of the first breakout stars of the international spice trade, the fragrant root is used in everything from Jamaican ginger beer to Thai curry paste to Scandinavian gingersnap cookies. Vietnamese cooks will throw a smashed knob of ginger into soups to perfume the broth or mince it up to mix with fish sauce (page 41) or Mỡ Hành Gừng | Ginger and Green Onion Sauce (page 47). To peel ginger, I like to use a sharp paring knife. If you're not super comfortable with your knife skills, scraping the thin skin off with a metal spoon will work,

too. Keep the skins, since they add a lot of flavor to stock.

GREEN ONIONS

During the pandemic, a lot of people got into growing green onions from discarded roots on their windowsills, though I wonder how many people have kept up the practice in the years since 2020. (They lose flavor over time, so hopefully no one's still nursing the same plant.) The cool thing is that a lot of folks learned it's not hard to maintain green onions. They regenerate quickly, and you can just snip the tops off to use as garnishes in other dishes. I cut the stalks differently depending on how I want to use them. For classic Mỡ Hành | Green Onion Sauce (page 47), I cut them into thin rounds; for garnishes that need a little more flash, I slice them on the diagonal, in what Chinese chefs call the horse's ear cut.

LEMONGRASS

People always ask me how they can best use lemongrass. It's a tricky herb, and I think that since it's so labor-intensive to prepare, it's tempting to underutilize it. But you have to use a lot to get the big citrus flavor that most recipes call for. The bunches of

lemongrass sold at grocery stores will yield too much for a single recipe, so I would prep them all at once and freeze for later. Make it all into dán sả (page 36), an easy-to-use paste that you can stir into soups and marinades. Some recipes call for bruising the stalk to release the flavorful oils inside, so here's how you do it. Roll a heavy rolling pin over the lemongrass stalk from top to bottom to squeeze out the base, which is the woodiest part. Throw out the woody bits, or save them for tea or stock. Continue to roll over the lemongrass stalk to bruise it—you can even smack it if you need to—like you're trying to even out a lumpy piece of pie dough.

MAKRUT LIME LEAVES

Known as chanh sấc in Vietnam, the Makrut lime grows throughout Southeast Asia. Its leaves have a cool hourglass shape and a gloriously evocative citrus smell. They're often used as a flavoring in curry pastes and soups, where regular citrus juice flavor might get muddled. Keep a batch of leaves in your freezer. If you can't find these leaves, swap in half a teaspoon of regular lime or lemon zest per leaf called for in the recipe.

YELLOW ONIONS

The yellow onion was the one vegetable I knew my family would almost always have in our pantry, no matter how dicey our food situation got. Meat was seldom available, and fish scraps were always a "maybe." Onions, though, were the building blocks of my staple meals. When I was a kid, I'd make instant ramen and add tons of chopped onion to the broth to add flavor and so I would actually feel satiated. Later on, in culinary school, one of my favorite recipes was French onion soup. Since onions were also cheap and easy to grow in France, the soup was considered to be peasant food. It was one of the few recipes in the culinary-school canon that I really saw myself in, and I have a soft spot for it to this day.

HERBS

Probably the most important inhabitants of my mom's garden were the herbs. Most were grown from seeds she swapped with relatives and neighbors. So many dishes in Miền Tây cuisine require a plethora of fresh herbs, and it just doesn't make economic sense to buy four or five bunches of different herbs that are going to go bad if you don't use them immediately. It's much easier to grow them yourself and cut sprigs and leaves off when you need them. Some, like chamomile and parsley, are easy to dry for later, whereas Thai basil is one of those plants that is most aromatic when cut immediately before use. The main herbs my mom grew were spearmint, diếp cá (fish wort), perilla, dill, Thai basil, and rau răm, and they made their way into lots of dishes she and my dad made. I use bitter and spicy rau răm, also known as Vietnamese coriander, a lot, but if you can't find it, swap in cilantro or Thai basil. Same with culantro, a feather-shaped herb that tastes like a punchier cilantro.

These days, you can find a lot of different herbs as starter plants at nurseries. Dill weed, spearmint, flat-leaf and curly parsley, and Thai basil are easy to find. Thai basil and fish wort are two that you can actually grow from cuttings, which is a great way to save money if you have leftovers from the store. If you don't have much outdoor space, some herbs, like perilla, will do fine in pots.

HYBRID BIRD'S EYE CHILES

The plants are packed in so close to each other in my mom's garden that all kinds of botanical freaks emerged over the years. One was the hybrid bird's eye chile, a super dark black pepper that she called "the crazy chile." We had no idea why it was so spicy, and the dark black and sort-of-greenish color made it seem almost unripe. Just a tiny bite of one would be enough to set your lips on fire. But you'll do okay without the crazy chile—the normal bird's eye chiles that you can get from the grocery store are more than adequate for the recipes in this book.

KUMQUAT

During Lunar New Year celebrations, you can pick up on the scent of kumquats and their blossoms wafting through many Vietnamese households. The kumquat tree's golden-orange fruits cheer us up in the winter, and we also use them in medicines and desserts like Sâm Bổ Lượng | Vietnamese Herbal Tonic Drink (page 169).

LISBON LEMONS

Unlike typical lemons from the grocery store, the ones from my mom's garden had a thicker rind and a lot more juice. A typical Lisbon lemon tree stands about 15 to 20 feet tall. Instead of squeezing them for their juice to use in nước chấm, my mom would peel the rinds off with a paring knife and cut the fruit into suprêmes. The pulp would give the dipping sauce body and texture, and I always loved how those little pearls of lemon juice would pop in your mouth. Of course, you can use a regular lemon in the same way.

PASSION FRUIT

In the late summers, the passion fruit vines in the garden would grow heavy with fruit the color of a black eye, their insides bursting with juicy golden pulp. The crunchy seeds are edible, so you can simply scoop the insides into your mouth or stir the pulp into a drink. Fresh passion fruits can be found in some produce markets, especially Mexican ones. Otherwise, you can find the pulp in the freezer section.

POMEGRANATES

Though mostly associated with Mediterranean food, pomegranates are huge in Southeast Asia, too. The Thai varieties aren't as ruby-red as their cousins in the Middle East—they're mostly yellow, with a pinkish blush. The seeds, too, tend to be lighter and almost translucent. While pomegranate seeds don't get much use outside of salad garnish in the United States, we'd usually dust them with Muối Ớt | Chile Salt (page 43) to amp up their puckery sweetness and eat them as a snack. My mom's plant is a dwarf that produces fruit that's way smaller than the typical softball-size ones, and she kept it around for medicinal purposes. Whenever I had a stomachache, she'd have me chew on pomegranate leaves to calm my stomach. It was so blindingly bitter, it'd give me cottonmouth in seconds! But within the hour, my stomach would chill.

SPECIALTY TOOLS

I'm not going to ask you to buy a bunch of one-hit wonders for these recipes, and that's not because I'm being a snob about it. If I asked my mom to buy a custom-size butter spreader for a recipe, she'd laugh in my face! One thing my parents taught me is that there are multiple ways to solve a problem: You can buy your way out of it, or you can MacGyver that shit with whatever you have on hand. I believe in you.

I'm going to assume you have some of the basics, including a sharp chef's knife, a sauté pan, a basic suite of utensils, mixing bowls, and pots of various sizes. With that out of the way, I will say that there are a few tools that are nice-to-haves (and they're relatively affordable). Trust, I'm not gonna be asking you to buy a whole popcorn cart or anything like that. If you'd rather pass, no biggie—but they will make cooking the recipes in this book easier.

ASIAN PEELER KNIFE
The Asian-style peeler knife is a lot bigger than the dainty peelers most chefs pack—the one I like has a super sharp five-inch blade. If you've ever struggled with peeling a winter squash, this is your guy. It's big, but easy to control with precision. Search online for "crude Asian peeler knife" and you'll find it. It's around $16 for one.

CIRCULAR CUTTING BOARD
I like a circular wooden board because it's actually more stable for heavy-duty tasks, like chopping chicken with meat cleavers and cutting through bone. But whatever you do, don't get a bamboo board—that material will just slaughter your knife edges. Season your cutting board with food-grade mineral oil about once a month to prevent it from cracking.

COCONUT SHREDDER
If you've never processed a whole coconut before, it's probably really intimidating to think about. But there are tools that a lot of folks, especially in the Pacific Islands, have refined over the years to make the work easier (and to save their wrists from the strain of scraping out a coconut). That includes the bench my parents used. That's right: It's a small wooden bench with something that looks like a cowboy's spur at the end. You sit on the bench facing the blade, then scrape the inside of a halved coconut to shred out the pulp. When I was a plump little kid, my mom would perch me next to her on the bench while she dealt with the coconut. There are other good coconut-shredding tools out there, like a tabletop scraper with a handy crank. Regardless of what you choose, you'll need some kind of scraping tool if you want to use fresh coconut at home.

COFFEE GRINDER
Remember in the spices section, when I said that there's no shame in buying pre-ground powders and blends? Well, if you've got the time and the wherewithal to deal with whole spices, an electric coffee grinder will really upgrade your spice game. The blends you make with this will be bursting with aromatic oils and will stay fresh longer. A coffee grinder is also great for grinding up dried herbs and shrimp. Keep a grinder in your cupboard just for spices so your coffee doesn't smell like cumin in the morning, and make sure to wipe it out between uses.

DEHYDRATOR
You can pick up a basic food dehydrator online or at a 99 Ranch or other well-stocked Asian market for roughly a hundred bucks and change, and it's essential for making things like Cá Khô | Fish Jerky (page 134) without any worries about food safety. I promise, it'll be the best Benjamin you've ever spent.

LARGE WOODEN MORTAR
A mortar and pestle are straightforward and classic, with a design that hasn't really changed over the centuries. A knife can't crush with the same amount of power, and a pestle can massage the flavors and oils of ingredients in a way a modern electric food processor can't. Plus, it doubles as a stress reliever.

STEAMER (METAL OR BAMBOO)
While you could get away with using a steam rack in a wok, if you're going to make dumplings (and other steamed dishes that need a flat surface), you need a dedicated steamer. If you get a metal steamer, pick one with handles that you can easily and quickly grab to safely pull the steamer basket off the pot of boiling water. When using a steamer, make sure you never let the water run out during cooking.

RECIPES FOR PANTRY STAPLES

The recipes in this section are the fundamentals, ingrained in me from decades of learning from my parents. From steaming rice (see page 34) to making a whole damn tasting menu of fish sauce dips, these are the building blocks for the recipes in the rest of the book. There are also some real in-depth techniques that will be extremely useful during the apocalypse, especially if you're someplace with lots of coconuts.

CƠM | RICE

Here, you'll find my master recipes for all the types of rice you'll need in this book. The key to understanding how rice works lies in getting a handle on its rate of absorption. It sounds really scientific when I say that, but I promise—practice will refine your internal timer so that you can get a feel for when to pull the pot off the stove before the rice scorches. The first two rice recipes call for an 8-quart, large pot, while the sticky rice recipe uses a rice cooker.

For all types of rice, rinse the grains at least three times before you cook them, or at least until the water runs clear. You can use the pot that you plan to cook with. Each time, flood the pot a few inches above the rice, then rub the grains against each other to get the starch off. Otherwise, the residual starch will make the rice granules stick together, and you'll end up with mushy rice. Rinsing is also the only way to remove any of the naturally occurring arsenic that may be in the rice. Don't waste the water, though! It's full of nutrients, and you can use it to water plants, especially houseplants that might need extra love.

CƠM TẤM
BROKEN RICE

Makes 5 cups

2 cups broken rice
2½ cups filtered water

In an 8-quart pot, wash the rice under running water. (See Cơm | Rice, above.) Then, allow the rice to soak for 20 minutes, allowing the granules to soften and bloom. Using a colander, drain the water, then put the rice back into the pot.

Add the 2½ cups water to the rice.

Set the pot over high heat and bring to a boil. Then turn the heat to low, cover with a well-fitting lid, and continue to simmer for 10 minutes.

Remove the pot from the heat and let stand, covered, for 10 minutes to allow the rice to continue absorbing moisture. Fluff the rice with a wooden spoon or fork before serving.

Note: It's a Vietnamese rule that when you cook broken rice, the amount of water you use should always be equal to the amount of rice plus an additional half cup of water. Easy to remember, right?

GẠO THƠM HOA NHÀI
JASMINE RICE

Makes 3 cups

1 cup jasmine rice
1¼ cups filtered water

In an 8-quart pot, wash the rice under running water. (See Cơm | Rice, above.) Using a colander, drain the water, then put the rice back into the pot with the 1¼ cups water.

Set the pot over high heat and bring to a hard boil. Then turn the heat to low, cover with a well-fitting lid, and let simmer for 15 minutes.

Remove the pot from the heat and let stand, covered, for 10 minutes to allow the rice to continue absorbing moisture. Fluff the rice with a fork or rice paddle before serving.

XÔI
STICKY RICE

Makes 6 cups

2 cups glutinous rice
1⅓ cups filtered water

In a large rice cooker pot, wash the rice under running water. (See Cơm | Rice, page 34.) In the same rice cooker pot, cover the rice with two inches of cold water and let it soak for 24 hours. (Time to relax!)

After 24 hours, drain the rice, then add the 1⅓ cups water. Hit the "cook" button on your rice cooker, et voila! Fluff the rice with a fork or rice paddle before serving. Let the leftovers cool before storing in the fridge for up to 3 days or in the freezer for a month.

DÁN ME
TAMARIND PASTE

Makes 2½ cups

On an instinctive level, all humans crave sourness, whether that comes from tart, foraged oxalis leaves or hard lemon candies. We all find it somehow, by any means necessary. In my mom's case, she reaches for lime, coconut vinegar, and tamarind to shower food with bright, mouth-puckering flavors. Tamarind's complexity makes it a favorite of my staple ingredients. It's one of the few fruits in the world that offers both sweet and sour tastes, with notes harmonizing the familiar flavors of lime, lemon, date, apricot, and caramel. It's an incredibly difficult ingredient to master in cooking because it can be quite sour—so sour that your tongue, if overwhelmed by the flavor, might interpret it as bitter. A novice cook might try to balance the bitterness with sugar, but an expert would pull in spices and alliums such as ginger, galangal, garlic, and chiles—or sometimes, even fish sauce.

One 8-ounce block tamarind pulp, cut into ½-inch chunks
2 cups warm filtered water

In a large bowl, combine the tamarind pulp and warm water. Cover the bowl with plastic wrap or a plate and leave on the counter at room temperature to soak until the tamarind pulp has softened, 1 to 2 hours. If it hasn't within 2 hours, give it another 30 minutes. (I know I shouldn't have to tell you this, but wash your hands thoroughly before the next step.)

Using your fingertips, squeeze any remaining chunks of tamarind pulp into smaller pieces. Set a fine-mesh sieve over another large bowl and, using a ladle, push the tamarind pulp mixture through it, leaving the seeds behind. Transfer the strained pulp into an airtight jar.

Store the tamarind paste in the fridge for up to 1 month.

NƯỚC SỐT ME
TAMARIND SAUCE

Makes ½ cup

Like I've said, I'm a total tamarind fanboy. When I go to Vietnam, this is the flavor I chase, whether it's in an extra-sour bowl of canh chua (page 89) or coating every nook and cranny of shell-on prawns (page 72).

1 tablespoon neutral oil (such as vegetable oil)
2 tablespoons minced shallot
1 tablespoon minced garlic
1 Thai bird's eye chile, minced
¼ cup Dán Me	Tamarind Paste (this page)
½ cup coconut water (no pulp)
1 tablespoon granulated sugar
½ teaspoon kosher salt
½ teaspoon MSG

Set a medium saucepan on high heat for 2 minutes. When it's warm, add the neutral oil and swirl the saucepan. When the oil is shimmering, add the shallot, garlic, and chile and cook until the mixture begins to soften. (You might want to crack a window so the chile doesn't mess you up.)

Add the tamarind paste, coconut water, sugar, salt, and MSG to the pan and let simmer for 1 minute, just to get the flavors to meld in the heat. Then turn off your stovetop and let the pan cool to room temperature.

Store the sauce in an airtight container in the fridge for up to 1 week.

DÀN SẢ

LEMONGRASS PASTE

Makes 1 cup

Lemongrass isn't the most convenient, easy-to-use herb in the world. The foot-long stalks you'll find at grocery stores often yield a lot more of the stuff than a single recipe needs; and it's so much work to process them that if you waste the leftovers, you're just playing yourself—for real. So, what to do? Use the leftovers to make lemongrass paste and freeze it. When you need that unmistakable hit of citrus, you'll be able to easily scrape the frozen lemongrass paste out of the jar and straight into your recipe, where it will instantly melt into the other ingredients. Lemongrass is pretty fibrous, so you'll need a powerful food processor or blender for this recipe.

Notes: Avoid choosing lemongrass with thicker stalks; they tend to be woodier. Be picky about any traces of mold on the stalk, which indicate that the lemongrass is old. Fresh lemongrass should have plenty of moisture, so check the tops to see if they're dry and brittle—again, that means old.

For any recipe that calls for minced lemongrass, you can sub this paste in a 1:1 ratio. If you're in a pinch, you can also find this in the freezer section of an Asian grocery store, but be aware that it might contain preservatives.

Two 1-foot-long lemongrass stalks, bruised (see page 29)

Using a sharp knife, finely mince the lemongrass crosswise. In a food processor or blender, pulse the lemongrass until smooth, 1 to 2 minutes. Using a thin rubber spatula or chopstick, transfer the lemongrass paste into an airtight glass jar.

Store the lemongrass paste in the freezer for up to 4 months, before the flavor starts to fade.

NƯỚC MÀU DỪA

COCONUT CARAMEL SAUCE

Makes 1 cup

Nước màu, or caramel sauce, is a staple ingredient found in most Vietnamese pantries for savory dishes, like braised fish (page 113), giving meats and braises a deep, toasty sweetness and a pleasant brown color. When kept on hand, the sauce can be used as a shortcut so you don't have to make a pan caramel on the fly for every recipe that calls for one.

Caramel sauce recipes vary by region, using different combinations of liquid and sweetener. In its most basic form, it's made with cane sugar and water. Other types of sugar you can use include honey, brown sugar, and palm sugar; for alternate liquids, there's coconut water or straight-up Coco Rico (see page 24). When you use a coconut-based liquid, the name of the recipe changes from nước màu to nước màu dừa—*dừa* means "coconut." I prefer this version because the coconut water adds some complexity to an otherwise plain, sugary element. You'll find that this technique is basically the same as the one for Nước Mắm Sánh Kẹo | Fish Sauce Caramel (page 37), though there's no fish sauce here. One quick trick: A drop of lemon juice used in this recipe helps prevent the sugars in the sauce from crystallizing.

2 cups granulated sugar

1 cup coconut water (no pulp)

1 drop lemon juice (optional)

In a large bowl, one that's wide enough to comfortably fit a 3-quart, heavy stainless-steel pot with handles, combine ice cubes and water to prepare an ice bath. Make sure you'll be able to easily perch the pot in the ice bath without having to hold it. Set up the ice bath in the sink so that it can overflow without making a mess.

In the stainless-steel pot, combine the sugar, coconut water, and lemon juice (if using). Place over medium heat and, using just the pot handles, gently swirl the pot until the sugar dissolves, darkens, and registers 380°F on a candy thermometer, 10 to 15 minutes. Be careful not to splash yourself, or you will be very, very sad.

Remove the pot from the heat and sink it immediately in the ice bath to prevent the mixture from over-caramelizing. Be very careful not to let any water get into the caramel—the temperature difference will make the mixture pop, and you could potentially take out an eyeball. Allow the caramel to cool to room temperature in the bath.

Store the caramel sauce in an airtight jar in the fridge for up to 6 months.

NƯỚC MẮM SÁNH KẸO
FISH SAUCE CARAMEL

Makes 2 cups

In some Vietnamese food circles, nước mắm sánh kẹo is considered a nước chấm recipe, a dipping sauce that uses caramel as a sweetener. I don't want to tell anybody they're wrong, but my family's recipe is definitely not that. In my family, we know it as a fish sauce caramel, littered with black peppercorns, that is used to marinate fish. Specifically, we use it to make Cá Khô | Fish Jerky (page 134). It's definitely not the same kind of caramel that you find in little cubes at a candy store. This stuff will wallop you in the face with salty, briny fish sauce power. One batch of this recipe should roughly correspond to one batch (12 ounces) of fish jerky, or 2½ pounds of fish.

2 tablespoons whole black peppercorns
2 cups granulated sugar
1 cup fish sauce

Place the peppercorns in a large plastic or cloth bag and lay it flat on the counter. Using a rolling pin, smack the peppercorns repeatedly until most are coarsely cracked. Just be careful to keep the peppercorns contained in the bag, or you'll randomly find pieces of them in your kitchen for the next year or so. (You can also use a mortar and pestle to crack the peppercorns—just don't zone out and accidentally turn them into powder.) Pour the peppercorns into a small bowl and set next to the stove.

In a large bowl, one that's wide enough to comfortably fit a 3-quart, heavy stainless-steel pot with handles, combine ice cubes and water to prepare an ice bath. Make sure you'll be able to easily perch the pot in the ice bath without having to hold it. Set up the ice bath in the sink so that it can safely overflow without making a mess.

In the stainless-steel pot, combine the sugar and fish sauce. Place over medium heat and, using just the pot handles, gently swirl the pot until the sugar dissolves, darkens, and registers 380°F on a candy thermometer, 10 to 15 minutes. (Please don't splash yourself!) Note that I don't use a spatula or spoon for this recipe because the caramel will just want to stick to it, and you'll end up with a crystallized mess.

Pour the cracked peppercorns into the pot and quickly swirl the pot by its handles again to mix them into the sauce.

Remove the pot from the heat and sink it immediately into the ice bath to keep the mixture from over-caramelizing. Be very careful not to let any water get into the caramel; the temperature difference will make it pop, and you could potentially get hurt. Allow the caramel to cool to room temperature in the ice bath.

Store the caramel in an airtight jar in the fridge for up to 6 months.

FISH SAUCE CONTAINS MULTITUDES

There are so many ways that fish sauce figures into Vietnamese culture, far beyond its use in the kitchen. Free divers, like the guys in my family, traditionally believe that rubbing fish sauce all over your lips and mouth before you jump into the water will help regulate your body's temperature. Some Viets like to talk about how fish sauce runs through their veins, and there's a whole cottage industry around making clothes that boost nước mắm to the level of the Supreme logo. I talk about the symbolism of fish sauce a lot with my friend Danny Tran, who owns Son Fish Sauce with his wife and fourth-generation fish sauce maker Albee Tran. Something he once said has stuck with me: "In Vietnam, we take fish sauce very seriously. Fish sauce is our identity."

Fish sauce is our identity—and it contains multitudes. There are the Two-Buck Chucks of fish sauce, and there are also some Dom Pérignons, and the difference is all about technique. Traditional Vietnamese fish sauce is made by fermenting black anchovies from the South China Sea and the Gulf of Thailand with salt from the same sea. The mixture is aged for twelve to sixteen months in large vats or wooden barrels that are made from local palms. This process captures a sense of place—so just like wine, fish sauce can have a strong element of terroir, meaning it tastes like the area it's from. (In the oyster business, "merroir" expresses a similar concept, but with the sea.)

Now for the Two-Buck Chucks—the lower-end fish sauces. If you're using fish and salt (or, say, bulk grapes) from all over the place, there's going to be a generic flatness to the flavor.

Cheaper fish sauce brands compensate for that flatness with additives, sugar, fillers, and even dyes, like caramel coloring. The stereotype that fish sauce stinks is mostly based on people smelling the cheap stuff, which is made from an anchovy mash, an "extract" that's already decaying—so of course it stinks.

In this particular way, I was privileged: The fish sauce my parents brought home from trips to Phú Quốc was the best of the best, so I knew the difference from a young age. In 2012, Phú Quốc fish sauce was even given European Union Protected Designation of Origin status, joining the ranks of Parmesan and Champagne. Earning this protective status will go a long way toward ensuring the economic future of Phú Quốc Island and prevent competitors from selling an inferior product under the same name.

Phú Quốc is the birthplace of Vietnam's centuries-old fish sauce industry, and my mom's side of the family has had their factory, Hưng Thành, since 1895. When I visited the factory, I got to walk among the towering wooden vats and smell the fish sauce at all stages of its life, from two weeks to a year, and the differences were stunning. I listened to the river-like sound of fish sauce being filtered from barrel to barrel and took small sips of it at various stages of aging. The aroma in the air wasn't necessarily fishy—it smelled more like aged soy sauce, or the plume of scent that's released when you bite into a shiitake mushroom. Like Son, Hưng Thành makes fish sauce the traditional way, from whole anchovies, and the complexity of its flavor—and that my mouth would water just from the smell of it—validated the superiority of those classic, age-old techniques.

EVERYDAY FISH SAUCE

Makes 1 cup

Nước chấm is a very general term for a sauce that is served as a staple condiment on Vietnamese dining tables. It has as many variations as leopards have spots, and each one highlights a different flavor: Some are saltier, some are spicier, and some have strong fruity notes. Generally speaking, Vietnamese folks—my mom included—lean on this quick and basic recipe for an everyday, all-around hitter that you can throw together at the last minute before a meal. Think of this version as the black baseball cap of sauces, the one that goes with everything, from eggs to salad to grilled meats. My mom has never served a meal without nước chấm—not even takeout from Burger King.

While it's very common for people to use fresh lime juice instead of vinegar in this recipe, vinegar is a more reliable pantry ingredient and can come in handy. Sometimes you can't get fresh lime, or maybe all the ones at the store suck for some reason. The Thai bird's eye chile adds a nice, subtle blossom of heat, but if you need to make it really mild for kids or the spice-averse, you can deseed the pepper or omit it entirely.

1 teaspoon minced garlic

1 teaspoon minced Thai bird's eye chile

2 tablespoons distilled white vinegar

2 tablespoons granulated sugar

¼ cup fish sauce

¼ cup lukewarm filtered water

In a small mixing bowl, combine the garlic and chile. Add the distilled vinegar to the bowl and allow the mixture to macerate for about 30 seconds—long enough that the vegetables "cook" in the vinegar. Add the sugar, fish sauce, and water and stir until the sugar dissolves.

Serve immediately or store the fish sauce in an airtight container in the fridge for up to 3 days.

FISHLESS DIPPING SAUCE

Makes 1 cup

Nước mắm has always been a staple in our household, as natural as the San Francisco fog. It's the workhorse of the Vietnamese pantry, but sometimes—gasp!—you run out. This is especially true for folks who don't have the luxury of living in places where fish sauce is easy to access. In the rare case when even my family's well of fish sauce ran dry, our good friend Maggi would tag in for the recipe. Made from fermented wheat and lighter than fish sauce in flavor, Maggi seasoning sauce, like bread and puff pastry, is one of those European imports that stuck around Vietnam after the colonial days. As a bonus, this recipe is totally vegan. Serve it with anything you'd use nước chấm for, such as Gỏi Bắp Chuối | Banana Flower Salad (page 158) or Bún Chả Giò Khoai Môn | Taro Spring Roll and Rice Noodle Salad (page 165), which can both be veganized easily.

1 teaspoon minced garlic

1 tablespoon minced shallot

1 lemon, suprêmed (see Note on page 43)

2 teaspoons sambal oelek (see page 22)

½ cup cold filtered water

½ cup Maggi seasoning sauce

2 tablespoons granulated sugar

In a small bowl, combine the garlic, shallot, and lemon suprêmes and let sit for a few minutes to macerate. The lemon juice will soften the vegetables a bit and mellow out their flavor. Add the sambal oelek and mix thoroughly to separate the chunky chile bits in the sauce. Stir in the water, Maggi seasoning, and sugar and mix until the sugar dissolves.

Serve immediately or store the dipping sauce in an airtight container in the fridge for up to 3 days.

NƯỚC MẮM DỪA
COCONUT FISH SAUCE

Makes 1 cup

Now we're getting fancy! This version of dipping sauce can be as complicated as you want it to be. Does the spirit move you to crack open a whole coconut (page 49) to make this? Go for it, homie. Just feel like using a carton of coconut water and reclaiming your time? Hell yeah—in that case, you can swap in defrosted frozen coconut meat, which is usually stocked at Asian grocers. You'll find the maximum-effort version of this sauce at a lot of the seafood restaurants in Phú Quốc, especially with blanched squid and salad-ish dishes like Gỏi Cá Trích | Herring Salad (page 60).

Note: If you're using whole coconut in this recipe, reserve the juice in one medium bowl and scrape out the meat into another medium bowl. You'll probably end up with more than the half cup of meat needed for this recipe, but you can freeze the extra and use it in something else—Bún Nhâm Hà Tiên | Coconut and Fish Sauce Rice Noodle Salad (page 65), perhaps?

½ cup minced coconut meat (see Note)

2 tablespoons minced shallot

2 teaspoons minced garlic

½ cup lemon juice or lime juice

1 Thai bird's eye chile, minced

3 tablespoons palm sugar

½ cup fish sauce

½ cup coconut water, from a carton or a young coconut

Place the coconut meat, shallot, and garlic in a small bowl, then pour the lemon juice over the mixture and allow it to macerate for 30 seconds. Add the chile to the bowl, then mix thoroughly. Add the palm sugar, fish sauce, and coconut water to the bowl, then mix until the sugar dissolves.

Serve immediately or store in an airtight container in the fridge for up to 3 days.

NƯỚC MẮM GỪNG
GINGER FISH SAUCE

Makes 1 cup

Nước Mắm Gừng is all about zippy ginger flavor, making it perfect for meat dishes like Bánh Hỏi Heo Quay | Woven Noodles with Crispy Pork Belly (page 217) and Cơm Gà Hải Nam | Hainanese Chicken and Rice (page 74). With so much minced ginger in the mix, this sauce should end up pretty chunky.

2 tablespoons minced ginger

1 teaspoon minced garlic

1 Thai bird's eye chile, minced

¼ cup lemon juice

2 tablespoons granulated sugar

2 tablespoons lukewarm filtered water

½ cup fish sauce

Add the ginger, garlic, and chile to a wooden mortar, then use the pestle to stir the mixture vigorously in a circular motion, scraping against the sides of the mortar to crush the ingredients. This will help release the oils. Add the lemon juice and allow the mixture to macerate for about 30 seconds.

Using a rubber spatula, scrape the mixture out of the mortar and into a small mixing bowl. Add the sugar, water, and fish sauce to the bowl, and mix the sauce until the sugar dissolves.

Serve immediately or store in an airtight container in the fridge for up to 3 days.

PINEAPPLE FISH SAUCE

Makes 1 cup

In this version of nước chấm, pineapple is the main character. The combination of coconut water and pineapple gives this sauce a refreshing tropical flavor, like a piña colada that also happens to taste like anchovies. It was on the table during the last meal I had with my maternal grandfather, my ông ngoại, before he died. I remember sitting at the table with him, watching his normally sharp features soften with pleasure as we dipped slices of poached herring into the sauce, the minced pineapple clinging to the pieces.

This sauce is great for adding brightness and dimension to "raw" dishes, including the ceviche-like Huyết Cá Tái Chanh | Tuna Bloodline Tartare (page 135) and Vietnamese beef carpaccio. For this recipe, you can substitute canned crushed pineapple in place of fresh pineapple—doing so will make the sauce more caramelly and "cooked." And as with the recipe for Nước Mắm Dừa | Coconut Fish Sauce (page 41), you have the option to use a whole young coconut along with its meat. Try it if you're feeling ambitious and want to make the ultimate luxury, head-to-toe Gucci version of the recipe.

½ cup minced coconut meat
2 tablespoons minced shallot
2 teaspoons minced garlic
½ cup lemon juice or lime juice
1 Thai bird's eye chile, minced
3 tablespoons palm sugar
½ cup fish sauce
1 cup minced fresh pineapple or canned crushed pineapple
½ cup coconut water

Add the coconut meat, shallot, and garlic to a small mixing bowl, then pour the lemon juice over the mixture and allow it to macerate for at least 30 seconds, so the aromatics "cook" in the acid. Add the chile to the bowl, then mix thoroughly. Add the sugar, fish sauce, pineapple, and coconut water to the bowl, then mix until the sugar dissolves.

Serve immediately or store in an airtight container in the fridge for up to 3 days.

TAMARIND FISH SAUCE

Makes 1 cup

Earthy and sour, this dipping sauce gets its character from tamarind paste. The tamarind's natural tartness offers a mouthwatering flavor enhancer and is ideal for romancing all the sour lovers out there. This is excellent as a dipping sauce for seafood, and is honestly fire with gamey meat dishes like Vịt Nướng | Roasted Hoisin-Glazed Duck (page 212).

Unlike the other fish sauces in this chapter, this recipe involves a little bit of active stovetop cooking, but it's not too difficult to pull off. You'll notice that even a short simmer gives the sauce a more mature, "cooked" taste.

1 teaspoon neutral oil (such as vegetable oil)
2 tablespoons minced shallot
2 teaspoons minced garlic
1 Thai bird's eye chile, minced
3 tablespoons palm sugar
½ cup fish sauce
¼ cup Dán Me	Tamarind Paste (page 35)
½ cup filtered water

Set a small saucepan over medium heat for 3 to 5 minutes, just until it gets a little toasty. Once it's warm, add the neutral oil and swirl the pot. When the oil is shimmering, add the shallot and garlic to the pot and stir immediately. Cook for 2 to 3 minutes, until the mixture softens and begins to get translucent. Add the chile and palm sugar to the pot and mix thoroughly to distribute.

Add the fish sauce, tamarind paste, and water to the pot. Increase the heat to medium-high and bring the sauce to a simmer. Stir continuously until the sugar dissolves, then take the pot off the heat and allow the mixture to cool to room temperature.

Serve immediately or store in an airtight container in the fridge for up to 10 days.

NƯỚC MẮM TỎI ỚT
CHILE FISH SAUCE

Makes 1½ cups

When I was growing up, this recipe was the epitome of fancy home cooking. It's not because it uses upscale ingredients—most of the components are pantry staples. It's the technique that makes it.

In culinary school, I learned how to suprême citrus (see Note), and the technique immediately felt familiar. It was something my mom had always done when making this sauce, though she never used a French name for it. The resulting pulpy wedges give this sauce extra heft, making it what I can only describe as delectable.

To me, one of life's great pleasures is dipping Gỏi Cuốn Cá Ngừ | Tuna Summer Rolls (page 152) into this fish sauce and watching the little bits of lemon pulp, minced shallot, garlic, and chile cling to the rice paper like barnacles on a ship. In my family, that little sensation is what we look forward to the most.

You can either bust up a fresh chile pepper and some minced garlic for this recipe or toss in 2 teaspoons of sambal oelek (see page 22) and skip the mortar and pestle . . . your choice.

Note: To suprême citrus, use a sharp paring knife to cut away the rind and pith, then cut the pulp segments out of the membrane. (Toss the juicy leftover membrane into a glass of sparkling water for a refreshing drink.)

1 tablespoon minced garlic
1 Thai bird's eye chile, minced
1 tablespoon minced shallot
1 lemon, suprêmed, membrane reserved (see Note)
1 can Coco Rico (see page 24)
½ cup fish sauce
2 tablespoons granulated sugar

Add the garlic and chile to a wooden mortar, then use the pestle to stir the mixture vigorously in a circular motion, scraping against the sides of the mortar to crush the ingredients. This will help release the oils.

Add the shallot to the mixture. Squeeze the membrane of the lemon over the bowl and allow the mixture to macerate for 30 seconds.

Using a rubber spatula, scrape the mixture into a small mixing bowl. Add the Coco Rico, lemon suprêmes, fish sauce, and sugar. Mix the sauce until the sugar dissolves.

Serve immediately or store in an airtight container in the fridge for up to 3 days.

MUỐI ỚT
CHILE SALT

Makes 3 tablespoons

In the night markets of Phú Quốc, you'll often see vendors selling cups full of cut fruit dusted with muối ớt. Salt and chile open up your tastebuds, enhancing the sourness of fruits like green mango, pineapple, and the local specialty: cà na. In the United States, you've probably already had something sort of like this in the form of Tajín. This chile salt can also be used as a spice rubs for proteins, such as fried sand dabs (page 99). Plus, this recipe makes just enough to marinate a whole chicken.

3 tablespoons kosher salt
1 Thai bird's eye chile

Add the salt and chile to a wooden mortar, then use the pestle to smash them together. Don't be gentle—you want to force out all the spicy chile juice and oils so they can mix it with the salt. Keep pounding the chile until the pieces are nearly disintegrated.

Serve immediately or store in your pantry in an airtight container for up to 1 month.

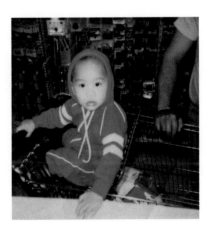

MUỐI TIÊU CHANH
SALT, PEPPER, AND LIME DIPPING SAUCE

Makes 2 tablespoons

This is the cousin to muối ớt: It hits similar parts of the tongue, but it uses lime juice and black pepper instead of Thai bird's eye chile. You'll often see it served in small sauce dishes alongside fried quail or steamed crab (page 208). It's also a common element in one of the most popular genres of Vietnamese cooking: nhậu, or drinking snacks, because that lick of spice really makes you crave a cold one after each bite. This single-size recipe makes enough for one small dipping vessel.

To make the sauce, you'll start with a spice blend of freshly toasted black peppercorns and two kinds of salt. You can make this blend in larger amounts and store it in your pantry for handy use. To turn it into a sauce, you add lime juice—do so right before serving. (At restaurants in Vietnam, they'll usually just give you the house spice blend along with lime slices so you can mix it right at your table.) And one small warning: When making the spice blend, especially if you're using the optional bird's eye chile, it can start to feel like you've maced your whole kitchen. Keep your windows open.

SPICE BLEND

3 tablespoons kosher salt

2 teaspoons flaky sea salt or coarse sea salt

1 tablespoon cracked black pepper

1 teaspoon MSG

⅛ teaspoon Thai bird's eye chile powder (optional)

Juice of 1 lime

To make the spice blend: Line a large baking sheet with parchment paper.

Set a large wok or frying pan over medium heat. When warm, add the kosher and flaky sea salts and pan-roast them, shaking the wok frequently to ensure even roasting, for 15 to 20 minutes. (This roasting technique, called rang muối, removes all moisture from the salt, thereby amplifying any spices introduced to the mixture. Don't skip this step!)

Add the black pepper to the salts, and toss the mixture to shuffle it in. Toast the mixture for 10 minutes more to allow the pepper to cook, then add the MSG and chile powder (if using) to the pan. Toss the mixture to evenly distribute the new additions and toast it for 5 minutes more. When 5 minutes are up, pour the spice blend onto the prepared baking sheet and let cool to room temperature.

Use immediately or store the spice blend in an airtight container in a cool, dry place for up to 3 months (or, honestly, up to a few years if you toss in a silica gel packet).

To turn the spice blend into sauce: In a small bowl, combine 1 tablespoon of the dry spice blend and the lime juice. Stir until the salt dissolves and serve.

MỞ HÀNH
GREEN ONION SAUCE

Makes 1 cup

Mỡ hành is a traditional staple condiment in Vietnamese cuisine, used as a garnish for rice, noodles, meats, and vegetables. In Phú Quốc, it manifests as the shimmering, emerald-colored sauce that's spooned over smoky grilled seafood, cutting through the briny flavors with the subtle sweetness of grilled green onions. At Vietnamese American barbecues, you'll see mỡ hành on grilled corn and pork chops: something about the savory oil works beautifully with the sweet-bitter flavors you get with any food that's been charred on a grill. If you like charred spring onions with your carne asada tacos, this sauce is the same flavor profile at work.

¼ cup neutral oil (such as vegetable oil)

2 cups chopped green onions, white and green parts

⅛ teaspoon MSG

Warm the neutral oil in a small pot over low heat. Once the oil starts to shimmer, add the green onions. Let the green onions sweat in the oil for 15 seconds, then immediately remove the pot from the heat. You only want the onions to wilt. Stir in the MSG, then set the pot aside and allow it to cool to room temperature.

Serve immediately or store the sauce in an airtight container in the fridge for up to 5 days.

MỞ HÀNH GỪNG
GINGER AND GREEN ONION SAUCE

Makes 1 cup

In this nontraditional version of mỡ hành, I've spiked the usual concoction with ginger and lemongrass, two zippy ingredients that add even more umami to the sauce. If you have a Microplane grater, use it to mince the ginger and garlic—the superfine pieces are ideal for making a more delicate sauce.

¼ cup neutral oil (such as vegetable oil)

2 tablespoons minced ginger

1 tablespoon minced garlic

2 cups thinly sliced green onion, white and green parts

1 teaspoon minced lemongrass

1 teaspoon fish sauce

½ teaspoon rice vinegar

¼ teaspoon kosher salt

¼ teaspoon granulated sugar

Set a medium saucepan on the stove over medium-high heat for 1 to 2 minutes. Once it's warm, pour in the neutral oil. When the oil starts to shimmer, add the ginger and garlic, and let those aromatics sweat for 15 seconds. Then, add the green onions and lemongrass. Let all of that sweat for another 15 seconds, then turn the heat down to medium.

Add the fish sauce, rice vinegar, salt, and sugar to the pot. Cook the mixture for 1 minute, then take the pot off the heat, set it aside, and allow it to cool to room temperature.

Serve immediately or store the sauce in an airtight container in the fridge for up to 5 days.

CỦ CẢI CHUA NGỌT
PICKLED CARROTS AND DAIKON

Makes 2 cups

I always keep my fridge stocked with these workhorse pickles, which are great for homemade bánh mì and rice noodle salads. They pair especially well with Sườn Chiên | Caramelized Pan-Fried Pork Chops (page 139).

¼ teaspoon kosher salt
½ teaspoon granulated sugar
1 cup rice vinegar
2 cups filtered water
2 garlic cloves, peeled
1 small sliver ginger
½ jalapeño, sliced
½ red onion, thinly sliced
1 carrot, peeled and cut into matchsticks
One 3-inch piece daikon, peeled and cut into matchsticks (about 4 ounces)

In a medium pot set over medium-low heat, combine the salt, sugar, rice vinegar, water, garlic, ginger, jalapeño, and red onion. Bring the mixture to a simmer and stir to dissolve the salt and sugar. Once dissolved, remove the pot from the heat.

Add the carrot and daikon matchsticks and submerge them in the liquid, using a small plate to weigh them down so they don't bob out of the liquid. Transfer to the fridge and steep them for at least 1 hour before using, but preferably at least a day. They'll get even more sour with time.

You can store the pickles with their pickling liquid in an airtight jar for . . . let's say a few weeks, though I've definitely enjoyed them at the 4-month mark. No shame!

NƯỚC CỐT DỪA TƯƠI
FRESH COCONUT MILK

Makes 3 cups

One of my earliest childhood memories is making fresh coconut milk with my mom. Being the hefty, plump elementary schooler that I was, my mom would have me sit on her coconut shredder bench to keep it steady while she scraped the coconut flesh out. Fresh coconut milk is one of my favorite flavors: It's rich, sweet, and savory, and there really is nothing else like it. But making it is a pain in the butt, in more ways than one. To make this, you'll need a Phillips-head screwdriver, a hammer, a coconut scraper (see page 32), and a nut milk bag or fine cheesecloth.

2 cups filtered water
2 old coconuts (see pages 65 and 67)

Add the water to a small pot and set over high heat. Bring it to a boil while you embark on this coconut journey.

Start by stabbing through the eyes of the coconut using a Phillips-head screwdriver. The "eyes" are located in a similar position on the coconut to the finger holes on a bowling ball. Your puncture holes should reach into the hollow interior of the fruit.

Drain the liquid out of the holes and through a fine-mesh sieve. Save it to drink later, as a little treat for all your hard work. Store that in the fridge for now—it's time to prepare for coconut demolition.

Wet a dishtowel or rag and form it into a small coil on your cutting board. Place the coconut in the center of the rag. This should keep it from rolling around too much. Hold the coconut in place firmly with one hand. With the other hand, use the hammer to confidently strike the coconut 3 or 4 times until it cracks in half. It goes without saying, but be extremely careful to not to hammer your own hand.

Once the coconut is open, rinse out the inside. Using your coconut scraper tool of choice, remove the flesh and collect it in a medium bowl.

By now, the water should be boiling. Lower the heat, bringing the water to a consistent simmer. If the coconut-opening process took longer than you thought, and you accidentally let all the water boil off, replenish it.

Repeat the stabbing, draining, and scraping process with the other coconut. Once both coconuts are scraped clean of flesh, put the hulls aside for some other arts and crafts project. Transfer the grated flesh into a blender.

Crank up the heat on the pot of water to get it to boil again. Once it reaches a rolling boil, turn it off. Blend the coconut flesh on low speed, then add the boiling water to the blender ¼ cup at a time. Blend for 10 seconds between each addition. When all of the water is integrated, turn the blender on high for 5 seconds to pulverize the mixture.

Pull out your nut milk bag and two medium bowls. Strain the coconut mixture through the nut milk bag into one of the bowls. Squeeze the pulp firmly with your hands to drain out all of the milk until it slows to a thin trickle. Congratulations, this batch is your first-press coconut milk—the good stuff!

You guessed it—next is the second press. Hold the bag over the second (empty) bowl. Twist the bag, using more force this time, to extract as much liquid as possible. This second-press batch is thinner, with less fat in it, but it's still way better than the canned stuff.

Save the coconut pulp to use as garnish for a salad, to mix into oatmeal and granola, or to eat with dessert. Reserve the first-press milk for use in its raw form for salads, like Bún Kèn | Curry Coconut Noodles (page 67). The second-press milk is best used in cooked dishes, like curry. Both types of milk can be stored in airtight containers in the fridge for up to 5 days.

CỦ HẸ CHIÊN
FRIED SHALLOTS

Makes ¾ cup

Sweet and intense, shallots are the aromatic of choice in multiple Southeast Asian cuisines: They form the base of Thai curry pastes; they pair really well with pickled cucumbers and grilled chicken; and, when fried, they become the ultimate multi-purpose condiment. If you have the luxury of time and space to do so, making freshly fried shallots is so worth the effort. (But if you don't, never feel bad about using the stuff from the jar!)

| 2 cups filtered water |
| 1 teaspoon kosher salt |
| 8 ounces shallots, peeled and thinly sliced |
| 2 tablespoons rice flour |
| Neutral oil (such as vegetable oil) for frying |

To take the astringent bite off of the shallots, you'll need to soak them. In a small bowl, combine the water and salt and stir until dissolved. Steep the sliced shallots in this brine mixture for 10 minutes. Drain the shallots in a colander, then spread them out on a paper towel–lined plate to drain excess moisture.

In a small mixing bowl, dredge the shallots with the rice flour. The rice flour acts as a buffer to keep the shallots, which have a lot of natural sugar in them, from burning instead of frying.

Line another plate with paper towels. Fill a medium pot with 3 inches of neutral oil and bring it up to 325°F over medium-high heat. Gradually add the shallots to the oil, but make sure to avoid crowding the pot—give them plenty of space to swim. Fry the shallots for 5 to 7 minutes, or until they become golden brown. As the shallots finish cooking, transfer them to the paper towel–lined plate to drain extra oil. Let them rest for at least 10 minutes.

Serve immediately or store the fried shallots in an airtight container in a cool, dry spot in the kitchen for up to a week. If they get soggy or lose their crisp, put them in the oven at 200°F and toast them for an hour.

NƯỚC LUỘC CÁ
FISH STOCK

Makes 4 quarts

Fish stock, rich with collagen from fish heads and bones, is the secret to incredible seafood soups and stews. Whether as a foundation for sauces or a simmering liquid, this stock imparts a distinct marine sweetness and essence that you really can't fake. Ask your local fishmonger for the bones and scraps of mild, lean white-fleshed fish, like halibut, sea bass, cod, and flounder. Alternatively, collect a stash of scraps in your freezer as you cook at home. For the most efficient use, freeze the stock in small portions. That way, you can just thaw out what you need for a recipe.

| 2 to 3 pounds white fish bones and heads |
| 4 quarts cold filtered water |
| 4 cups ice cubes |
| 2 large onions, cut into 1-inch chunks |
| 4 garlic cloves, smashed with peels |
| One ½-inch knob fresh ginger, peeled and sliced into coins |
| 1 bunch green onions, white parts only |

1 lemongrass stalk, bruised (see page 29)

3 Makrut lime leaves

About 10 whole black peppercorns

2 tablespoons fish sauce

2 tablespoons kosher salt

1 tablespoon granulated sugar

1 teaspoon MSG

Start by placing the fish bones and heads in a large bowl and rinsing them under cold running water to wash off all the blood and gunk. When the water in the bowl looks mostly clear, drain it.

Fill a large stock pot with the cold filtered water, then toss in the ice, fish scraps, onions, garlic, ginger, green onions, lemongrass, Makrut lime leaves, and peppercorns. Set the pot on the stove on low heat.

Stir in the fish sauce, salt, sugar, and MSG. Let the pot slowly come up to a bare simmer, with just a few bubbles, which should take about an hour. (You definitely don't want a roaring boil; if it boils, the stock will taste super fishy.) On low heat, bringing the stock to a simmer should take about an hour. Once simmering, remove the stock from the heat.

Strain the stock through a fine-mesh sieve into a gallon-size container (you can use another pot). Discard the solids. Use immediately or let the stock cool completely, then transfer to an airtight container or containers. The stock will keep in the fridge for up to 3 days or in the freezer for up to 2 months.

NƯỚC LUỘC GÀ
CHICKEN STOCK

Makes 4 quarts

In my opinion, the most important parts of the chicken are its bones. Whenever I cook something that uses a whole chicken, whether it's poached with rice (page 74), confited (page 194), or barbecued (page 210), I stash the bones in a bag in the freezer so that I can make stock. This is one of the basic techniques you can employ in order to maintain a low-waste kitchen. Plus, you'll get bonus thrifty points for squeezing as much value as you can out of your groceries. Over the years, I've discovered that this recipe serves as a great foundation for incorporating random scraps from the fridge, like mushrooms, dried-out parsnips, and fennel greens.

2 to 3 pounds chicken bones

4 quarts cold filtered water

4 garlic cloves, smashed with peels

One ½-inch knob fresh ginger, peeled and sliced into coins

1 lemongrass stalk, bruised (see page 29)

3 Makrut lime leaves

About 10 whole black peppercorns

4 carrots, cut into 1-inch chunks

4 celery stalks, cut into 1-inch chunks

2 large onions, cut into 1-inch chunks

2 tablespoons fish sauce

2 tablespoons kosher salt

1 teaspoon MSG

1 tablespoon granulated sugar

Preheat the oven to 400°F and line a baking sheet with foil. Spread the chicken bones evenly on the baking sheet. Roast for 30 minutes, or until they start to brown and they'll fill the kitchen with a mouthwatering scent. Set the bones aside.

Fill a large stock pot with the cold filtered water and add in the garlic, ginger, lemongrass, and Makrut lime leaves. Drop in the chicken bones and peppercorns, and then bring the pot to a simmer over medium-high heat. When the broth starts to simmer, add in the carrots, celery, and onions and let the pot come back up to a simmer.

Turn the heat to medium and simmer the stock for an hour. As that happens, use a spider strainer or large spoon to skim off any foamy scum that rises to the surface of the liquid. After an hour, the stock should be a nice, light brown color. (Or a more golden color, if the bones aren't roasted.) Strain the broth through a fine-mesh sieve into a gallon-size container. Now you can discard the solids.

Wipe out the pot to make sure there are no solids left in it. Pour the strained stock back into the pot and season it with the fish sauce, MSG, salt, and sugar. Taste the stock and add more of the seasonings as needed. To help meld the flavors together, return the pot to the stove and bring the broth back up to a simmer over medium-high heat. Turn off the flame and use immediately or let the stock hang out for at least 2 hours at room temperature to cool off. Once cooled, transfer to an airtight container or containers. The stock will keep in the fridge for 5 days or in the freezer for up to 3 months.

WE ARE FROM
PHÚ QUỐC ISLAND

My family's story begins in Phú Quốc Island. Its waters are thick with sea turtles, dolphins, and, of course, anchovies, the backbone of the island's famous fish sauce industry. Phú Quốc includes one huge, 222-square-mile island and twenty-one much smaller ones sprinkled around the Gulf of Thailand. Seventy percent of the main island, where my family is from, is covered in forested mountains, with most people living on the coasts and working as fishermen. When you fly in, you can't help but stare at the white- and peppermint-painted houses and the long docks that jut out into the sea. From up on high, the fishing boats attached to the docks look like the teeth of a serrated knife.

It's easy to romanticize the place and to focus in on the warmth of the sea as it rushes around your ankles, the faint tap-tap-tap of fishing boat motors stirring to life just before sunrise, and the tang of vinegar-washed herring and coconut meat on your tongue. From a young age, I was enamored with the island's beauty, but what really got me was how it brought me closer to understanding the people I loved.

In Phú Quốc, everything begins and ends with the sea. "We don't feel right if we can't see the ocean at least once a week," my dad would tell me. I might have thought that was a weird over-exaggeration when I first heard him say it, but the reality of the statement became clear when I was ten years old and my parents started bringing me and my sister to the island to visit our relatives. Everyone there has a relationship to the ocean, whether they're running tour boats for snorkelers, heading out at dusk to fish for squid, or cooking lemongrass-stuffed whelks over coals at the night markets. I got to hear so many stories from my aunts and uncles about my normally not-so-talkative dad, who I didn't know had a reputation among local sailors as the guy who always dove into stormy waters to save people from sinking ships, just like my grandfathers before him. In bed, still fussy from jetlag, my sister and I would often wake up to the sound of our uncles getting ready to go fishing before sunrise.

The minute they were old enough to get away with working on fishing boats, my dad and his brothers put in the back-breaking work to support their family by joining bigger crews or selling their own catches at the market. My dad's older sister took what they caught and helped support the family with her talent in the kitchen, developing a recipe for Bánh Canh Chả Cá | Fish Cake and Tapioca Noodle Soup (page 69) that she could sell from a stall right outside their house. As soon as she was old enough to handle a pestle, their younger sister started pitching in to make the fish cakes for the soup, pounding minced mackerel by hand until it was silky smooth. They did this for decades, until their bodies broke down and they literally couldn't cook anymore. But before that happened, I remember studying their movements as a child, hypnotized by their mastery of their craft.

As you'll see in this chapter, so many of Phú Quốc's greatest culinary contributions were born from the sea. Fish sauce, nước mắm, is one of the island's treasures—so of course, we have many ways of preparing it, including as a dipping sauce thick with coconut meat (page 41) and a flavor base for brothy bowls of Bún Nhâm Hà Tiên | Coconut and Fish Sauce Rice Noodle Salad (page 65). There are also a handful of dishes that have become famous in their own right, including Gỏi Cá Trích (page 60), an unforgettable, ceviche-like herring-and-coconut salad, and Bún Kèn (page 67), a dish of rice noodles swimming in fresh coconut milk and curry. The flavors and recipes in this chapter all stem from my memories of Phú Quốc: walks through the night markets, beachside grill-outs, and hectic and fun meals with family members I rarely got to see. I hope they give you a real sense of this island and its people, who continue to inspire my reverence for the ocean.

WHERE TO EAT ON PHÚ QUỐC ISLAND

Bún Kèn Út Lượm
42 Đ. 30 Tháng 4, TT. Dương Đông,
Phú Quốc, Kiên Giang, Vietnam

This iconic soup spot has been serving the definitive version of Bún Kèn | Curry Coconut Noodles (page 67) since 1980. The rich coconut-curry broth is a stunner, and you're definitely gonna want to slurp it all up after you finish the rice noodles.

Dương Đông Night Market
128 Đường Bạch Đằng, TT. Dương Đông,
Phú Quốc, Kiên Giang, Vietnam

Yeah, it's a little touristy, but the night market is absolutely worth checking out. You'll find local goods like green peppercorns and dried fish for sale, and you can fill up on barbecued local seafood at any one of the many hawker stalls.

Bánh Canh Phung 7 Chả Cá
27 Đường Bạch Đằng, TT. Dương Đông,
Phú Quốc, Kiên Giang, Vietnam

My mom would always take me to this spot for her favorite version of Bánh Canh Chả Cá | Fish Cake and Tapioca Noodle Soup (page 69). Here, it's served with silky cubes of pig's blood and chewy strips of Chinese-style fried dough.

GỎI CÁ TRÍCH
HERRING SALAD

Serves 4

In Vietnam, Phú Quốc Island is synonymous with premium fish sauce, but there's another thing it's famous for: Gỏi Cá Trích, a remarkable, mouthwatering salad of brined herring mixed with coconut meat, palm sugar, and toasted peanuts. Oh, and there's fish sauce in it, of course. The most well-known restaurants that serve this dish in Phú Quốc are perched right on the docks, "floating" on the ocean, so you know that the herring are as fresh as they come.

The semi-raw fish salad is full of intense, punchy flavors, which makes it well-suited to eat in a summer roll. You'll often see it served with baskets filled with herbs, rice noodles, and rice paper so you can make your own. And it's this dish—the moistness of the oily brined herring, the uneven crunch of peanuts and coconut in each bite—that Phú Quốc natives crave the most in diaspora. For people like my parents, it's the equivalent of pure comfort food.

To select fresh herring, use your senses. Smell the fish—it should smell like the ocean. Feel the skin to check for presence of slime, a good sign of freshness. Look for bright red gills—dark red gills are a sign of decomposition. The eyes should be clear, full, and bulging, with black pupils. If they're dry, sunken, and cloudy, the fish has already begun to rot. The best herring have thick bodies and light pink bellies.

Note: If there are no directions for cooking the rice vermicelli, because sometimes prepackaged noodles can be wack like that, follow my technique. First, soak the noodles in cold water for 15 minutes. While the noodles soak, get a large pot of water boiling over high heat. When the water and noodles are ready to go, cook the noodles for 5 to 8 minutes. Like pasta, check the noodles as they progress and stop when you get to that bouncy, tender tex-ture. Drain the noodles in a colander in the sink, then rinse with cold water to stop their cooking and to remove excess starch. Set the colander of noodles over a large bowl and cover the noodles with a damp cloth to prevent them from drying out.

---

4 ounces dried rice vermicelli

---

3 tablespoons fish sauce

2 tablespoons palm sugar

Cook the rice vermicelli according to the package directions (see Note). Set aside.

Make a fish sauce mixture for the herring. In a small pot over medium heat, combine the fish sauce and palm sugar and bring to a simmer, stirring to distribute the sugar. Once the sugar dissolves, remove the pot from the heat and set aside to cool.

Now, brine the herring. Line a baking sheet with paper towels. In a large bowl, combine the ice cubes, water, and salt. Stir until the salt dissolves, then submerge the herring fillets in the brine solution for 5 minutes. If needed, use a plate to keep the herring below the surface of the brine. When 5 minutes are up, lay the fillets out on the prepared baking sheet to drain excess moisture.

BRINED HERRING

1 cup ice cubes

4 cups cold filtered water

2 tablespoons kosher salt

5 whole medium herring (about 1½ pounds total), filleted (see page 88)

1 yellow onion, sliced

5 Makrut lime leaves

½ cup grated fresh coconut (see page 49) or frozen and defrosted coconut meat

¼ cup toasted and chopped peanuts

1 butter lettuce head, leaves separated

1 bunch cilantro, thick stems removed

1 bunch mint, leaves picked

1 English cucumber, cut into 3-inch spears

Nước Mắm Dừa | Coconut Fish Sauce (page 41) for serving

One 12-ounce package rice paper wrappers (see page 23)

Next, assemble the salad. In a large bowl, combine the brined herring fillets, the cooled fish sauce mixture, and the onion. Bruise the lime leaves by slapping them in your palm to release the oils in the leaves and make them more aromatic. Sprinkle the leaves on top and stir gently with a spoon to evenly distribute the ingredients.

When you're about ready to eat, using a slotted spoon, transfer the herring salad to a large salad bowl or serving dish. You'll want to leave excess juices behind to prevent sogginess—adios! Garnish the salad with the grated coconut meat and peanuts.

For the ideal gỏi cá trích eating situation, arrange the rice vermicelli, lettuce, cilantro, mint, and cucumber on a central serving platter alongside the bowl of herring salad. Prepare a shallow rimmed dish with cold water for dipping the rice paper wrappers, and divide the Coconut Fish Sauce among four dipping bowls. Using the rice paper wrappers, let your dinner pals build their rolls as they like. (See page 77 for more instructions on how to get rolling.)

GỎI XOÀI XANH KHÔ MỰC
GREEN MANGO AND DRIED SQUID SALAD

Serves 4

Around January of each year, crates of green mangos start popping up at South and Southeast Asian markets. The crunchy unripe fruit is a sucker punch of sourness that tastes best when paired with a pop of salt. People dip wedges of it in spicy Muối Ớt | Chile Salt (page 43), but I like it best with mouth-watering strips of dried squid. At Phú Quốc's night markets, dried squid is displayed in massive stacks that look almost like piles of flip-flops. They're a popular drinking snack on their own, but I do think they really shine in more composed dishes like this salad. For this recipe, pick out the hardest, most unripe green mango you can find. A specialty mango shredder (otherwise known as a julienne peeler, the kind with a rippled blade) is also essential here.

---

4 cups cold filtered water

½ teaspoon kosher salt

2 green mangos

4 ounces dried squid, shredded into bite-size pieces

¼ cup toasted peanuts, coarsely chopped

1 bunch rau răm, leaves picked

1 bunch mint, leaves picked

½ cup Nước Mắm Tỏi Ớt | Chile Fish Sauce (page 43)

Eating too much straight-up green mango is a surefire way to upset your stomach, but a quick brine is a solid preventative measure to mellow it out.

To make a brine for the mango, combine the water and salt in a large bowl. Peel the green mangos and use the specialty shredder to cut the flesh into strips. Do this directly over the bowl so that the strips fall right into the brine. (Work smarter, not harder!) Allow the green mango to soak in the brine for 30 minutes, then drain it in a colander. Squeeze the mango flesh to remove any residual liquid.

Now, assemble the salad. Return the mango to the large mixing bowl and add in the squid, along with most of the peanuts, rau răm, and mint. Pour in the Chile Fish Sauce and mix the ingredients thoroughly to dress the salad. Garnish with the remaining peanuts, rau răm, and mint and serve immediately.

CON SÒ ƯỚP CHAO
GRILLED SCALLOP WITH FERMENTED TOFU

Serves 5

In 2001, I went on my second trip to Vietnam. I was seventeen—practically an adult!—and this time, I wasn't tethered to my parents. One night, my cousins woke me up a few hours past midnight to go to the beach. According to my cousins, this was the perfect time for hunting crustaceans, and we carried only a lighter and jar of spicy fermented bean curd. While one cousin built a small fire pit on the beach, the rest of us foraged. We smeared wild mollusks with fermented tofu and grilled them, savoring the way the nutty caramelized tofu mingled with the smoke. I'll always associate that flavor with that first electrifying taste of independence.

Note: Use fresh scallops for this recipe if possible. Look for dry-packed scallops, which aren't stored with preservatives. You don't have to remove the feet from the scallops, but if you don't want to eat that chewier part right now, you can freeze them to use in a dish, such as the rice porridge on page 94. You'll also need five 9-inch wooden double skewers—or ten 9-inch wooden skewers soaked in water to prevent burning.

2 pounds large U-10 scallops or smaller scallops

3 tablespoons spicy fermented bean curd (I recommend Lao Gan Ma)

2 tablespoons toasted and chopped peanuts for garnish

2 tablespoons sliced green onions, green parts only, for garnish

If using a barbecue grill, preheat it now. If using a broiler, set the tray about 6 inches below the heating element. Five minutes before you're ready to cook the scallops, preheat the broiler.

Rinse the scallops quickly under cold running water to remove any grit, then pat dry with a paper towel. Add a few drops of oil to the scallops and lay them oil-side down on a foil-lined baking sheet. Smear about ½ teaspoon of the fermented bean curd on each one. Skewer them through their sides; you'll want to end up with four scallops on each skewer. (If you're using individual skewers, double up on them for each set.)

If grilling: Brush your grill with oil to prevent your scallops from sticking to it. Grill the skewers for 2 minutes, then flip and grill for 2 minutes more, watching closely to prevent burning.

If broiling: Transfer the baking sheet with the skewered scallops to the preheated broiler and cook for the same length of time, watching closely to prevent burning.

Plate the skewers and garnish with the peanuts and green onions. Reminisce about the beach while serving.

BÚN NHÂM HÀ TIÊN
COCONUT AND FISH SAUCE RICE NOODLE SALAD

Serves 4

Hà Tiên is the closest Vietnamese coastal province to Phú Quốc Island, and it's the origin of one of my favorite dishes, bún nhâm. When I was a kid, I'd savor the immediacy of all the herbs that came right from the garden.

Served cold, bún nhâm's base is a mixture of rice vermicelli with fresh bean sprouts, raw cucumbers, and crunchy shredded cabbage and banana flower. (If you can't source fresh banana flower, look for the jarred or bagged pre-brined version, which you can simply slice into thin pieces.) What gives this dish its unique taste is the spicy-sour dressing of Nước Mắm Tỏi Ớt | Chile Fish Sauce mixed with cold, soothing coconut milk.

---

8 cups cold filtered water

---

4 teaspoons kosher salt

½ cup lemon juice or distilled vinegar

---

1 banana flower

½ green cabbage

¼ cup dried shrimp

One 16-ounce package dried rice vermicelli, cooked (see Note on page 60)

---

1 cucumber, cut into matchsticks

---

1 bunch perilla, leaves picked and roughly torn

---

1 bunch mint, leaves picked and roughly torn

---

4 ounces mung bean sprouts

½ cup Nước Mắm Tỏi Ớt | Chile Fish Sauce (page 43)

½ cup Nước Cốt Dừa Tươi | Fresh Coconut Milk (page 49) or canned coconut milk

---

½ cup grated fresh coconut (page 49) or frozen and defrosted coconut meat for garnish (optional)

Prepare two brines for the banana flower and cabbage. Fill two large bowls with about 4 cups of the water each. Add 1 tablespoon of the salt and the lemon juice to one bowl; add just 1 teaspoon of the salt to the other. Stir both mixtures to dissolve the salt.

Now it's shreddin' time! Start with the banana flower. Peel away and discard any bruised, blemished, or dried petals. If you're using an Asian peeler (see page 32), hold the flower in your non-dominant hand, blossom pointing downward, positioned over a cutting board or bowl. Starting from the top, use the peeler to shave the blossom away from you at an angle, rotating the flower as you go. Eyeball about 4 cups' worth of shaved blossom, then stop. (You can stash the leftover blossom in a bag in the fridge for about a week.) Put the shredded blossom into the bowl of water, salt, and lemon juice and set aside. Let it sit for 15 minutes, then drain it.

Next, shred the cabbage. Peel away and discard any blemished leaves, then use a peeler or knife to shred into thin slices, the same way you sliced the flower. Add the shredded cabbage to the other bowl of water and salt and let sit for 15 minutes, then drain it.

Next, prep the shrimp floss. Put the dried shrimp in a coffee grinder, then pulse until the shrimp is torn into fine threads. You can do this step ahead of time, too. Just keep the shrimp floss in an airtight container in the fridge and use it within a week.

Remove the cabbage and banana blossom from their respective brines and squeeze out any excess brine, like you're squeezing a sponge. Put the wrung-out cabbage and blossom in a colander set over the sink. Once finished, you can discard the brine.

When you're ready to assemble the salad, divide the rice vermicelli among four large salad bowls. Arrange the cabbage, banana blossom, cucumber, perilla, mint, and mung bean sprouts on top of the noodles. Drizzle each bowl with 1 ounce of the Chile Fish Sauce and 1 ounce of the coconut milk. Garnish the bowls with a heaping teaspoon of shrimp floss and the grated coconut meat (if using) and enjoy immediately.

BÚN KÈN
CURRY COCONUT NOODLES

Serves 6

2 tablespoons shrimp floss (see page 65)
3 tablespoons minced lemongrass
4 Makrut lime leaves, minced (optional)
One 2-inch knob fresh ginger, peeled and minced
4 garlic cloves, minced
1 shallot, minced
1 tablespoon minced fresh turmeric
1 teaspoon turmeric powder
1 teaspoon sa tế (see page 22)
1 teaspoon chrouk metae or sambal oelek (see page 22)
2 tablespoons fish sauce
2 tablespoons granulated sugar
1 teaspoon kosher salt
1 teaspoon MSG
1 tablespoon shredded coconut meat
2 pounds halibut fillets, cut into 1-inch squares
1 cup coconut cream
⅛ teaspoon cracked black pepper
1 tablespoon neutral oil (such as vegetable oil)
2 cups Nước Cốt Dừa Tươi | Fresh Coconut Milk (page 49) or canned coconut milk
8 cups coconut water
8 cups Nước Luộc Cá | Fish Stock (page 50)
One 16-ounce package dried rice vermicelli, cooked (see Note on page 60)
3 cups shredded banana flower or red cabbage (see page 65)
½ English cucumber, cut into matchsticks
2 bunches diếp cá (fish wort) leaves or Thai basil
2 bunches mint leaves, leaves picked
8 ounces mung bean sprouts
1 cup toasted and chopped peanuts

Every year in July, the Bay Area's Hội Đồng Hương (Council) of Phú Quốc holds a community gathering at Lake Cunningham Park in San Jose. And at this event, Phú Quốc natives come together and host the most awesome fucking cookout. In the United States, we're a tiny minority within a minority, so to gather everyone up—and to fill the park with islanders and the scents of coconut milk and grilled seafood—is a powerful thing. The most popular dish at the party is one of Phú Quốc's icons: bún kèn.

Bún kèn is a gorgeous ensemble of rice noodles, topped with a ladleful of aromatic coconut fish curry and garnished with fresh herbs like bean sprouts, mint, and cucumber. The island's street vendors, most famously Út Lượm, serve the turmeric-tinted orange curry with ground fish, which takes on the bouncy texture of scrambled egg or tofu. Fresh herbs and a variety of shredded vegetables make each bowl a riot of colors and flavors. All of the ingredients that make up the culinary DNA of Phú Quốc, from fish sauce to coconut to the spices that came through the Silk Road, are in this dish, so it's no wonder that homesick natives pine for it.

First up, make the spice paste. In a large wooden mortar, pound the shrimp floss, lemongrass, lime leaves, if using, ginger, garlic, shallot, turmeric, turmeric powder, sa tế, chrouk metae, 1 tablespoon of the fish sauce, the sugar, salt, MSG, and shredded coconut meat until the mixture is thoroughly melded together. This should take around 5 minutes, or less if you're hella swole.

Then, marinate the halibut. Place about half of the spice paste in a shallow bowl, along with the remaining 1 tablespoon fish sauce. Add the halibut, coconut cream, and black pepper. Use your hands to mix everything together carefully, so as to not shred the fish. Let the mixture marinate for at least 15 minutes, but no longer than 30 minutes.

Now, start on the curry. Set a stock pot over medium heat for 3 minutes, then add in the neutral oil. When the oil starts to shimmer, dump in the rest of the spice paste and sauté for 3 minutes. At this point, the mixture should really start releasing its aromas. Add the coconut milk, coconut water, and fish stock to the pot and bring the curry to a gentle simmer. You should start tasting it for balance now; season the curry with salt, sugar, and fish sauce to taste, erring on the side of more flavorful.

When you're done adjusting the seasoning, return the broth to a higher simmer and add the marinated halibut. Let the fish poach for 15 minutes, then turn the heat to its lowest setting—just enough to keep the soup hot.

To serve, divide the rice vermicelli among six large soup bowls. Use a ladle to eyeball about ½ cup of curry into each bowl, taking care to pour it all over the noodles. Arrange the shredded banana flower, cucumber, diếp cá, mint leaves, and mung bean sprouts in each bowl, then sprinkle them with the peanuts. Serve immediately.

FISH CAKE AND TAPIOCA NOODLE SOUP

Serves 6

Bánh Canh Chả Cá is a special recipe on my dad's side of the family. My dad's older sister, who we called Cô Hai (Auntie Two), supported the family through her mastery of this dish, selling it to neighbors right outside of the family home for decades. And Cô Sáu (Auntie Six), the younger sister, would make the fish cakes for it. Some of my most cherished memories are of watching the two of them work: Cô Hai slicing the tapioca noodles by hand with a cleaver and Cô Sáu rhythmically kneading minced fish into soft, springy fish cake dough. Both aunties have since passed away from cancer, but their sisters and the younger generation still know the recipe by heart. I have yet to find a bowl that is just as carefully prepared as theirs.

Like Gỏi Cá Trích | Herring Salad (page 60), Bánh Canh Chả Cá is a Phú Quốc Island delicacy. To perfect this dish is to master the noodles and fish cake. The noodles should always be made fresh, since slurping them down—tasting the sweet and saline broth clinging to the strands—is key to the experience. And as Cô Sáu knew all the way down to her bones, chả cá, the fish cake, is incredibly labor intensive. It requires tremendous skill and finesse to pound the fish with a stone mortar and pestle for two hours without straight-up passing out—but the result of all that work is a cake with a pleasurable, marshmallow-like chew. And all that without any fillers or binder: just fish, seasoning, and a whole lot of elbow grease.

In Phú Quốc, cá thu, or king mackerel, is the traditional choice for this dish, but albacore tuna offers a delightful alternative. To make your soup đặc biệt or extra special for holidays or esteemed guests, consider the optional additions of poached shrimp, squid, and pork riblets. Each ingredient can be poached separately in a pot of the broth, simmering for 5 minutes to infuse their unique flavors. These additions transform a simple bowl into a lavish feast. For the fish cakes, while hand-pounding is traditional, a KitchenAid stand mixer simplifies the process. If time is short, pre-made fish cakes from your local Asian grocery are a fine substitute—a secret best kept from my aunts!

Note: You'll need a KitchenAid stand mixer for both the fish cakes and the noodles in this recipe, including the paddle and dough hook attachments. You'll also need a wide and flat soup ladle and a cooling rack.

CHẢ CÁ (FISH CAKE)

1 pound king mackerel or albacore tuna fillet

¼ cup sliced green onions, white parts only

1 teaspoon minced garlic

1 tablespoon granulated sugar

Kosher salt

⅛ teaspoon cracked black pepper

Neutral oil (such as vegetable oil) for frying

CONTINUED

Ideally, you have a whole crew working on all the elements of this recipe together so that everything is ready at the same time. That's how my cousins and aunties do it! But if you're flying solo, start with the fish cake.

Lay the fish fillet on a cutting board. Using a metal spoon, hold it so that the edge is adjacent against the fillet. Gently scrape the spoon over the flesh, using light pressure to pull it away from the connective tissue. Discard any gristle. Scrape the flesh into a stand mixer bowl.

Use a mortar and pestle to crush the green onions, garlic, and sugar into a paste. Add this mixture to the stand mixer bowl with the fish, along with 1 teaspoon salt and the black pepper.

NOODLES

Filtered water

2 cups tapioca starch

¼ cup rice flour, plus more for sprinkling

Neutral oil (such as vegetable oil)

BROTH

4 cups filtered water

2 pounds pork knuckle bones

4 garlic cloves, smashed and peeled

8 cups Nước Luộc Cá | Fish Stock (page 50)

1 jicama, peeled and cut into large chunks

1 medium (8-inch) daikon, cut into large chunks (about 2½ cups)

2 carrots, cut into large chunks

1 cup coarsely chopped yellow onion

1 bunch sliced green onions, white parts only

2 tablespoons fish sauce

1 tablespoon kosher salt

2 tablespoons granulated sugar

1 teaspoon Knorr hạt nêm or MSG

1 pound king mackerel or albacore tuna fillet, cut into 1-inch chunks

Fit the stand mixer with the paddle attachment and beat the fish cake mixture on the high-speed setting for 15 to 20 minutes, or until it becomes smooth and elastic and starts to pull away from the edges of the bowl. Transfer the mixture to another bowl, cover it, and stash it in the fridge until you're ready to start frying. Wash the stand mixer bowl so it's ready for noodle-making.

Once the fish cake mixture is ready, it's time to fry. Fill a cast iron or other heavy pot with 3 inches of the neutral oil and set it over medium-high heat. Once the oil reaches 325°F on a probe thermometer, brush the inside of a wide and flat soup ladle with just enough neutral oil to form a thin coat to prevent sticking and scoop half an ounce of the fish cake mix into it. Use another spoon to flatten the mix against the ladle. Submerge the ladle in the oil for 3 minutes, frying the fish cake, then use a large spoon to release the fish cake from the ladle. Once released, continue to fry the fish cake for 3 minutes more on each side, or until it is golden brown all over.

Remove the fish cake from the oil and transfer it to a cooling rack. Sprinkle it with salt. Repeat the frying process with the rest of the mixture, topping off the oil when it gets low and keeping an eye on the temperature to make sure it stays around 325°F.

Now, move on to making the noodles. The first step is to make the dough. Fill a teakettle with filtered water and bring it to a hard boil. In the clean stand mixer bowl, combine the tapioca starch and rice flour. Use the paddle or whisk attachment to incorporate them. Then switch to the dough hook attachment, and run the mixer on its slowest setting. Gradually add 4½ cups of boiling water to the flour mixture.

Once the noodle dough starts clumping up, increase the mixing speed to medium. Mix the dough until it pulls away from the sides of the bowl and becomes elastic and smooth. Remove it from the bowl and lay it out on a flat, clean surface like a cutting board. Dust the dough lightly with additional rice flour.

Roll out the noodle dough. Use a rolling pin to flatten the dough into a ⅓-inch-thick rectangle. Cut the rectangle into ⅓-inch-thick strips; it doesn't matter how long they end up. Sprinkle more rice flour over the noodles and fluff them up to prevent sticking, then immediately stash them in an airtight container before they have a chance to dry out (which can happen quickly). Keep them in this container until right before you're ready to cook them.

GARNISH

½ cup sliced green onions,
green parts only

8 ounces mung bean sprouts

¼ cup culantro, chopped

½ cup cilantro, chopped

½ cup Củ Hẹ Chiên | Fried Shallots
(page 50) or store-bought fried shallots

Black pepper

⅓ cup fish sauce

6 Thai bird's eye chiles, sliced

1 lime, cut into 6 wedges

To cook the noodles, bring a large pot of water to a boil over high heat. Add the tapioca noodles in small batches. Stir each batch aggressively to prevent the noodles from sticking. Cook them for 2 to 3 minutes or until they become translucent, soft, and chewy.

Right after cooking, rinse each batch of noodles in a colander under cold running water. Let them drain, then drizzle neutral oil over them to prevent sticking and keep them in an airtight container. (Don't refrigerate them! They can sit at room temperature until you're ready to eat, but they have to be used the same day.)

To make the broth: Fill a large pot with the measured-out water and bring to a boil over high heat. Blanch the pork bones and garlic for 5 minutes. Top it off with the fish stock, then add the jicama, daikon, carrots, yellow onion, and green onions. Bring the pot back up to a simmer and skim any impurities off the surface. Let it simmer for 45 to 60 minutes, or until the vegetables are all tender, then remove them from the pot. In the spirit of not wasting too much, my aunties would serve the heartier vegetables on a side plate since they've soaked up a lot of flavor. Season the broth with the fish sauce, salt, sugar, and hạt nêm and let it simmer again. Skim it again, then let it keep simmering for 30 minutes more. Turn the heat to its lowest setting—just enough to keep the soup hot.

Once the broth is ready, line a plate with a paper towel. Drop the king mackerel straight into the hot broth and use the ladle to keep it submerged for 3 to 5 minutes, or until the pieces are opaque and cooked through. Use a slotted spoon to transfer the fish to the paper towel–lined plate and set aside.

Spring into action to finish the soup. Divide the noodles among six soup bowls. Cut the fish cakes into ¼-inch-thick slices and fan them out all fancy over the noodles. Plop 2 tablespoons of the poached fish into each bowl. Garnish the bowls with the green onions, mung bean sprouts, culantro, cilantro, fried shallots, and black pepper. Mix the fish sauce with the chile pepper slices and serve it on the side with the lime wedges.

TÔM RANG ME CHUA NGỌT
TAMARIND BLACK TIGER PRAWNS

Serves 4

2 pounds Vietnamese black tiger prawns or U-15 (jumbo) white Gulf shrimp, whole with heads

2 cups cold filtered water

1 cup ice

½ teaspoon kosher salt

1 teaspoon lemon juice

1 cup Nước Sốt Me | Tamarind Sauce (page 35)

1 bunch Thai basil, leaves picked

Toasted and chopped peanuts for garnish

In the night markets of Phú Quốc, prawns are grilled and topped with Mỡ Hành | Green Onion Sauce (page 47) and peanuts or stir-fried with Nước Sốt Me | Tamarind Sauce. This recipe takes that same spirit of simplicity and applies it to a really incredible prawn that is farmed in mainland Vietnam: the black tiger prawn. Despite their unusually large size, black tiger prawns are tender, with a pleasant and sweet flavor.

Outside of Vietnam, you can source live black tiger prawns from nicer seafood markets. They're not cheap, so I urge you to maximize the experience by cooking them with their shells and head still attached. There are a few big benefits to doing this: The meat won't overcook as easily, the shell provides nutrition that will transfer over to the meat, and the oils in the prawn head and shell will moisten the dish and lend it that irreplaceable, umami-rich prawn flavor.

To keep the prawns as fresh as possible, give them a nice ice bath. Fill a medium mixing bowl halfway with ice water and put the prawns in it. Then, clean the prawns. Using sharp kitchen scissors, cut a shallow incision down its back, then gently pry open the flesh to expose the vein. Remove the vein and rinse the prawn under cold running water to remove any leftover grit. Put the cleaned prawn back in the ice bath. Throughout this process, take care to keep the prawn shells and heads attached.

In another medium mixing bowl, make a brine by stirring together the water, ice, salt, and lemon juice. Once combined, submerge the cleaned prawns in the brine for 5 minutes. In the meantime, line a baking sheet with paper towels. Once 5 minutes are up, remove the prawns from the brine and place them on the paper towels. Remember, you're on a tight timeline to keep the prawns fresh: You can store this tray in the fridge for a maximum of 10 minutes until you're ready to cook.

To cook, set a large frying pan over medium heat. Pour the tamarind sauce into the frying pan and add 12 of the Thai basil leaves. Bring the pan to a simmer, then add the prawns.

For the next step, you're going to alternate between covering the pan with a lid and cracking it open to baste the prawns with the sauce. To baste, uncover the pan and tilt it to one side to create a pool of sauce. Use a large spoon to scoop up some of the sauce and drizzle it over the prawns. When you're finished basting, re-cover the pan. Baste the prawns like this three times in the next 5 minutes, then flip the prawns and repeat. (If you're using smaller Gulf shrimp, cut the cooking time in half.)

After 5 minutes, take the prawns out of the pan and transfer them to a large serving platter. Allow the sauce to keep simmering in the pan for 5 to 10 minutes, or until it becomes thick and glazelike. Take this time to tear up the rest of the basil leaves by hand. Pour the sauce over the prawns and garnish the dish with the peanuts and the rest of the basil. Serve immediately.

CƠM GÀ HẢI NAM
HAINANESE CHICKEN AND RICE

Serves 4

You're probably like, hold up, dude—Hainanese chicken and rice in a Vietnamese cookbook? Perceive it, friend. Yes, this deceptively simple-looking plate of chicken and rice originates from China: namely, its largest "island," Hainan. But the dish became known to the Vietnamese around the turn of the twentieth century, when Southeast Asia received an influx of immigrants from Hainan, including my grandpa, who settled in Phú Quốc. This is my family's version, made by my grandparents, my parents, and me. It's nothing fussy—just an all-around, comforting plate of poached chicken and rice.

I'll be honest that I prefaced this recipe with that context because Americans—even Vietnamese Americans!—are always trying to step to me about this dish, saying that it's wrong to include it in conversations about Vietnamese food. As if Vietnam weren't a multicultural society made of millions of immigrants, including my own grandfather from Hainan. To freeze our cultures in time capsules is to erase the beautiful stories that complicate and shape us. So face it, haters: Hainanese chicken and rice can be Vietnamese, too. Sorry! It's in the book.

POACHED CHICKEN

5 teaspoons kosher salt

12 cups cold filtered water

One 3-pound whole organic chicken

4 cups Nước Luộc Gà | Chicken Stock (page 51) or store-bought stock

One ½-inch knob fresh ginger, sliced into ⅛-inch coins

2 garlic cloves, smashed with peels

¼ teaspoon turmeric powder (optional)

1 stalk fresh lemongrass

¼ teaspoon fish sauce

½ teaspoon granulated sugar

First, make a brine for the chicken. In a large bowl, combine 3 teaspoons of the salt and 8 cups of the water. Submerge the chicken in the brine for 5 to 10 minutes. After brining, rinse the chicken under cold water until the water runs mostly clear. Remember to disinfect your hands and the sink after doing this. Set it on a baking sheet or meat-designated cutting board.

This next step is technically optional, but I promise that it'll make poaching the chicken way easier. You're basically going to make some handles that you can use to maneuver the whole chicken while it poaches. Using a pointed chopstick, skewer the bird through the right side of its back, so that the point exits between the thigh and tail. Do the same with a second chopstick on the left side, going the opposite way through. The thick ends of the chopsticks should poke out of the bird by a few inches, and you can use them as handles to maneuver the chicken. Alternately, you can use metal poultry hooks, like the kind they have at Chinese barbecue spots. If you skip this step, lifting the cooked chicken out of its hot poaching liquid could get pretty spicy—like, *Raiders of the Lost Ark* face-melting spicy—so be careful.

With your chicken skewered, you can start poaching. In a large pot, combine the chicken with chicken stock, the remaining 4 cups water, the ginger, garlic, turmeric powder (if using), lemongrass, fish sauce, sugar, and the remaining 2 teaspoons salt. Bring the pot to a simmer over high heat, then turn the heat down to medium. Continue to cook the chicken at a low simmer for 15 minutes. In the meantime, prepare an ice bath that will fit the chicken.

CONTINUED

SEASONED RICE

2 cups jasmine rice

1 teaspoon kosher salt

1 teaspoon fish sauce

GARNISH

1 iceberg lettuce head, halved (optional)

1 bunch mint, leaves picked (optional)

2 Roma tomatoes, quartered into wedges

4 Persian cucumbers, sliced into coins

1 cup Nước Mắm Gừng | Ginger Fish Sauce (page 41) for serving

When 15 minutes are up, adjust the heat to medium-low, just to keep the poaching liquid warm. Remove the chicken from the broth and shock it in the ice bath for 10 minutes to help the skin firm up. Place the chicken back in the pot and increase the heat to medium to bring the liquid back up to a simmer. If the liquid isn't at least 2 inches above the chicken, top off the pot with more filtered water. Keep the pot at a low simmer for 35 minutes, or until the chicken is cooked through. Check by sticking a probe thermometer into the thickest part of the flesh, usually the upper thigh toward the bone, for 15 seconds. If the chicken is done, the internal temperature should sit at around 165°F for 30 seconds straight.

While the chicken is simmering, set a cooling rack on top of a baking sheet. Once cooked through, remove the chicken from the broth and set it on a cooling rack. Allow the chicken to cool at room temperature for 30 minutes. Meanwhile, keep the poaching liquid warm over a low flame so that it's still hot by the time you're ready to eat.

While the chicken cools, make the rice. In a medium pot, rinse the jasmine rice until the water runs clear. (See page 34 for detailed washing instructions.) Strain the aromatics out of the reserved chicken broth and discard. Measure 3 cups of the poaching liquid and pour it into the pot of rice, along with the salt and fish sauce. Bring the pot to a simmer over medium heat. As soon as it simmers, turn the heat down to low. Stir the rice with a spoon, cover the pot with a tight-fitting lid, and cook on low heat for 15 minutes, uninterrupted. After 15 minutes, take the pot off the heat and give the rice a stir. Put the lid back on and let the rice hang out off the heat for 15 minutes more. Give the rice another stir to fluff it up. Replace the lid and keep it covered until right before eating, to prevent it from drying out.

Now, butcher the bird. Using a sharp knife, carefully detach the wings, breasts, legs, and thighs from the cooled chicken. Try to keep the skin attached to the meat. Use a meat cleaver to cut the leg and thigh pieces into neat slices. Slice the chicken breasts and arrange all the meat on a platter. Make it as fancy as you want.

For serving, you have the option to either leave the rice in the pot to stay warm or move it onto a large serving plate. In either case, it's best to cover the rice until it's time to eat to keep it from drying out. Distribute the Ginger Fish Sauce into individual small bowls for each guest. Keep the hot chicken broth in a central bowl or pot on the table, with a ladle for guests to add broth to their rice as desired. You could also serve the broth in small bowls for individual sipping. Place the garnishes, such as tomato wedges and cucumber slices, either directly on the serving plate with the rice or separately, to add fresh vegetables to the meal.

CÁ TRÍCH NHÚNG GIẤM
VIETNAMESE FISH SHABU SHABU

Serves 4

My last meal with my maternal grandfather, a lifelong pescatarian, was Cá Trích Nhúng Giấm. We sat together on a quilt in his home in Phú Quốc, wrapping poached herring in rice paper and dipping the rolls in fish sauce. His body was worn down after a long battle with cancer, and he didn't have any teeth left. But even so, his face lit up with pure joy as he ate this dish that touched his soul and grounded him in his home. I'll always remember that. For this recipe, you'll need an Instant Pot or tabletop burner so you can freshly poach the herring as you eat.

8 whole herring, cleaned and filleted (see page 88)

HOT POT BASE

1 tablespoon neutral oil

2 tablespoons minced shallot

1 tablespoon minced garlic

2 cups sliced yellow onion

1 tablespoon minced lemongrass

4 Makrut lime leaves

One 15-ounce can crushed pineapple

2 cups coconut vinegar or white wine vinegar

¼ cup granulated sugar

1 tablespoon fish sauce

8 cups coconut water

2 tablespoons kosher salt

SUMMER ROLLS

4 ounces dried rice vermicelli, cooked (see Note on page 60)

24 butter lettuce leaves

24 sprigs mint leaves

24 sprigs cilantro

2 English cucumbers, sliced into thin, 4-inch-long wedges

½ cup Nước Mắm Tỏi Ớt | Chile Fish Sauce (page 43) for serving

One 12-ounce package rice paper wrappers (see page 23)

Cut each herring fillet on the diagonal into 5 or 6 equal bite-size pieces. Set the pieces on a plate and keep refrigerated until you're ready to cook.

Get started making the hot pot base. Set a medium pot on the stove over medium heat. Allow the pot to heat for 2 to 3 minutes, then add the neutral oil. Once the oil starts to shimmer, add the shallot, garlic, onion, lemongrass, and lime leaves and stir. Sweat the aromatics for 1 minute, or until the garlic starts to brown slightly. Next, add the crushed pineapple, coconut vinegar, sugar, and fish sauce to the pot. The mixture should be nice and juicy. Keep it cooking for 15 to 20 minutes, or until those juices start to simmer, then add the coconut water and salt. Bring the mixture up to a simmer to get the flavors to meld, then turn the heat down to its lowest setting. You just want to keep the hot pot base warm while you get everything else set up.

Arrange the noodles, lettuce, mint, cilantro, and cucumbers on a platter at your dinner table. Divide the Chile Fish Sauce among four small dipping bowls. Make sure each person has a large plate, chopsticks (or a fork), and a rimmed plate or medium bowl filled with water for hydrating the rice paper wrappers.

If you're using a hot plate, set it up at the table and transfer the pot of hot pot base to the burner. If you're using an Instant Pot, set it up in the middle of your table and transfer the base to the pot. Set the Instant Pot to "Sauté" mode and adjust the heat so that the broth simmers gently.

Poach the herring as you eat: It just takes 30 seconds to a minute for each piece to cook, so each person should be able to get into a rhythm of poaching, wrapping, eating, and talking smack during the meal.

Now let's get to rolling. Moisten a rice paper wrapper and lay it flat on your plate. Add the following ingredients in horizontal rows, starting 1½ inches from the bottom edge of the rice paper wrapper: 2 tablespoons rice vermicelli, 2 butter lettuce leaves, a sprig of mint, a sprig of cilantro, and a piece of cucumber.

Fold the sides of the wrapper toward the center, then partially pull up the bottom edge to wrap the ingredients in an initial layer of rice paper. There should still be 2 to 3 inches of wrapper left open at the top of the wrapper. Place 2 to 3 slices of freshly poached herring at the bottom of that open end, then roll the rest of the way up to trap the fish meat in the outer layer of the roll. Dip the roll in the Chile Fish Sauce and enjoy immediately.

**WE ARE
OCEAN PEOPLE**

So many of the stories I've heard about my family are also—in a way—about the ocean. In my mom's memories of her late father, he's a legendary free diver who broke local records for holding his breath underwater. Long after he retired, people still talked about the time he single-handedly saved a family of fishermen from drowning when their ship sank. And even though my dad left Vietnam as a young man, it seems like he also made a huge impression on the local fishing scene. His sisters and their neighbors would tell me about my dad's escapades as a sea captain in his youth, when he'd guide crews through dangerous waters to catch the fish they depended on for a living.

And for my parents, fish has always been their love language. When they first got to know each other as teenagers at that Phú Quốc fish market, my lovestruck dad was too shy to court my mom when she visited his makeshift stall; instead, he communicated his feelings by saving her the biggest, prettiest fish every day. (After a few heart-thumping conversations about fish, my mom ended up being the one to finally pull the trigger.) Fifty years later, they still get pretty sappy while cooking and eating Phú Quốc–style seafood dishes together.

It doesn't feel accurate to say that my family and our people "lived by" the sea. Instead, we have always been a part of it, and it a part of us. During the lean times of French occupation and war, my parents' families turned to the ocean and its many gifts—fish, whelks, salt, and seaweed—to survive. That was a feeling that endured even after my family left Phú Quốc Island: In the United States, the ocean was our lifeline.

Even though we were supposedly living in the land of abundance and opportunity, the reality was that hunger haunted my family throughout my life. Thanks to white flight and generations of governmental neglect of Oakland's largely working-class, Black, and immigrant neighborhoods, residents like my family and I had extremely limited options for decent food. For decades, whole neighborhoods were subjected to redlining by banks that deemed them too "risky" for investment, which meant that supermarkets and other community resources ended up relocating to wealthier and whiter residential areas. There were few, if any, places where we could buy fresh vegetables or meat, but plenty of ways to get drugs, liquor, cigarettes, and fast food. To be honest, there still aren't many options to this day. All that meant I spent my formative years living with the low-frequency, ever-present background hum of hunger.

So, when my dad managed to lug home scraps from his fishmonger job—Styrofoam coolers packed with sweating ice and bags of fish heads, bellies, and other scraps—we treated them like treasure chests overflowing with glittering gold coins and rubies. In that way, I caught a backdoor view of the fish that made its way into the Bay Area's high-end restaurants. I was able to get a sense of seasonality, too: For instance, I always knew that springtime meant herring.

In the hands of my parents, each morsel of fish could truly become anything—a stew, hot pot, a meaty topping for rice, jerky, or any kind of feast they could imagine. In addition to offcuts of hamachi, tuna, and salmon, my dad brought home cheap whole fish, roe, scallop guts, and swordfish tails. Nothing was off the table. My dad even ate the tough, papery gills; I've gotta admit that I was never that hard-core. Just like it did in Phú Quốc Island, the ocean kept my family alive in Oakland. We would never dare let its gifts go to waste.

To reflect the gill-to-fin cooking methods I grew up with, I've structured the recipes in this chapter by the parts of a fish, from the head to the tail. And if you've never dealt with anything but the fillet, I've included a step-by-step whole fish butchering and cleaning guide.

Salmon skin scaled and removed from the loin

TOTAL FISH DOMINATION

Starting at a young age, I watched my dad break down fish after fish with the fluidity of a dancer, his sharp knife reducing them to perfectly neat pieces in just a few strokes. That's why I'm confident that I learned from the best in the game. Breaking down a whole fish might seem intimidating if you've never done it before, but starting from scratch is worthwhile for a few reasons. One, it's so much more affordable than only buying precut fillets at the grocery store; and two, you'll gain access to delicious parts of the fish that aren't usually sold on their own in stores. Plus, if you're ever stuck on a deserted island, the skill will also (literally) serve you well.

For this guide, I'll walk you through how to break down and prep a big fish, like salmon, and a smaller fish, like herring. In both cases, you'll need a sharp and flexible fillet knife, a cutting board, and a pair of fish tweezers or pliers to remove any bones. A horse comb-style fish scaler is a nice-to-have for removing scales from bigger fish, but you can also get away with using a standard chef's knife.

Scaling the salmon at Water2Table, Pier 45, Fisherman's Wharf, San Francisco

LARGE FISH—SALMON

Peep these directions for bigger fish, like salmon, branzino, red snapper, and sea bass. You can ask a fishmonger to remove the fish's scales for you, but I encourage you to try it yourself. It's a good skill to have. The scales are gonna go flying off of the fish, so do this in a place where it's safe to make a mess.

Place the salmon on the cutting board with the head facing away from you. Hold the tail end of the fish with one hand and use a fish scaler or the dull edge of a chef's knife to scrape the scales off the skin of the fish, starting from the tail end and moving toward the head. Use long, firm strokes, applying enough pressure to remove the scales, but not so much that you damage the skin.

Work carefully to remove all the scales from the skin, paying special attention to the nooks around the fins, belly, and head. Once you've removed all the scales, rinse the fish under cold water. Pat it dry with paper towels and put it back on the cutting board.

With the salmon's belly facing you, use a fillet knife to make a ¼-inch-deep cut along the belly, starting from the fish's anus and continuing all the way up to its gills. (The anus is on the belly side of the fish, usually an inch or so up from the tail fin.) Be careful not to puncture the internal organs as you make this cut.

Use your fingers to gently pry open the belly cavity and expose the internal organs, then use a spoon to remove them. You'll want to remove all the organs, including the liver and kidneys, as they can spoil quickly and taint the flavor of the fish. Dispose of them—or, like my mom, bury them deep in your backyard to enrich the soil. Once you have removed the organs, rinse the fish inside and out under cold water to remove any remaining blood or debris.

Next up is the fun part. (What am I saying? Every part is the fun part!) Lay the fish on its side and make a perpendicular cut behind the gills; stop when you hit the hard vertebrae. With the blade running parallel to the cutting board, slice the fish from head to tail, cutting through the rib bones, to remove the first fillet. Keep the blade as close as possible to the central "cord" of bone as you cut—this will ensure you get the most meat off the fish. To keep the fillets pretty, try to avoid sawing back and forth with your knife. Instead, cut in long, smooth strokes. Flip the fish over and repeat on the other side. Set the fillets aside for now.

Lay the fish frame on the cutting board with its head facing you. Use sharp kitchen shears or a knife to sever the head from the spine. Keep the head for canh chua (page 89), or grill it with a sprinkle of chile salt (page 43). Set aside the salmon skeleton, or "frame," for stock (page 50) or frying (page 92).

Grab one of the fillets and put it on the cutting board. Run your fingertips along the center-top of the fillet, starting from the tail end. You should

Removing the salmon head

From top to bottom: salmon belly, frames, and skin-on fillet loin

feel small, thin bones sticking out of the flesh, almost like splinters or thorns—those are the pin bones. Use fish tweezers to grip the end of one pin bone and gently pull it out of the flesh, following the direction it's pointing toward to avoid disturbing the flesh as much as possible. If a pin bone breaks, use the tweezers to burrow into the flesh and pull it out. Repeat the process to remove all the pin bones, working your way down the fillet. You can check for stragglers by running your fingers along the fillet in different directions—or, use a flashlight to illuminate the bones.

Locate the rib bones, which are bigger than the pin bones and run along the bottom (cavity side) of the fillet. You can cut them off in a nice cluster. Use a fillet knife to make a ¼-inch cut along the tops of the rib bones, then use a gentle sawing motion to carefully cut them away from the flesh. Keep the blade as close to the bones

as possible so that you don't lose any meat, and try not to cut through the bones, either. Once you've cut all the way to the rib bones, use the tip of the knife to pry them away from the flesh gently. Use your fingers to double-check the fillet for any lingering bones.

Next, locate the belly of the salmon. It's the flattest and fattiest part of the fillet, and it runs along the bottom of the body. You can identify it by its lighter, peachy-orange color; to remove it, cut 2 to 3 inches up from the fillet's bottom edge. Continue cutting along the belly until you get a nice long piece. Be sure to remove any residual fins, bones, and scales. Repeat the deboning and belly removal processes with the other fillet piece.

When the fillets are all cleaned up, cut them into portion-size pieces (standard portion size is around 6 ounces,

which comes out to 2 to 3 portions per pound, but it really depends on what you want to do with the fish). Generally, check the recipes you're using for guidelines. Regardless, make sure you cut with the fillets skin-side down and try to slice with one smooth motion instead of sawing for the prettiest results.

If you plan to use the fillets within 3 days, refrigerate them in a non-airtight container lined with a linen towel (or paper towels) to suck up any fish juice. The bottom layer of fillets should be skin-side down, and the top layer (if you're stacking) should be skin-side up: If the skin touches the flesh, it'll degrade faster. Swap out the towel for a fresh one every day. To freeze the fillets, put them in an airtight container or freezer bags and use within a month.

Butterflied salmon head

Salmon loin cut into fillets

SMALL FISH—HERRING

You can use this method for fish like herring, sardines, anchovies, and mackerel. Butchering a bunch of small fish is for sure a lot of work, but once you get a rhythm going, it'll go fast. In your sink, use the edge of a spoon or a fish scaler to scrape the herring from the tail to the head, until all scales are gone. Imagine petting a cat the wrong way. Rinse the fish under cold running water to remove its excess scales. Repeat with the rest of the herring.

To fillet the fish, use a sharp paring knife or kitchen scissors to make an incision in the fish's poophole, located on its underside near the tail end. Try not to think too much about how that might feel. Make a ¼-inch-deep incision along the belly, being careful not to cut into the guts—basically trying to slice open a package without damaging the stuff inside. Pull the guts out and discard them. Open the fish up and flatten it out, skin-side down. Use your fingers to gently pull the spine up and out, along with the rib bones and head. Cut off the tail fin and slice the fillets in half so you have two equal pieces from each fish. (If you want, you can keep the spines and fry them for a snack.)

Once you have all your fillets cut, it's time to clean them up. Brush your fingers along the fillets to feel for pin bones and use fish tweezers to pluck them out. To make sure you don't lose too much meat in the process, press gently on the flesh around the bone as you pluck it out. If you don't have tweezers, you can also cut them out with a knife: Make two slices on either side of the line of pin bones at an angle parallel to them. You'll want to be able to get them all out in one swoop; otherwise, you won't get as much meat. Use immediately.

Herring, whole and fillets

For the finest in sustainable seafood from local San Francisco fishermen, visit Four Star Seafood's chef-curated marketplace at www.fourstarseafood.com. Discover pristine flavors and support our local fishing community.

CANH CHUA ĐẦU CÁ HỒI
HOT POT–STYLE SALMON HEAD SOUR SOUP

Serves 4

Canh chua is often incorrectly translated as "sweet and sour soup," but the literal translation is actually sour soup. If you grew up eating Warheads and your tastebuds are all blown out, you might think there's only one kind of sour. But canh chua is all about keeping different sources of sourness—tomato, pineapple, and tamarind—in balance. Since its flavors are great at complementing rich flavors, canh chua can handle a variety of proteins, including fatty fish like salmon. Salmon heads are especially ideal for this, because the head is rich in gelatin and houses extra-delicate meat in the throat, cheeks, and jaw.

As a rule in my home while growing up, the fish wasn't dropped into the broth until we were ready to eat. If you let the fish languish in the broth while you mess around before dinner, the flavor is just ruined. My parents would yell, "Dinner time! Come and eat now before the fish gets too fishy in the canh chua!" So for best results, treat this basically like hot pot by setting up a portable burner or Instant Pot on the dinner table, and have the garnishes ready to add in along with the salmon head. Time it so that the fish finishes cooking just as everyone's sitting down.

Note: The herbs on the garnish list are what my family uses, but feel free to swap in something easier to find, like cilantro, tarragon, or parsley for the ones you can't source.

CANH CHUA BASE

1 tablespoon neutral oil (such as vegetable oil)

½ cup minced shallot

¼ cup minced garlic

1 tablespoon minced lemongrass

1 teaspoon thinly sliced Thai bird's eye chile or serrano pepper

5 Makrut lime leaves

2 tablespoons minced fresh yellow turmeric

1 teaspoon turmeric powder

3 tablespoons fish sauce

1 tablespoon granulated sugar

2 Roma tomatoes, cut into chunks

2 tablespoons Dán Me | Tamarind Paste (page 35)

First, make the canh chua base. Set a sturdy, medium-size pot over medium heat for 2 to 3 minutes. Add the neutral oil, and once the oil starts to shimmer, add the shallot, garlic, lemongrass, chile, and lime leaves to the pot. Use a spoon to stir the mixture constantly to sweat it.

In a minute, or once the garlic starts to smell toasty, add the turmeric, turmeric powder, fish sauce, sugar, tomatoes, and tamarind paste to the pot. Cook the mixture, stirring occasionally, for 15 minutes, or until the liquid starts to simmer. At that point, add in the fish stock and raise the heat to medium-high, so that the whole mixture comes to a simmer. You'll smell all the aromas melding together. Then, turn the heat to its lowest setting—just enough to keep the soup hot until you're ready to eat.

Place the fish head in a bowl that'll fit it and rinse it under cold running water until the water looks mostly clear. Take the head out of the bowl and put it on a cutting board, then using a large knife, split it into two symmetrical halves, with an eye on each side. Enjoy the flashback to dissection lab in high school biology. Set aside.

Then, set the table. If you're using an Instant Pot, set it in the middle of the table and pour in the Canh Chua broth. Set the Instant Pot to "Sauté" mode and adjust the heat level so that the broth comes to a simmer. If you're using a butane burner or a hot plate, set the pot of Canh Chua Base onto it and bring it to a simmer.

CONTINUED

HOT POT-STYLE SALMON HEAD SOUR SOUP, CONTINUED

12 cups Nước Luộc Cá | Fish Stock (page 50) or filtered water

1 salmon head

GARNISH

1 pound mung bean sprouts

1 bunch ngò ôm (rice paddy herb), chopped

1 bunch cilantro, chopped

1 bunch dill

1 stalk bạc hà (elephant's ear plant), peeled and chopped

4 cups shredded banana flower (see page 65)

1 cup sliced okra

1 cup pineapple chunks

2 tablespoons fried garlic (see page 21)

2 tablespoons julienned Thai basil

Steamed rice (see page 34) or cooked rice vermicelli (see Note on page 60) for serving

Sliced Thai bird's eye chile, for serving

Now deal with the salmon head: Add the salmon head pieces to the soup, gently so you don't burn yourself, then immediately follow that with the mung bean sprouts, rice paddy herb, cilantro, dill, elephant's ear plant, banana flower, okra, pineapple, garlic, and basil. Poach the salmon for 5 to 8 minutes, basically until the meat becomes fully opaque. Remove the head and transfer it to a platter. Assign the person with the nimblest fingers to head breakdown duty. Make sure all the flesh and gelatin are removed from the head. Don't forget the cheek! That's the best part. Discard the inedible parts.

Scoop the herbs out of the soup with a slotted spoon and set them on the plate next to the salmon meat. To serve, ladle however much soup you want into a bowl and garnish with the meat, vegetables, fruit, and herbs. Enjoy immediately with rice and fresh chiles on the side.

XUONG CÁ HỒI CHIÊN GIÒN
FRIED SALMON FRAMES

Serves 4

I ate a lot of salmon growing up, but it's not like we were digging into fat, juicy fillets with asparagus and lots of lemon butter every night. We ate the heads, gills, bones, tails, and other parts that Westerners didn't know how to eat. It almost felt like we were getting away with something, the way my parents transformed "scraps" into our favorite dishes. The secret of how to turn discarded salmon carcasses into something that rivaled bacon felt like some Vietnamese Illuminati shit.

In some stores, for instance H Mart, you'll find de-filleted salmon carcasses, or frames, wrapped up and sold in a cooler next to the seafood counter. Otherwise, ask the fishmonger directly. You won't need the head for this recipe. If you like, you can stash it in the fridge in an airtight container or bag it for another recipe, like canh chua (page 89) or Nước Luộc Cá | Fish Stock (page 50).

1 salmon frame (about 1½ pounds)

2 cups all-purpose flour

½ cup rice flour

½ cup cornstarch

½ teaspoon kosher salt

Neutral oil (such as vegetable oil) for frying

Steamed rice (see page 34) for serving

Sriracha or Nước Mắm Chấm | Everyday Fish Sauce (see page 40) for serving

First, prepare the salmon frame. Separate the salmon head if it's still attached to the carcass and reserve for another use. Cut the frame into 4-inch pieces, or whatever size makes sense for your frying pan.

Now, dredge the frame. Add the flour, rice flour, cornstarch, and salt to a wide, shallow bowl and whisk with a fork to combine. Dredge each piece of salmon in the flour, turning and pressing lightly to coat. Shake off the excess flour like you're drying a Polaroid. Set the dredged fish pieces aside on a large plate.

To fry, set a large frying pan over medium heat. Allow the pan to heat through for 3 minutes, then add 2 inches of neutral oil. Once the oil reaches 325°F on a probe thermometer, you're ready to fry. When cooking, work in batches and be careful not to crowd the pan too much, or your frame pieces will fry all wonky. Gently add a few pieces of fish to the pan, and use tongs or long cooking chopsticks to keep them submerged in the oil. Don't let them touch the bottom, though, or they'll scorch. It's a delicate dance! Fry the fish for 4 to 5 minutes on each side, until the pieces turn golden brown all over.

While the fish are frying, line a serving dish with paper towels. Transfer the finished pieces to that plate and let the excess grease drain off. Whenever you pull a batch of fish out of the oil, replenish the supply with some fresh oil. Serve the frame pieces hot with steamed rice and Sriracha.

LƯỜN CÁ HỒI ÁP CHẢO
CRISPY SKIN PAN-ROASTED SALMON FILLETS

Serves 4

Of course, a whole fish isn't just the head and the bones. We're here for fillets too. We didn't eat this "prime" cut of the fish too often when I was growing up, and if we did, it was usually in the form of smaller pieces that we threw into porridges or soups. I really learned to love pan-fried fillets later, after I started working at restaurants. So, this recipe is a melding of those restaurant-style dishes and the flavors that I typically ate at home. I recommend serving this salmon with steamed rice (see page 34) or with salad. You can even use it to top a curry or stew. For this recipe, you'll need a thin fish spatula and a large spoon for basting.

Four 5-ounce salmon fillets, skin on
⅛ teaspoon kosher salt
2 tablespoons neutral oil (such as vegetable oil)
1 tablespoon minced ginger
1 tablespoon minced lemongrass
2 tablespoons unsalted butter
1 teaspoon thinly sliced chives for garnish
1 teaspoon toasted sesame seeds (see page 19) for garnish

Set a large cast-iron skillet over medium-high heat. Allow the skillet to heat through for 3 to 5 minutes.

Meanwhile, pat the fish fillets dry with paper towels and season them on both sides with the salt. Once the skillet is hot, add in the neutral oil to the pan. After about a minute, the oil should start to shimmer.

At this point, it's time to add in the salmon. Tilting the pan away from your body, gently lay the salmon fillets in the skillet, skin-side down. Place each piece in the skillet starting with the part closest to you so that the salmon doesn't splash oil in your direction. For added protection, wear a long-sleeved shirt that you hate.

Using a metal spatula (or a chef's press tool if you're fancy), press down firmly on the fillets to ensure that the skin is flat against the hot surface of the pan for 1 to 2 minutes. This will ensure the skin crisps up evenly.

Now, start on the pan sauce. Add the ginger, lemongrass, and butter to the edge of the pan. Once the butter melts, tilt the pan to the side and use a large spoon to scoop up the melted butter and baste it over the fish. Repeat this for 3 to 4 minutes, or until the edges of the fish start to get brown and crispy. Now you're basting like a restaurant chef!

Gently flip the fillets over using the spatula. If a piece is sticking to the pan, flip your spatula over and use the sharp edge to gently nudge the piece free. I'll be honest, though. Sometimes, despite your best efforts, the skin wants to stick, and you might tear it. In that case, forgive yourself and keep going: It's still gonna taste great. Let the salmon cook on the other side for 1 to 2 minutes more, or until the edges start to brown and crisp.

In the meantime, line a plate with paper towels. When the edges have started to brown and crisp, remove the fillets from the pan and transfer them to the paper towel–lined plate to drain excess oil.

To serve, remove the paper towels and garnish the fish with the chives and sesame seeds. Serve immediately.

CHẢO CÁ
FISH AND SEAFOOD PORRIDGE

Serves 4

This dish is my equivalent to chicken soup—my comfort food, in more ways than one. Branzino, clams, and squid add a deep, briny quality to a porridge scented with ginger, garlic, and lemongrass. It's easy to imagine a fisherman digging into a bowl of this after a long, cold morning out at sea. It's a plunge into steamy bathwater, a polar fleece blanket for you to bury your face in.

I ate this porridge a lot growing up, but it was a little different each time, depending on the season and what fish were popular (and cheap). Whatever odds and ends we had joined up with a scant bit of rice and turned into this soul-warming concoction. When I crack open the clams to let their liquor seep into the rice and sip this broth, I'm reminded that working people are the world's best innovators. Like the mish-mash of sea creatures in cioppino, this is a true fishmongers' dish, with all the humility, honesty, and earning-your-keep that comes with that label.

Once you have filleted the fish, you can reserve the bones and heads to make Nước Luộc Cá | Fish Stock another day.

2 pounds whole sea bass or branzino, gutted, filleted, and scaled, with fillets cut into 1-inch pieces (see page 85)

½ teaspoon minced ginger

1 tablespoon minced garlic

3 tablespoons fish sauce

⅛ teaspoon cracked black pepper

1 cup broken rice

2 tablespoons neutral oil (such as vegetable oil)

¼ cup diced shallot

12 cups Nước Luộc Cá | Fish Stock (page 50)

1½ pounds littleneck clams (see Notes on page 163)

½ pound Monterey squid, cleaned

1 tablespoon coconut sugar

GARNISH

¼ cup Củ Hẹ Chiên | Fried Shallots (page 50) or store-bought fried shallots

¼ cup cilantro leaves

¼ cup sliced green onions, white and green parts

First, marinate the fish. In a medium mixing bowl, mix the fish fillet pieces with the minced ginger, 1 teaspoon of the garlic, 1 tablespoon of the fish sauce, and the black pepper. Let it sit at room temperature to marinate for 5 to 10 minutes. It seems like a lot of seasoning, but this super-aromatic mixture is what'll ultimately perfume the broth.

While the fish is marinating, get started on the rice. In a fine-mesh colander, wash the rice until the water runs clear. Drain the rice. In a medium pot over medium heat, warm the neutral oil. Add the washed rice, shallot, and the remaining 2 teaspoons garlic, stirring frequently with a spoon to prevent browning. Keep on low heat for 3 minutes, or until you start to smell the toasted aromatics.

Now, turn that rice into porridge. Add the fish stock to the pot of rice and bring the pot to a simmer over medium-high heat. Add the clams to the pot and cook for 5 to 8 minutes, or until their shells open. At this point, you should alternate between covering the pot with a lid and stirring so that the rice doesn't stick to the bottom, like you're making oatmeal or grits.

Once the clams have opened, add the marinated fish and squid and cook for another 5 minutes, stirring gently to avoid breaking up the fish. Season the porridge with the coconut sugar, the remaining 2 tablespoons fish sauce, and more salt to taste.

To serve, divide the porridge among four bowls and garnish with the fried shallots, cilantro leaves, and sliced green onions.

BỤNG CÁ HỒI SỐT CÀ CHUA
TOMATO-BRAISED SALMON BELLY

Serves 4

In the '90s, there wasn't much consumer demand for salmon belly. The juicy, fatty bellies were culinary outcasts during the long-lasting anti-fat diet dogma of the decade. In the end, the dieters' loss was my family's gain. My parents braised salmon belly in a sweet-and-sour tomato sauce that complemented its natural richness. Like pork belly, another cut that became trendy in the United States after years of living in relative obscurity, this cut of salmon is a legit luxury in the right hands.

1½ pounds salmon belly, cut into 2- to 3-inch strips

Kosher salt

⅛ teaspoon cracked black pepper

2 tablespoons neutral oil (such as vegetable oil)

1 tablespoon minced garlic

¼ teaspoon minced lemongrass

4 Makrut lime leaves

½ cup diced yellow onion

1 cup cherry tomatoes, halved

½ cup coconut water

¼ teaspoon MSG

2 teaspoons granulated sugar

1 green onion, green parts only, sliced on the diagonal for garnish

Steamed rice (see page 34) for serving

Pat the salmon belly pieces dry with paper towels to remove excess moisture, then season them on both sides with ¼ teaspoon salt and the pepper. Line a plate with paper towels and set it aside.

Set a large cast-iron frying pan over medium-high heat. Give the pan 3 to 5 minutes to heat up, then add in the neutral oil. Heat the oil for 1 minute, until it starts to shimmer. Now, it's time to fry. Tilting the pan away from your body to prevent splattering yourself with oil, gently lay the salmon belly pieces in the oil, skin-side down. Place each piece in the pan starting with the part closest to you so that the salmon doesn't splash oil in your direction.

Using a metal spatula, press the salmon belly pieces down firmly to ensure that the skin makes contact with the hot surface of the pan for 1 to 2 minutes. This ensures a crispy skin and will prevent the fish from curling up as the skin loses moisture. (If there's no skin, don't worry about this part, since without the skin it won't curl up. Just make sure you get a nice sear for extra flavor.) Transfer the salmon belly pieces to the paper towel–lined plate to drain any excess oil. The salmon doesn't need to be cooked all the way at this point.

Keeping the pan on medium-high heat, get started on the sauce. Quickly add the garlic, lemongrass, lime leaves, onion, tomatoes, and coconut water to the hot pan. Sauté the mixture over high heat for 2 to 3 minutes, until the tomato halves have nearly disintegrated. Add the MSG and sugar, plus more salt to taste. Bring the sauce to a simmer.

Once the sauce is simmering, gently lay the pieces of salmon belly on top of the tomato mixture. Use a large spoon to carefully baste the salmon belly with the tomato sauce. Then let it braise for another 3 minutes, or until the sauce returns to a simmer again. When the sauce reaches a simmer, remove the pan from the heat and transfer the braised salmon belly and the sauce into a wide, shallow serving bowl, being careful not to let the pieces of fish break apart. Garnish with the green onions and serve immediately with rice.

TRỨNG CÁ TRÍCH TẢO BẸ
HERRING ROE ON KELP

Serves 4

One of the really cool similarities between Phú Quốc Island and the San Francisco Bay Area is the yearly herring run, when the sea glimmers with the silvery scales of herring returning to the rivers to spawn. On Phú Quốc Island, you don't even have to look at the water to know the herring have arrived in town. Tables all over the island will be filled with platters of Gỏi Cá Trích | Herring Salad (page 60), which takes full advantage of the oily fish's rich flavors.

But for millennia, herring has also been a staple food for indigenous people on the West Coast. As the herring migrate north along the Pacific coast in the springtime, they lay thick clumps of eggs on kelp, or kombu. Herring roe has long been a key part of indigenous aquaculture, encouraging communities to plant kelp forests on the shoreline so that they can gather more eggs.

Along with his love for nori, my dad picked up a taste for this type of roe from his Japanese coworkers, who call it komochi konbu. In my family, this delicacy, with its crispy and spongy texture and briny flavor, often found its way into our summer rolls alongside another herring dish—Cá Trích Nhúng Giấm | Vietnamese Fish Shabu Shabu (page 77). This ingredient is hyper-seasonal, so ask your fishmonger to check on availability in the spring. You just might get lucky!

You can eat this as a snack, with steamed rice (see page 34), or wrapped in summer rolls.

8 ounces herring roe on kelp

Line a tray with paper towels. On a cutting board, cut the roe into 4 by 1-inch slabs, and put the pieces in a large bowl. Rinse the roe under cold running water for 5 minutes to desalinate them. Transfer them to the paper towel–lined tray to drain excess water from the roe.

That's it! It's ready to serve.

CÁ BON CHIÊN MUÔI SÁ ỐT
FRIED SAND DABS WITH LEMONGRASS AND CHILE SALT

Serves 4

Muối Ớt | Chile Salt isn't just a condiment for adding zip to fresh fruit, though that's usually how you'll encounter it on the streets of Phú Quốc. If you add lemongrass, it becomes an amazingly fragrant seasoning for fried poultry and fish. That mix of chile heat, salt, and citrus is unbeatable—especially if you're drinking a beer with your fish.

You can use all sorts of fish with this recipe, though I suggest flatfish like sand dabs and rex sole for their delicate flavor. They're affordable in Northern California, which is why my family ate them a lot, and they take really well to pan-frying. Small oily fish, like herring or smelt, also fry well. You'll need a fish spatula for this recipe.

4 whole sand dabs
2 tablespoons Muối Ớt	Chile Salt (page 43)
2 tablespoons minced lemongrass
2 cups all-purpose flour
½ cup rice flour
½ cup cornstarch
½ teaspoon kosher salt
Neutral oil (such as vegetable oil) for frying

Cut off the heads of the fish by slicing diagonally from the area right above the eyes to the midpoint of the belly. Use your knife to carefully scrape out the guts from the cavity of the fish. This isn't surgery, but you don't want to get gut nastiness everywhere. You can also snip the tail and fins off, but I like to leave them on—they crisp up like potato chips in the fryer.

Get the spice blend ready. Pour the chile salt into a small mixing bowl, add the lemongrass, and stir to combine. Sprinkle the spice blend onto the fish, and make sure to season inside the cavity as well. We want it to be beautiful inside and out! Let the fish sit at room temperature for 10 minutes so the spice blend can soak in.

Make the dredging mixture. In a wide, shallow bowl combine the all-purpose flour, rice flour, cornstarch, and kosher salt. Dredge each fish in the mixture, turning and pressing lightly on each side. Shake off the excess flour and place the fish on a platter to hang out while you get the oil hot.

Now, it's time to fry. Set a large frying pan over medium heat and fill it with 1 inch of neutral oil. Bring the oil to about 350°F on a probe thermometer. (Keep additional neutral oil on hand so you can keep topping up the pan as you cook.) While the oil heats up, line a large plate with paper towels.

Working with one fish at a time, tilt the pan away from your body to prevent splattering and gently place one dredged fish into the oil, holding it by the tail. Shallow-fry the fish for 4 to 5 minutes, until browned on one side. With the fish spatula, carefully turn the fish over, once again away from your body to avoid splashing yourself with oil. Here's my rule: Pretty much every movement you make should be with the intent to prevent oil from splashing on you. I'm not saying you should be terrified of the oil, but it's good to keep in mind how much it can mess you up!

Fry the fish on the other side for 4 to 5 minutes, until it becomes crisp and golden brown. Transfer to the paper towel–lined plate. Repeat this process to fry the remaining fish, replenishing the oil in the pan if it's looking sparse. Remove the paper towels before serving. Serve hot, and be mindful of the bones.

Variation: You can add 1 tablespoon grated fresh turmeric and 1 tablespoon granulated sugar to the dredging mixture to give the fish an earthier flavor.

CÁ VƯỢC NƯỚNG GIẤY BẠC
FOIL-BAKED WHOLE SEA BASS

Serves 4

I went on a lot of fishing trips with my dad, who'd wake me up before dawn to help him lug fishing gear to his secret spots around the San Francisco Bay. And on each trip, he and his friends would always tell tales about the elusive California white sea bass, a sleek, glittery fish that could grow to almost 5 feet long. That was the trophy they aimed for, and I know they'd want me to tell you that, on very rare occasions, they did manage to land a few big ones. When you catch a prize fish like this, you'd better have a fail-proof recipe ready to do it justice.

My family's recipe is the result of many dining table debates with other family members. Each family had their own secret technique for a so-called prize fish, but in general, it involved slathering the fish in fermented chile paste, tons of aromatics, and fish sauce before baking or grilling. When it comes to flaky fish like the white sea bass, cooking it whole is a good way to keep it from falling apart. This preparation is great as a filling for summer rolls (see page 152).

Note: Yes, fish bones can be annoying to deal with. But if you understand the anatomy of the fish you are eating—namely, where the bones are— you can avoid them. When serving a whole fish, you can forgo the whole bone-seeking rigmarole by making a couple of cuts along the major muscle sections of the fish. From there, you can use a chopstick (or spoon) to pull the flesh away from the bones. Allocate that flesh onto a separate plate for serving. This technique is standard protocol in my family, and it's saved us a lot of headaches.

3 pounds whole sea bass or branzino, scaled and gutted (see page 85)

2 tablespoons chrouk metae or sambal oelek (see page 22)

1 teaspoon minced lemongrass

1 teaspoon minced ginger

1 tablespoon fish sauce

2 teaspoons granulated sugar

1 lemongrass stalk, bruised and cut into 4-inch segments (see page 29)

Preheat the oven to 350°F.

First, butcher the fish. Place your fish on a cutting board or plate and use a sharp knife to make multiple cuts through the flesh at 45-degree angles, down to the bone. Make your incisions 1 to 1½ inches apart, starting from the pectoral fin and tail. Do this on both sides of each fish.

Make the chile paste marinade. In a small bowl, combine the chrouk metae, lemongrass, ginger, fish sauce, and sugar. Slather the chile marinade all over the fish, including in the cavity and in the cuts you made. Stuff the cavity with half of the lemongrass stalk segments.

Now, wrap the fish. Place a sheet of aluminum foil on top of a baking sheet. You're just using the baking sheet to stage the foil, so don't press it around the edges of the baking sheet. Line up the remaining lemongrass segments in a horizontal line along the center of the foil, then place the marinated fish on top of them. Gently fold the top and bottom edges of the foil over the fish, then fold the left and right edges toward the center to seal them.

Transfer the foil-wrapped fish on the baking sheet to the preheated oven and bake for 15 to 20 minutes, or until steam starts really billowing out of the foil. When finished, the eyes of the fish should also be firm and opaque. Serve immediately. If the lemongrass is young and tender, you can eat the segments with the fish, too.

WE LIVED
THROUGH WAR

If you're gonna talk about Vietnamese food and culture, you have to talk about the suffering, too. I know it's not easy dinner conversation for most people. Ironically for me, the people in my life who came face-to-face with the hardest times in our history, with war, were the least likely to share their stories. But I think talking about the awful stuff is so important in order to see the whole picture of who we are and where we come from.

So many dishes around the world are richer for their context. In Cambodia, tarantulas, known as aping, have been a part of Khmer cuisine for as long as anyone can remember, but their popularity boomed during the Khmer Rouge military regime, when famine sent citizens into the jungles to forage for food. One of South Korea's most famous modern dishes is budae jjigae, or "army stew," a post-war recipe whose key ingredients, Spam and American cheese, were smuggled out of United States army bases by hungry locals.

We don't just inherit specific dishes from war; it brought in new ways of cooking, too. My earliest memory in the kitchen is the first time I was enlisted to wash rice. My mom held the pot and showed me the motions first, using her hand to scrub the grains in the water, but my little fingers were too clumsy to strain it without letting a few pieces drop down the drain.

"You're being wasteful!" my mom would say, furious. Those lost grains were a slap in the face to a woman who, as a small child living in colonial-era Phú Quốc, was responsible for retrieving her family's rice rations in the wake of a famine that killed an estimated half a million to two million Vietnamese. Dropping a bowl of rice, losing a few grains, was a matter of life and death. Later, my dad would tell me about how he used to stretch a dozen grains of rice into a tea that would last him for days. If he was lucky, he'd be able to supplement it with an anchovy he caught. I never experienced those beyond-harsh conditions firsthand, but I still felt them indirectly, in the desperate undertone of a spoken reprimand, or the bare, smooth surface of a completely eaten pot of rice.

For the average person, war isn't about heroic, badass shit—it's hunger. It haunts you.

The recipes in this chapter are all touched by Vietnam's wars, in one way or another. Cơm Chay Mỡ Hành Gừng | Scorched Rice with Ginger and Green Onion Sauce (page 109) documents the brilliance of cooks who managed to turn precious grains of burnt rice into a now-treasured street food. The recipes for Cá Kho Tộ | Clay Pot Catfish (page 113) and Rau Muống Xao | Stir-Fried Water Spinach (page 110) are, at least apocryphally, tied to what soldiers ate in warzones. I've also decided to put the book's phở recipes in this chapter because the soup, while famous as an icon of Vietnamese food, has also been symbolic of post-war scarcity, food rationing, and the fragility of life under Việt Cộng rule.

And just like budae jjigae and aping, these dishes are still popular—not necessarily because of their utility, but because they're damn delicious. Though war and all of the misery it carries with it should be a thing of the past, I don't want people to forget about it either. Dishes like the ones in this chapter don't just tell us about what our ancestors went through; they also reassure us that, whatever comes, humanity will find a way to survive—and we'll find pleasure and comfort wherever and however we can.

SCORCHED RICE WITH GINGER AND GREEN ONION SAUCE

Serves 4

1 tablespoon neutral oil
(such as vegetable oil)

2½ cups day-old cooked Cơm Tấm | Broken Rice (page 34)

1 cup Mỡ Hành Gừng | Ginger and Green Onion Sauce (page 47)

¼ cup fresh coconut pulp or shredded fresh coconut for garnish

¼ cup squid floss or pork floss for garnish

2 tablespoons toasted and chopped peanuts for garnish

When you're hungry, it doesn't really matter if the apple is ugly or if the rice is kinda burnt—you're gonna eat it anyway. And sometimes, that necessity can lead to fondness or even something revelatory. Take this cơm chay, for example. Some Vietnamese home cook scraped up the scorched rice at the bottom of their pot and, with a little bit of seasoning and know-how, made it into a full-fledged Dish with a capital D. Nowadays, people scorch their rice on purpose just to make it.

When rice is scorched in this way, it takes on a nutty flavor and gains a fantastic crunch. No wonder folks in places as disparate as Korea, Iran, and Spain have versions of the same.

Note: This dish is all about leftover rice. Make sure to cook the broken rice the day before you start so it can cool and dry out a bit overnight. To help it along, you can spread out the rice in a thin layer on a rimmed baking sheet. If you already have leftover rice, lucky you. You can go ahead and start scorching.

Pour the neutral oil into a medium non-stick or cast-iron pan set over medium heat. Once the oil is shimmering, add in the day-old rice and use a spatula to flatten it, maximizing its contact with the hot surface of the pan. The rice should cover the entire surface of the pan.

Turn the heat to low, and let the rice cook for 20 to 25 minutes, continuously pressing the rice down to maintain contact with the hot surface of the pan. When the bottom of the rice is scorched and crispy, turn off the heat and carefully flip the rice out of the pan. To do this, place a plate that is slightly larger than the pan upside down over the top of the rice. Hold the plate steady as you quickly flip the pan over. The crispy part of the rice should be facing up.

To serve, use the spatula or scissors to cut the scorched rice into 8 pieces, then top each piece with a spoonful of the Ginger and Green Onion Sauce. Finally, garnish with the coconut pulp, squid floss, and toasted peanuts. Eat with your hands, as though it were a plate of nachos.

RAU MUỐNG XÀO
STIR-FRIED WATER SPINACH

Serves 4

There's a story that I like to think about whenever I eat water spinach, a vegetable beloved in Southeast Asian cuisine for its tender shoots. Rumor has it that it played a key role in the Second Indochina War, sustaining Việt Cộng soldiers who traveled up and down the Ho Chi Minh Trail, an important military supply route. American forces bombed the hell out of the trail, leaving massive craters that quickly filled with fresh water during monsoon seasons. They also indiscriminately sprayed 20 million gallons of Agent Orange, a destructive chemical herbicide, over crop fields and vegetation. According to the story, the Việt Cộng avoided starvation by filling the craters with fast-growing water spinach and catfish, turning them into little ecosystems. Water spinach grows quickly—up to 9 feet per day when conditions are right—so it's easy to imagine it literally feeding an army.

3 pounds water spinach

3 tablespoons neutral oil (such as vegetable oil)

1 tablespoon minced garlic

3 tablespoons minced dried shrimp

1 Thai bird's eye chile, sliced

1 tablespoon fish sauce

¼ teaspoon kosher salt

Steamed rice (see page 34) to serve

First, prep the spinach. Cut the water spinach into fourths, and don't worry about being exact—you just want it to be able to fit in your pan. In a large, clean bowl or directly in the sink, rinse the water spinach thoroughly to remove any grit, then drain it in a colander and set aside.

Now, get started cooking. Set a wok or large skillet over high heat for 1 to 2 minutes. Once the wok is hot, add 1 tablespoon of the neutral oil. When the oil is shimmering, add in the garlic and dried shrimp. Toast the aromatics for about 30 seconds, until they start to turn golden brown. Remove the shrimp and garlic from the wok and set aside.

Add the remaining 2 tablespoons neutral oil to the wok, and give it a few seconds to heat up. Once the oil is shimmering, add the water spinach and chile to the wok and toss the mixture 2 to 3 times. (If you're using a large skillet rather than a huge wok, you might need to cook the water spinach in batches. If this is the case, keep the chile in the skillet throughout.) Season the greens with the fish sauce and salt, then keep tossing the spinach until it cooks down to about a third of its original mass, about 5 minutes.

To serve, garnish the spinach with the reserved garlic and dried shrimp and enjoy with rice.

CÁ KHO TỘ
CLAY POT CATFISH

Serves 6

Regardless of whether the stories about crater "farming" on the Ho Chi Minh Trail are true (see the headnote on page 110), braised catfish is still one of the most iconic recipes in Vietnamese cuisine. Its main components are staples in Vietnam—fish sauce, palm sugar, peppercorns, and catfish—and they taste so good after a steamy session in a clay pot.

If you're looking for Vietnamese catfish in the United States, be aware that here, it's got a different name: basa. It's basically the same as American catfish.

Note: Clay pots are great for slow, low-heat braises and ideal for delicate, heat-sensitive ingredients such as rice and fish. I highly recommend looking for your own clay pot at a local Asian market or online. Just make sure that your pot doesn't have any cracks and that it's glazed on the inside. When you plan to use the pot, wash it thoroughly and soak it in cold water for 24 hours to ensure that it won't crack during cooking. Of course, if you don't have a clay pot, cooking this recipe in a Dutch oven will work, too.

3 pounds catfish steaks, sliced 1½ inches thick

3 tablespoons fish sauce

1 teaspoon cracked black pepper

2 tablespoons neutral oil (such as vegetable oil)

½ cup minced shallot

1½ tablespoons minced ginger

2 teaspoons minced garlic

½ cup Nước Màu Dừa | Coconut Caramel Sauce (page 36)

1 Thai bird's eye chile, bruised

2 cups coconut water

2 tablespoons sliced green onions, green parts only, for garnish

Steamed rice (see page 34) for serving

Pat the catfish steaks with a paper towel to remove excess moisture. They don't have to be totally dry; just make sure they're not wet. Season the catfish with the fish sauce and black pepper and set aside (room temperature is okay).

Set a clay pot or Dutch oven on the stove over medium-high heat. Allow the pot to heat through for 2 to 3 minutes, then add in the neutral oil. When the oil starts to shimmer, add the shallot, ginger, and garlic to the pot. Cook the mixture for 1 minute, or just until the garlic begins to get toasty and a little bit brown at the edges.

Pour in the Coconut Caramel Sauce, then swiftly (but gently) place the seasoned fish steaks in the pot in a single layer. Adjust the heat to high and allow the steaks to cook for 1 to 2 minutes on each side. After you've flipped the steaks and they've taken on a light brown color, add the chile and coconut water. Bring the mixture to a simmer.

Once the mixture reaches a simmer, cover the pot and turn the heat to medium-low. Allow the fish to braise for 20 minutes, until the catfish is tender and cooked through. To serve, garnish the catfish with the green onions and serve immediately with rice. This dish will also keep well in an airtight container in the fridge for dinner the next day, at which point the flavor will be more caramelly and a bit fishier.

BÁNH TÔM
PRAWN FRITTERS

Serves 4

In an essay for the online magazine *Catapult*, writer Hoang Samuelson goes into how sweet potatoes were key to her family's survival in post-war southern Vietnam: When the rice crop failed disastrously in the 1970s, Samuelson's mother planted sweet potatoes to supplement their diet. The sweet potato came to Vietnam by way of the Philippines in the late sixteenth century. Farmers and everyday people embraced the crop for its high yield and its ability to thrive in relatively nutrient-poor soil, making it a reliable standby during times of scarcity.

Local cooks figured out a ton of ways to use sweet potatoes, but the most delicious modern use of the vegetable is this recipe, which combines shredded sweet potatoes with shell-on shrimp. Both ingredients are coated in a tempura-like batter and deep-fried, with the sweet potatoes forming a little "basket" for the shrimp. These crunchy parcels are wrapped in lettuce, then dipped in a spicy and sweet nước chấm. For this recipe, you'll need a wide and flat soup ladle and a cooling rack.

Note: If you're working with frozen shrimp, you'll need to fully defrost them overnight in the fridge in advance of making this recipe. Additionally, if you're making pickles specifically for this recipe, you'll need to do so one day in advance.

PRAWN FRITTERS

2 pounds fresh or frozen and defrosted U-15 (jumbo) white shrimp, whole with heads

2 eggs

1 cup seltzer water

½ cup rice flour

½ cup all-purpose flour

¼ cup tapioca flour

1 teaspoon kosher salt

1 teaspoon turmeric powder

1 teaspoon baking powder

2 sweet potatoes, peeled and cut into matchsticks (about 3 cups)

Neutral oil (such as vegetable oil) for frying

Start by preparing the shrimp. First, line a baking sheet or a tray with paper towels. Then make an ice bath by filling a medium bowl with cold water and ice; a chilly bath will keep them fresh longer. Add the shrimp to the ice bath to rinse them off. Once rinsed, remove the shrimp from the water and set them on the paper towel–lined baking sheet to drain excess moisture.

To devein the shrimp, make an incision in the shell, following down the spine, and use a toothpick or sharp skewer to pull out the dark, stringy organ. To do this, pierce the shrimp through the soft part of its body, between the head and the first segment of shell, and gently pull up on the toothpick to lift out the vein. If the vein breaks, repeat the process in several places. It's finicky work, but it's worth it to not eat shrimp doo-doo. Store the deveined shrimp in the fridge until you're ready to cook.

Next, make the tempura-like batter. Grab a medium mixing bowl and crack the eggs into it. Add the seltzer water to the bowl, then whisk the mixture together like you're making scrambled eggs. Carbonated water, a secret ingredient in a lot of tempura recipes, makes the batter crispier when you fry it. Add the flours, salt, turmeric powder, and baking powder and whisk until smooth. Drop the sweet potato matchsticks into the batter and mix them in gently. Set aside while you get your fry setup ready.

CONTINUED

PRAWN FRITTERS,
CONTINUED

GARNISH

1 head iceberg lettuce, washed and leaves detached

2 bunches mint

1 English cucumber, sliced into coins

1 cup Củ Cải Chua Ngọt | Pickled Carrots and Daikon (page 49), liquid drained

¼ cup Nước Mắm Tỏi Ớt | Chile Fish Sauce (page 43) for serving

Fill a cast-iron pot or Dutch oven with 2 to 3 inches of neutral oil and set over medium heat. Once the oil reaches 325°F on a probe thermometer, you're ready to fry.

Assembling the fritters is a little more complicated than simply tossing the battered vegetables into the pot, but a wide and flat soup ladle will help a lot. Brush the inside of the ladle with just enough neutral oil to form a thin coat to prevent sticking. Spoon 2 tablespoons of the battered sweet potatoes into the greased ladle and use the shape of the ladle as a guide to press the mixture into a vaguely cuplike shape. This is the literal cradle for your sweet lil' shrimp. Place one shrimp in the sweet potato cradle, then drizzle a tablespoon of batter over it to tuck it in.

Hold the ladle close to the surface of the hot oil. (If you hold it higher up, you'll risk the fritter splashing down into the oil, which trust me, could hurt.) Use a large spoon to gently dislodge the fritter from the ladle and release it into the oil. Fry the prawn fritter for 5 minutes on one side, then use chopsticks or tongs to flip it over and fry it for 5 minutes more, until golden brown. Transfer the fritter to a cooling rack and season it to taste with salt (remember that you'll be dipping these in fish sauce later, so go light).

Repeat until you finish the batter and shrimp. You should have the right ratio of shrimp to sweet potatoes, but if you have extra sweet potatoes, they're just as good fried without the shrimp, too. Consider those to be bonus fritters.

To serve, transfer the fritters to a platter, and arrange the lettuce leaves, mint, cucumber slices, and pickled vegetables on a large plate. Divide the Chile Fish Sauce among four bowls. To eat, grab a lettuce leaf. Place a fritter, a few mint leaves, one or two pieces of cucumber, and a pinch of pickles inside the leaf and wrap together. Dip the package into Chile Fish Sauce between each bite. It takes some finesse to not make a mess while you eat, but I promise that I won't judge you for it.

BÁNH PHỞ
PHỞ NOODLES

Serves 6

Most people outside of Vietnam have only known phở made with dried rice noodles; but in Vietnam, plush, silky, freshly made noodles are the norm. Just like corn tortillas in Mexico and pasta in Italy, every neighborhood seems to have at least one vendor making noodles from scratch. If you're lucky enough to find fresh noodles where you are, your soup will be better for it. Otherwise, I'm also including my dried noodle rehydration hacks, which result in a better and almost-fresh texture.

DRIED NOODLE VARIATION

One 16-ounce package dried phở noodles, small or medium thickness

Neutral oil (such as vegetable oil) to prevent sticking

First, soak the noodles. Place the noodles in a medium bowl and cover them with cold water. Let them soak for up to 4 hours at room temperature or overnight in the fridge. After the soak, they should have softened just a bit.

Next, cook 'em. Bring a medium pot of water to boil over high heat. Drain the noodles and add them to the pot. Stir them occasionally to prevent sticking—nothing's worse than an uncooked clump of noodles. After 5 minutes, start checking the noodles to see if they're tender enough to bite through. The timing will vary by the brand, but it shouldn't take longer than 10 minutes.

Drain the noodles in a colander in your sink and rinse them thoroughly with cold water to get rid of any excess starch. Coat them in a few drops of neutral oil to keep them from sticking together. Use them as soon as you can—within a day or so—because they'll only get stickier with time.

FRESH NOODLE VARIATION

28 ounces fresh phở noodles

Neutral oil (such as vegetable oil) to prevent sticking

For fresh noodles, you can go straight to cooking. Fill a medium pot about three-fourths of the way with water and bring it to a boil over high heat. In the meantime, unwrap the noodles and separate the bundle as much as you can so they don't become one giant mass in the pot.

Blanch the noodles in the boiling water for just 15 to 30 seconds, then immediately drain them in a colander in the sink. Rinse them thoroughly with cold water to get rid of the excess starch. Coat them in a few drops of the oil to keep them from sticking together. Use them as soon as you can—within a day or so—they'll only get stickier with time.

PHỞ GÀ MIỀN NAM
SOUTHERN-STYLE CHICKEN PHỞ

Serves 6

You could write a whole book about Vietnamese society under the Việt Cộng regime—and I know people have—but a single bowl of phở gà will also tell you a lot about that history. Vietnam had already gone through a series of famines under French colonial rule, but after the war, even more food shortages came out of the forced collectivization of the agriculture and fishing industries, worsened by the mass destruction of fertile land by Agent Orange.

People made it work however they could in those times. Real rice noodles and good meat could be found for steep prices in the thriving black markets, but you shopped at your own peril. In British journalist Graham Holliday's book, *Eating Viet Nam*, a woman who grew up in Hanoi explains why the chicken version of phở gained popularity in the post-war years. Neighbors were incentivized by the government to sell one another out, so grilling, baking, and roasting your black-market meat was out of the question. Gently, quietly poaching chicken for phở gà—keeping the windows shut tight, of course—was one way to keep your head down.

The style of phở in this book is the southern way of doing it. While northerners tend to prefer their soups straight-up, we southerners pile on the garnishes: fresh herbs, spicy sauces, fresh citrus, and chile peppers.

Note: This recipe will be a little easier if you have a spice bag or cheesecloth for the loose spices, but it's not a deal-breaker. You'll just have to fish out the spices with a slotted spoon or small strainer.

4 quarts cold filtered water

Kosher salt

One 3½-pound organic chicken

1 yellow onion, unpeeled

One 1-inch knob fresh ginger, unpeeled

1 garlic head

½ teaspoon whole fennel seeds

5 whole star anise pods

6 whole cloves

3 cinnamon sticks

1 tablespoon whole black peppercorns

4 quarts Nước Luộc Gà | Chicken Stock (page 51) or store-bought stock

¼ teaspoon turmeric powder

2 tablespoons granulated sugar

First, you'll brine the chicken. Find a big pot—one that's large enough to fit your whole chicken plus a good amount of water. Fill the pot with 8 cups of the water and 2 tablespoons kosher salt. Stir until the salt dissolves, then submerge the whole chicken in the pot and let it brine for 15 to 20 minutes. This is a trick from my mom: It makes the chicken juicier and the broth clearer in the end. Drain the pot, then rinse the chicken under cold water until the water runs clear. Remember to disinfect your hands and the sink after doing this. Stash the whole chicken in the fridge until you finish the next few steps. Clean the pot and hang onto it for later.

While the chicken is brining, broil the aromatics. Adjust an oven rack to the top position and set the oven to low broil. Allow the broiler to preheat for 5 minutes. Slice the onion and ginger into 1-inch chunks—no need to remove the peels. Separate the cloves from the head of garlic, again without removing the peels—the peels add flavor to the stock. Put the ginger, onion, and garlic in a small oven-safe tray or pan and broil them 6 inches from the heating element for 5 to 7 minutes. (Don't use oil or you'll make the soup greasy.) Shake the pan to rustle the pieces around and expose the un-charred sides, then broil them for 5 to 7 minutes more. Your oven might take more or less time to blacken the aromatics, so keep an eye on them. Once all sides of the aromatics are charred, set aside.

CONTINUED

The Memory of Taste

SOUTHERN-STYLE CHICKEN PHỞ,
CONTINUED

1 tablespoon MSG

¼ cup fish sauce

1½ packages dried or fresh phở noodles, cooked (page 117)

GARNISH

1 bunch Thai basil

1 bunch culantro or cilantro, leaves picked

¼ cup sliced green chile peppers (jalapeño or serrano)

1 lime or lemon, cut into 6 wedges

9 ounces mung bean sprouts

1 cup Nước Mắm Gừng | Ginger Fish Sauce (page 41) for serving

½ yellow onion, thinly sliced, for serving

½ cup sliced green onions, white and green parts, for serving

Now you'll toast some spices for the broth. Set a medium, heavy frying pan over medium heat. Allow the pan to heat through for 1 to 2 minutes. Once it's hot, add in the fennel seeds, star anise pods, cloves, cinnamon sticks, and black peppercorns. Turn the heat to low and toast the spices, shaking the pan frequently, for 5 minutes, until fragrant. Remove the pan from the heat, and when the spices are cool enough to handle, tuck them into a cheesecloth sachet or spice bag.

At this point, we'll get started on the broth in earnest. Return the brined chicken to the large pot from earlier. Fill the large pot with the chicken stock, the remaining 8 cups cold water, the charred aromatics, and the sachet of toasted spices, as well as the turmeric powder and 2 tablespoons salt. Place the pot over medium heat and bring the contents to a simmer. Don't let it get to a rolling boil or the broth will get cloudy. If that happens, it's not the end of the world, it just won't look like phở. Simmer the broth, uncovered, for 40 minutes.

To check the chicken for doneness, remove it from the pot, making sure the liquid in the chicken's cavity drains out into the pot. (Otherwise you're just stealing flavor from the phở and setting yourself up for a mess in your kitchen.) Stick a probe thermometer into the thickest part of the chicken, which is usually the upper thigh. If the chicken is done, the internal temperature should sit at around 165°F for 30 seconds straight.

Once the chicken is done, you can set the chicken on a cutting board or big plate to cool, and continue to cook the broth over medium heat for another hour. Again, the broth should be at a gentle simmer, not boiling. If you can, enlist a buddy to skim and discard any frothy scum that rises to the surface of the broth while you do the next step.

It's time to carve the chicken! Use a sharp 6-inch knife to remove the breast from the bone by cutting lengthwise through the chest. Aim to be slightly off-center, since the breastbone is right in the middle, and you can't cut through that. Carefully use the knife to "peel" the breast meat off of the bone using long strokes. Set the two breast pieces on a plate and transfer it to the fridge until you're almost ready to eat. Remove the leg quarters by dislocating the thigh bone from the main body and slicing through the gap. Return the leg quarters to the broth, along with the remainder of the chicken carcass. Once the broth has simmered for 30 minutes more, remove the chicken quarter pieces from the broth and allow them to cool on a cutting board or plate.

Strain the broth through a fine-mesh sieve into a clean, medium pot. Set the pot on the stove and season it with 1 teaspoon salt, the sugar, MSG, and fish sauce. Don't just trust me on this one, since the flavors of your ingredients might be different from mine: Taste the broth to make sure you like it, and if you don't, adjust the seasoning by adding more fish sauce.

Adjust the heat to medium and bring the broth back to a simmer. Once simmering, turn the heat to low, just to keep the broth hot while you prep the bowls for serving.

To prepare the garnishes for serving, arrange the Thai basil, culantro, green chile peppers, lime wedges, and mung bean sprouts on a platter. Divide the Ginger Fish Sauce among six dipping bowls.

Pull the chicken breasts out of the fridge and slice them against the grain into ¼-inch-thick pieces, being careful to keep the skin attached. Using your fingers or two forks, shred the meat off of the cooked chicken legs.

When ready to serve, divide the prepared phở noodles among six large soup bowls. Add 3 to 4 slices of chicken breast and a generous pinch of shredded dark meat from the legs to each bowl. At this point, you can crank up the heat on the broth to get it to a nice boil, then ladle 2 to 4 cups of broth into each bowl, depending on the size of the bowl. Top with the sliced yellow onion and a sprinkle of the green onions. Serve alongside the platter of garnishes so each person can customize their phở, and the small dipping bowls of the Ginger Fish Sauce for folks to dunk pieces of chicken meat in as they eat.

PHỞ BÒ MIỀN NAM
SOUTHERN-STYLE BEEF PHỞ

Serves 6

There are lots of stories about where phở came from: Some say it was an early French-Vietnamese fusion dish; others trace it to the crossing-the-bridge noodles eaten by Yunnanese immigrants from China. But one thing we do know is that phở started out as a regional northern Vietnamese dish, and until the French brought European cattle breeds to the country, the soup was made with water buffalo meat.

Beef phở, made with the offcuts of French cows, reigned. But during the food shortages and social paranoia of post-war Vietnam, the soup you could get (at least out in the open) was practically dishwater, made with just the crummiest ingredients possible. The rich, mouthwatering flavor of phở bò quickly became a distant, but fond memory.

Nowadays, you'll once again find it everywhere, especially in the Vietnamese diaspora. For those in my parents' generation who endured the scarcity of those years, beef phở is more than comfort food—it's a long sigh of relief. For this recipe, you'll need a cheesecloth or spice bag, a 10-quart stock pot, and ten hours of your life.

---

3 pounds beef bones, such as femur or knuckle

2 pounds beef brisket

3 beef tendons (about 6 ounces)

5 quarts cold filtered water

7 tablespoons kosher salt

1 pound beef tripe

4 quarts beef stock or bone broth

1 yellow onion, unpeeled

One 1-inch knob fresh ginger, unpeeled

1 garlic head

½ teaspoon whole fennel seeds

5 whole star anise pods

6 whole cloves

3 cinnamon sticks

1 tablespoon whole black peppercorns

3 tablespoons granulated sugar

1 tablespoon MSG

¼ cup fish sauce

2 packages beef balls (optional; I recommend Lao Thai Nam)

First, you'll clean the bones, brisket, and tendons under cold running water in a sink or large bowl for 5 minutes. You're just getting any extra grime off of the ingredients.

Next, blanch the beef. Fill a large pot with 12 cups of the water and 3 tablespoons of the salt. Bring the pot to a simmer over medium heat, then add the bones, brisket, tendons, and tripe. Once the water returns to a simmer, blanch for 10 minutes. (The meat does not need to be fully cooked.) While that's happening, use a spider skimmer to remove any foam that rises to the surface of the water. Remove the pot from the heat, then put a large colander in the sink. Drain the bones and meat into the colander, then rinse them with cold running water for 5 minutes to get off the rest of the scum.

At this point, we'll get started on the broth in earnest. Clean the large pot to get all the impurities and grime out of the interior. Then add in the beef stock and the remaining 8 cups water, and return the bones, brisket, and tendons to the pot. Add the tripe to the pot at this point as well.

Now, prepare to broil the aromatics. Place an oven rack in the top position and set the oven to low broil. Allow the broiler to preheat for 5 minutes. While that's happening, coarsely chop the onion and ginger—no need to remove the peels. Separate the cloves from the head of garlic, again without removing the peels—the peels add flavor to the stock. Put the ginger, onion, and garlic in a small oven-safe tray or pan and broil them 6 inches from the heating element for 5 to 7 minutes. (Don't use oil, or you'll make the soup greasy.) Shake the pan to rustle the pieces around and expose the un-charred sides, then broil them for 5 to 7 minutes more. Your oven might take more or less time to blacken the aromatics, so keep an eye on them. Once all sides of the aromatics are charred, put them in the large pot of broth.

GARNISH

1 bunch Thai basil or Genovese basil

1 bunch culantro or cilantro, leaves picked

¼ cup sliced green chile peppers
(jalapeño or serrano)

1 lime or lemon, cut into 6 wedges

9 ounces mung bean sprouts

1½ (16-ounce) packages phở noodles,
cooked (page 117)

6 ounces Bò Tái | Thinly Sliced Steak
(page 125)

½ peeled yellow onion, thinly sliced,
for serving

½ cup sliced green onions, white and
green parts, for serving

Hoisin sauce, Sriracha, and sa tế
(see pages 21 and 22) for the table

Next you'll toast some spices for use in the broth. Set a medium, heavy frying pan over medium heat. Allow the pan to heat through for 1 to 2 minutes. Once it's hot, add in the fennel seeds, star anise pods, cloves, cinnamon sticks, and black peppercorns. Turn the heat to low and toast the spices, shaking the pan frequently, for 5 minutes, until fragrant. Remove the pan from the heat, and when the spices are cool enough to handle, tuck them into a cheesecloth sachet or spice bag and add the whole thing to the broth.

Add 2 tablespoons of the salt, 1 tablespoon of the sugar, and the MSG to the pot and bring the mixture to a boil over high heat.

Once the mixture reaches a boil, turn the heat to medium-low and let it simmer for 10 hours—that's right, 10 hours. You'll have to baby the broth a little while this happens.

For the first 7 hours, check in every 15 minutes and skim off any of the impurities that rise to the surface of the liquid using a spider skimmer. Look for the greasy stuff, plus any gray-brown foam. After 7 hours, remove the spice bag and the beef bones and discard them. Prepare an ice bath in the sink. Remove the brisket and tendons from the pot and rinse them under cold running water for 5 minutes, then submerge them in the ice bath for 5 minutes, until cooled completely. Transfer the brisket, tendons, and tripe to a plate and refrigerate.

When the broth has been simmering for a total of 9 hours, add the beef tripe back to the pot. Season the broth with the fish sauce, as well as the remaining 2 tablespoons salt and remaining 2 tablespoons sugar. At 10 hours, add in the beef balls (if using). Prepare an ice bath in the sink. At this point, you can once again remove the beef tripe and rinse it under cold running water for 5 minutes, then submerge it in the ice bath for 5 minutes, until cooled completely. Transfer the tripe to a plate and refrigerate until you're almost ready to eat.

Let the broth continue to simmer for another half hour, and give it one final pass with a spider skimmer to get out any last bits of scum. Adjust the heat to the lowest setting, just to keep the broth hot while you prep the bowls.

Next, slice the meat for serving. Using a sharp knife, cut the tendons on the diagonal into ⅛-inch-thick slices. Do the same with the tripe. Cut the brisket into ⅛-inch-thick slices, cutting against the grain. Halve or quarter the beef balls (if using), according to your preference.

To prepare the garnishes for serving, arrange the Thai basil, culantro, green chile peppers, lime wedges, and mung bean sprouts on a platter.

Crank up the heat to return the broth to a boil before serving. Divide the noodles among six large soup bowls and add the brisket, tendons, tripe, and beef balls (if using) to each. Ladle 2 to 4 cups of hot broth into each bowl, depending on the size of the bowl. Top with the sliced yellow onion and a sprinkle of the green onions, and serve alongside the Bò Tái and the platter of garnishes so each person can customize their phở. Pass the sauces around the table.

BÒ TÁI
THINLY SLICED STEAK

Serves 6

Bò tái is pure luxury: It's a declaration that you've got beef that's so pretty and delicate, you can serve it raw. Sometimes you'll see it served as a dish all on its own, like Italian carpaccio, with a heavy sprinkle of lime juice and herbs to add flavor to the beef. Otherwise, you'll see it either in or next to a bowl of Phở Bò Miền Nam | Southern-Style Beef Phở (page 122), with broth that's hot enough to quickly cook the beef when you dunk it in. For this recipe, I like to use sirloin flap steak, also known as bavette, because it's pretty affordable and has a rich flavor that I love. But you can also use tenderloin or even filet mignon if you're feeling fancy.

---

6 ounces sirloin beef flap

Using a long, sharp knife, trim all the fat and gristle from the surface of the steak. Look for the grain, or the lines indicating the direction of the muscle fibers: Plan to cut perpendicular to those lines—against the grain—so the pieces aren't chewy.

Now, prep to slice. Lay a sheet of plastic wrap on your counter (this is where you'll place the pieces of cut steak). Hone your knife to make sure it's razor-sharp, then use it to cut super-thin slices of the beef—the thinner, the better. If the steak's been sitting out for a bit and feels too slouchy to cut precisely, here's a hack: Stick it in the freezer for half an hour to an hour to stiffen it up before you try again. As you cut the steak, place each piece of steak on the plastic wrap in a single layer. Then cover the pieces with another piece of plastic wrap.

Ahh, yes . . . it's time to tenderize. Grab a rolling pin or wine bottle and gently tap on the slices to turn them buttery soft. Repeat with the rest of the beef if you have more to cut.

At this point, the beef can be served. If you're not serving it immediately, you can keep the slices tightly wrapped in the fridge, ideally for up to 30 minutes before serving to prevent oxidization. You can also freeze the slices by separating them with wax paper into single-slice layers and placing them in an airtight container for up to 3 months.

XÔI XOÀI THÁI
THAI-STYLE STICKY RICE WITH MANGO

Serves 4

For people like my parents, the fall of Saigon to the Việt Cộng in 1975 was apocalyptic. "All of a sudden, we weren't allowed to go to school or work," my mom told me. "We were scared for our lives, so we left." In the dark of night, they dodged Việt Cộng soldiers on Phú Quốc Island and my dad took over a fishing boat, stuffed to the limit with a few dozen family members and friends. After a couple weeks of bobbing and weaving through the Gulf of Thailand to try and outsmart the Việt Cộng, as well as some pirates, they found their way to a Thai refugee camp. They were there for nine months.

That's when the story would usually get less detailed. Maybe because it was too painful; maybe because they starved. Desperate, my mom sewed for work, which brought in the equivalent of 88 cents a day. It was barely anything. But she told me that when the money came in, she would find a street vendor and treat herself to a warm mound of sweet sticky rice topped with slices of mango. In the thick of those bitter times, the dish gave her the comfort she needed to keep going. She still makes it at home to this day.

Note: For this recipe, silky-smooth Ataulfo mangos are best. A ripe one will have a bright, golden-yellow skin and should feel slightly soft to the touch, but not mushy or bruised. If it's too hard, it's not ripe yet. Check that the stem end is dry and shriveled—that's good! You can also check a mango by giving it a good sniff. If it's got a sweet and fragrant aroma, it's ready.

2 cups glutinous rice, soaked overnight and drained

1⅓ cups filtered water

3 fresh pandan leaves, or 1 vanilla bean pod

1 cup grated fresh coconut (see page 49) or frozen and defrosted coconut meat

1 cup Nước Cốt Dừa Tươi | Fresh Coconut Milk (page 49) or canned coconut milk

One 1-inch knob fresh ginger, sliced into coins

⅓ cup granulated sugar

1 teaspoon kosher salt

1 Ataulfo mango

4 teaspoons toasted sesame seeds (see page 19)

In a rice cooker, cook the glutinous rice with the water and pandan leaves. You don't need a cooker with a fancy "sticky rice" setting. My parents always just use the "Cook" button, so that should work well enough for you. Once it's done, stir in half of the grated coconut and let it cook for 5 minutes more.

Meanwhile, prepare the coconut milk mixture. Add the coconut milk to a small pot with the ginger, sugar, and salt. Warm the pot over low heat, keeping a watchful eye—if the mixture boils or scalds, it'll separate and look and taste like crap. The moment you see the slightest indication of bubbles (which you'll notice after 10 to 15 minutes), turn off the heat. Strain the coconut milk through a fine-mesh sieve and set it aside.

Prepare the mango: Rinse the mango under cool water to remove any dirt or debris on the skin. Use a sharp knife to slice off the stem end of the mango, creating a flat surface. Stand the mango up on a cutting board so that it's resting on the cut side. Hold the mango steady with your non-dominant hand while you slice off one side of the fruit, cutting as close to the vertical seed as possible. Repeat on the other side.

Use a knife to make crosshatched cuts into the flesh of each mango half without cutting through the skin. It should create a grid of 1-inch mango cubes. Use your fingers to invert the skin so that the cut pieces pop outward, then carefully cut out the crosshatched mango flesh. You should end up with about a cup's worth of cubed mango.

Repeat with the remaining mango half. If there's any meat still around the seed, cut it away in long slices. (Or, gobble it over the sink like a rabid monkey—your choice.)

To serve, set out four small bowls and divide the sticky rice among them. Top the rice with the cubed mango and coconut milk, then sprinkle the remaining grated coconut and the sesame seeds over the top. Serve immediately.

Variation: Swap the mango for ½ cup dried black-eyed peas to make a classic Vietnamese dessert, xôi chè đậu trắng. Soak the peas in a bowl of water for 4 hours; then drain the water and simmer them in a pot with 3 inches of water until they're tender, 1 to 3 hours, then drain. Once the sticky rice is finished, fold the drained peas right into the rice cooker.

WE ARE
INAUTHENTIC
AS HELL

While there are a ton of recipes in this book that are real-deal, straight outta Phú Quốc–style dishes, I don't want you to think that my family and I only eat one kind of cuisine. Vietnam might have been the blueprint, but the Bay Area was and is a major influence on how we ate. It's logical to adapt to what's around you—that's the foundation of farm-to-table cuisine, right?—but it's also good to remember that it's a luxury to be choosy about the authenticity of your ingredients. To be honest, the whole debate around authenticity strikes me as the pinnacle of nonsense bourgie thinking. When you're trying to nourish your family however you can, does it really matter if you're using lemons instead of limes in your phở? I'm not trying to speak for all Vietnamese people—that's a losing game if I've ever seen one. But what's important to me is fostering more openness in general to the infinite variations in the cuisine. To me, that flexibility is what defines diaspora cooking, and it reflects the reality of living frugally and sustainably. To me, anything that my parents cook counts as Vietnamese food.

Because when it comes to food, my parents are probably the most open, unbiased people I know. We wrapped fish sauce-spiked tuna tartare with nori (page 135) thanks to the influence of my dad's Japanese coworkers. My family got to taste a wide variety of fish and seafood thanks to my dad's fishmonger job, even if it was all basically rejects and leftovers. On top of that, pretty much any sea creature that my dad could reel out of the San Francisco Bay was turned into Phú Quốc–style jerky (page 134) and Cá Vược Nướng Giấy Bạc | Foil-Baked Whole Sea Bass (page 101). When we lived in Oakland, my mom often traded ingredients with a Korean neighbor, who luckily happened to be fluent in Vietnamese after working as a ginseng merchant in Vietnam. She introduced us to kimchee, crispy fried anchovies, and simmered burdock root and brought my mom to the local Korean market, where my sister and I would chow down on kimbap while they shopped. (Our neighbor set me up well for my eventual meeting with the love of my life, Jean, who seduced me with kimchee.) The way we ate, our home cuisine, was an accumulation of those and other influences: our neighbors, friends, community, and culture.

A diaspora is a community of people who live apart from their place of origin, and it's a word that I learned from my friend and fellow chef, Reem Assil. (I highly recommend her book, *Arabiyya: Recipes from the Life of an Arab in Diaspora*, for her take on this.) In diaspora, smaller communities of people come together and make do, just like my parents did, creating culture and traditions that aren't exactly the same as the old way, but are still just as beautiful. Before I learned about the concept of diaspora, I only associated my parents with their identities as refugees—as people who escaped from war. I didn't realize it at the time, but it was a term that kept them in the shadow of their violent displacement. So "diaspora" really got my brain churning: It allowed my parents to be more than just the most traumatic days of their lives. Instead, they were part of a community of people who were leading their own lives in whatever way made sense for them. They could be imperfect, complex, and most importantly, inauthentic as hell.

KHỔ QUA XÀO
STIR-FRIED BITTER MELON AND EGGS

Serves 4

Oh, bitter melon. Its name might seem intimidating, especially to people who might not be used to seeking out bitter or sour flavors in their food, but it only takes a little bit of work to make it delicious. The fruit cries out for balance, issuing a challenge to embrace it despite its astringency. In this recipe, much of the melon's bitterness is drawn out using a time-tested soaking method. Toasted garlic and oyster sauce bring their own understated sweetness into play, while the fattiness of the beaten eggs provides a mellow backup track for all the big flavors.

Note: If you're new to the art of shopping for bitter melons, here are some tips. Your ideal should be heavy and firm; if it's soft and mostly yellow, that means it's too ripe. Look for small, mostly green melons with longer grooves and smaller lumps: Large lumps translate to bigger seeds and less actual flesh.

4 bitter melons (see Note)

4 cups filtered water

Juice of 1 lemon

1 tablespoon plus ¼ teaspoon kosher salt

4 garlic cloves, smashed and peeled

1 tablespoon sesame oil

2 tablespoons oyster sauce

⅛ teaspoon cracked black pepper

⅛ teaspoon granulated sugar

4 eggs, beaten

Steamed rice (see page 34) for serving

Nước Mắm Chấm | Everyday Fish Sauce (page 40) for serving

First, prep the bitter melons for brining. Slice them in half lengthwise and use a spoon to remove the seeds. Flip them onto their cut sides and slice them on the diagonal into ¼-inch-thick slices. Places the pieces in a medium bowl and rinse them thoroughly under cold running water. Drain that water, then pour in the filtered water, lemon juice, and 1 tablespoon of the salt. You're going to soak the melon in this mixture to cut back on the bitterness so it doesn't show up in the final dish. Soak the bitter melon for at least 15 minutes, then drain the liquid and set the bowl aside. (If you really, really don't like bitter flavor, you can soak the melon for a whole hour.)

The next step Is a simple stir-fry. Set a large wok or cast-iron pot over medium heat and allow it to heat up for 5 minutes. Once it's hot, add the garlic and sesame oil to the wok. Once the garlic starts to look toasty at the edges, add in the bitter melon and turn the heat up to high. Cook the melon, stirring frequently, for 4 to 5 minutes, or when the melon starts to turn a shade darker. Pour in the oyster sauce, pepper, sugar, and the remaining ¼ teaspoon salt and stir to mix. Keep cooking the melon for 15 minutes more, or until the pieces are tender. If the ingredients start to scorch a little before the melon is cooked, add a splash of water to deglaze the wok.

In the last 2 minutes of cooking, add the eggs and fold gently to incorporate. Stop cooking when the eggs are done to your liking. I like them on the crispier side, but you can stop earlier if silky scrambled eggs are your jam. To serve, divide the melon and eggs among four bowls and serve alongside steamed rice and Everyday Fish Sauce.

CÁ KHÔ
FISH JERKY

Makes 12 ounces of fish jerky

Despite moving thousands of miles away from his home, my dad never stopped fishing. He'd always do it in spurts, when the spirit moved him, getting up in the early morning to take advantage of the high tide lapping at the banks below the Bay Bridge, which connects Oakland and San Francisco. When I turned 8 years old, I begged him to take me along just to get out of our grimy apartment. Though it was a welcome change in environment, this wasn't sunny Malibu Beach, okay? I'd be busting my face stumbling along the rocky shore, shivering from the sprays of freezing bay water, and fishing for mudskippers with the kid-size pole my dad gave me. If we got hungry, we'd try to start a fire and roast some frozen calamari bait as a snack. And often, I'd see him pull in incredible hauls—200-pound bat rays, their door-size wings slapping salty water into our faces as they fought the line. My dad would process those bad boys right there on the rocky shore.

Though skates and other ray-type fish are enjoyed as a delicacy around the world, they're harder to find in stores in the United States. If you're not as handy with a hook and line as my dad, you can of course use other fish in this jerky recipe: sole, rockfish (cheap!), tilapia, catfish, carp, and bass species like branzino. Look for lean fish with white flesh. Stay away from fatty fish like salmon or tuna, since they'll go rancid more quickly and you'll find your time has been wasted. For best results, use a dehydrator for this recipe.

2½ pounds boneless, skinless fish fillets

2 cups Nước Mắm Sánh Kẹo | Fish Sauce Caramel (page 37)

If you can find them, use skinless fish fillets, ideally less than ¼ inch thick. If they're thick boys, use a sharp knife to butterfly them into thinner pieces and cut them into 3 by 2-inch segments. Set the fish aside.

Microwave the Fish Sauce Caramel for about 30 seconds, until it becomes soft and spreadable. Using the back of a spoon or a basting brush, generously slather the caramel on both sides of each piece of fish.

Place the fish on a dehydrator rack, evenly spaced out to ensure the strips of jerky dry at the same pace. Set the dehydrator to 155°F and leave it be for 8 hours. When it's finished, the fish should have lost about 70 percent of its weight.

Keep the jerky in ziplock bags in the freezer for up to a year.

HUYẾT CÁ TÀI CHANH
TUNA BLOODLINE TARTARE

Serves 4

8 ounces minced yellowfin tuna bloodline

¼ cup finely diced pineapple

½ cup finely diced celery

4 Thai basil leaves, minced

1 teaspoon minced cilantro

1 teaspoon minced dill

1 tablespoon Củ Hẹ Chiên | Fried Shallots
(page 50) or store-bought fried shallots

1 tablespoon toasted and chopped peanuts

¼ teaspoon minced serrano pepper

1 teaspoon Dán Me | Tamarind Paste
(page 35)

¼ teaspoon rice vinegar

¼ teaspoon lemon juice

1 teaspoon coconut sugar

⅛ teaspoon toasted sesame seeds
(see page 19)

½ teaspoon kosher salt

2 teaspoons fish sauce

⅛ teaspoon cracked black pepper

Scant ⅛ teaspoon sesame oil

12 cilantro sprigs for garnish

12 dill sprigs for garnish

Full-size roasted nori sheets,
cut diagonally, for wrapping

As a chef, the dream is to have at least one dish in your repertoire that can tell your whole story in just a few bites. This is one of mine. It's an adaptation of a dish that my parents would make, and it expresses so much about the way I grew up. It starts with the "unusable" bloodline of a tuna loin and turns it into a sort of poke with tropical, Phú Quốc–style flavors: fresh herbs, pineapple, peanuts, and fish sauce. Normally, my parents would make this from tuna pieces that were unsellable because they had too much of the bloodline in them; for this recipe, I lean into it and use bloodline exclusively. Bright pineapple tempers the stronger flavors of the meat, and I've added celery just because it gives the tartare extra crunch without adding excessive moisture. The way we ate it at home, wrapped in nori, was loosely inspired by sushi, though my parents adapted the technique to fit their mostly Vietnamese pantry. All of these elements in combination create a dish that says it all. I'm proud of it, and I hope you'll enjoy.

Note: Fishmongers often dispose of bloodline because it's highly perishable and not as aesthetically attractive, but this recipe shows that when fresh, the stuff has the potential to be pretty tasty. To get your hands on bloodline, try calling your local fishmonger early in the day to see if they can save some fresh ones for you. They'll probably be surprised, but odds are they'll be glad to give it to you for free, or at least for cheap. Barring that option, you can simply order regular tuna loin and ask the shop not to cut out the bloodline.

Before you get started with the recipe, place a medium metal mixing bowl in the freezer to chill for 30 minutes.

While the bowl is chilling, set a fine-mesh sieve over a bowl to drain the pineapple pieces for 15 minutes to remove excess moisture. This will keep the tartare from getting too juicy. (You can save the juice for Nước Mắm Khóm | Pineapple Fish Sauce on page 42, or just knock it back—chef snack!)

Once the bowl is nice and chilly, remove it from the freezer and add in the tuna, pineapple, celery, Thai basil, cilantro, dill, fried shallots, peanuts, serrano pepper, tamarind paste, rice vinegar, lemon juice, coconut sugar, and sesame seeds. Fold everything together using a spoon or rubber spatula, then season the mixture with the salt, fish sauce, black pepper, and sesame oil. Gently toss the tartare one last time to ensure the seasoning is evenly distributed, then give it a taste and adjust the seasoning to your preference.

Garnish the tartare with the cilantro and dill sprigs. Keep the bowl in the fridge until right when you're ready to eat, and make sure that you use it the same day you make it.

In the spirit of my parent's dining table, set the bowl of tartare and a plate of nori in the center of the table so folks can build their own handrolls. Use one hand to hold a triangle of nori, and the other to scoop a heaping spoonful of tartare onto it. Loosely roll up the nori, forming a cone-shaped roll and enjoy.

GINGER-BRAISED CHICKEN

Serves 4

The offcuts of chicken were staples of my parents' kitchen, and one of my favorite ways to enjoy them was in this dish, which my mom made from chicken wings. The wings are simmered with shallot, lemongrass, Makrut lime leaves, and plenty of ginger, and the gelatin in the chicken breaks down and combines with a rich coconut caramel sauce to create a deeply savory braising liquid. While you could do this recipe with bone-in chicken thighs, the wings really offer the best of all worlds here, especially if you're like me and love chewing on bones and gelatinous skin.

2 pounds whole chicken wings

1 tablespoon fish sauce

1 teaspoon minced garlic

2 tablespoons granulated sugar

1 teaspoon kosher salt

2 tablespoons neutral oil (such as vegetable oil)

2 tablespoons minced shallot

1 tablespoon minced lemongrass

2 Makrut lime leaves

2 tablespoons Nước Màu Dừa | Coconut Caramel Sauce (page 36)

4 ounces fresh ginger, peeled and cut into slender matchsticks (about 1 cup)

3 to 4 cilantro sprigs for garnish

¼ cup sliced green onions, white and green parts, for garnish

1 Thai bird's eye chile, minced, for garnish (optional)

Steamed rice (see page 34) for serving

Disassemble the wings by cutting through the joints with a sharp knife. Each should separate into three sections: flat, drumette, and wingtip.

Make the marinade. In a large bowl, combine the fish sauce, garlic, sugar, and salt. Toss the wings in to incorporate, massaging a bit to ensure they are thoroughly coated, and let them marinate for 30 minutes at room temperature.

Now, you can start the process of braising. Set a large, heavy pot over medium heat. Allow the pot to preheat for 3 minutes, then add in the neutral oil. When the oil starts to shimmer, add the shallot, lemongrass, 2 lime leaves, and the Coconut Caramel Sauce. Allow the mixture to simmer for a minute, then add in the marinated chicken, along with any extra chicken juice and marinade goodness.

Stir everything together and continue simmering for 30 minutes. Add the ginger and increase the heat to high to return to a simmer. Lower the heat so the pot is barely at a simmer and cover it with a lid. Let the mixture cook for 15 minutes, or until you're able to easily pierce through a flat piece of chicken using a chopstick.

You'll know the chicken is done when the internal temperature of a wing reaches 165°F on a probe thermometer, though really, it's impossible to overcook chicken wings. Remove the lid and let cook for 15 minutes more so that the liquid reduces by a third.

Transfer the braised chicken wings into a wide, shallow bowl and garnish with the cilantro, green onions, and chile (if using). Serve with a side of steamed rice.

SƯỜN CHIÊN
CARAMELIZED PAN-FRIED PORK CHOPS

Serves 4

Nothing makes me more nostalgic than the sounds and smells of a pork chop being fried in a pan, sizzling in pork fat and filling the kitchen with the irresistible aromas of caramelized garlic, lemongrass, and oyster sauce. Sure, I was always excited about the big hunk of pork I was gonna get to eat, but even more tantalizing was the pan sauce, made from the fond—the bits of browned pork and marinade that stuck to the pan. My parents would add pasta or day-old rice to the hot pan of pork drippings, infusing the starch with all the flavors that might have otherwise gone to waste. You can eat these chops as-is and simply pour the extra juice over them, or you can do as my parents did: You'll find the recipe for a pasta version, Nui Sườn Chiên, and a variation with rice, Cơm Sườn Chiên, on page 140. Note that this recipe involves an overnight marination period, so plan accordingly.

MARINADE

3 tablespoons fish sauce

3 tablespoons oyster sauce

1 teaspoon minced ginger

1 teaspoon minced garlic

1 teaspoon minced shallot

1 teaspoon minced lemongrass

¼ cup sliced green onions, white and green parts

1 teaspoon Chef Tu Phở Seasoning or five-spice powder (see page 19)

1 tablespoon granulated sugar

2 tablespoons orange marmalade or honey

1 teaspoon sesame oil

4 bone-in pork chops, cut ½ inch thick

2 tablespoons neutral oil (such as vegetable oil)

Combine the fish sauce, oyster sauce, ginger, garlic, shallot, lemongrass, green onions, phở seasoning, sugar, marmalade, and sesame oil in a large bowl and mix thoroughly. Add the pork chops to the bowl with the marinade, then give them a nice 5-minute massage, as if the pig's been working real hard lately. Place the bowl in the fridge to marinate for at least 8 hours or overnight. Half an hour before you plan to start cooking, take the bowl out of the fridge and allow it to rest at room temperature for 30 minutes.

Then, get started cooking the pork chops. Set a large, heavy frying pan over medium heat. Give the pan 3 minutes to heat through, then add in the neutral oil. Once the oil starts to shimmer, tilt the pan away from your body and gently lay the pork chops in the pan. Place each chop in the frying pan starting with the part closest to you so that the pork doesn't splash oil in your direction. (If the pan's too small for all four pork chops, do this step in batches.)

Fry the pork chops for 5 minutes on each side, or until they register an internal temperature of 145°F on a probe thermometer. Remove the pan from the heat and transfer the pork chops to a cooling rack or cutting board and set the pan aside. Rest the pork chops for a few minutes.

Now it's time to choose your own pork chop adventure: Stay where you are to enjoy as-is, or turn to page 140 to find out what happens when you add pasta or rice. Note that the latter two recipes will use the pan drippings from the pan of pork chops, so don't wash it out yet!

NUI SƯỜN CHIÊN
CARAMELIZED PAN-FRIED PORK CHOPS AND MACARONI

Serves 4

One thing that might surprise a lot of non-Vietnamese people is the prevalence of pasta in our cooking. Our word for it, "nui," is a loanword from the French word for noodle, "nouille," but Viets mostly use it to talk about macaroni and other short pastas, not longer noodles. In Vietnam, pasta appears in stir-fry dishes and brothy soups. In the homeland, pasta is usually made from rice flour, and you'll even run into it at street food stands that sell soup. But in the diaspora, many of us just stick to the dried durum wheat pasta that's easily found in supermarkets. That's what we're using here. Note that this recipe requires you to prepare Sườn Chiên | Caramelized Pan-Fried Pork Chops ahead of time. You've been warned!

---

8 ounces dry elbow macaroni

2 tablespoons unsalted butter

½ cup filtered water

Sườn Chiên | Caramelized Pan-Fried Pork Chops (page 139)

Sliced cucumber for garnish

Whole cherry tomatoes for garnish

Cook the macaroni al dente according to directions on the box, then drain it in a colander in the sink. Rinse the cooked noodles with cool water to remove excess starch and let the pasta rest for 5 minutes.

Warm the pan of pork drippings from the sườn chiên over medium heat for 3 minutes, then add in the cooked macaroni, butter, and water. Stir to combine—the pasta will absorb all of the wonderfully savory, caramelly juices in the pan. Turn the heat to low and continue cooking the pasta for 5 minutes or until the liquid is mostly absorbed. Remove the pan from the heat and divide the pasta among four plates.

Use kitchen scissors to cut the pork chops against the grain into pieces that you can pick up with chopsticks (that's a tip I picked up from my wife, Jean, also used by Maangchi, the Korean recipe blogger). You don't want to lose all that precious meat juice, so cut the pork chops directly over the plates if you can. Garnish with the cucumber and tomato and serve immediately.

Cơm Sườn Chiên Variation: Instead of pasta, throw 2½ cups of day-old broken rice (page 34) into the drippings. As the rice cooks, it'll absorb all the pork drippings. Keep cooking the rice for 5 minutes, or until the moisture is mostly absorbed. If the rice seems too dry, add a splash of water to the pan and let it cook for another minute or until absorbed.

BÁNH CHUỐI NƯỚNG
MOM'S BANANA BREAD PUDDING

Serves 6

Like any sophisticated lady, my mom loves buttery, flaky French pastries, and to her, croissants are king. She always scrimped and saved the cash to buy them, but not from the places where the cashiers called them "kwah-saunts." Nope, we got our real-deal, trés magnifique croissants by the dozen from the Costco bakery, with hors d'ouevres of $1.50 Polish dogs and bottomless sodas. I'm not kidding when I say that getting a Costco card moved us up the economic and social ladder. But uh, we weren't actually members, technically speaking. It was more that the people who checked the membership cards couldn't really tell Asians apart, and let's just say we took advantage of it.

When our Costco croissants got too old to eat fresh, my mom would turn them into this amazing bread pudding, which she'd cook in our crappy little toaster oven. Her banana of choice was the lady finger banana, which is somehow custard-like but still firm, and so, so sweet. This recipe is pretty much her exact technique, though I've scaled it up to fit the average home oven. You'll need a 6-inch round cake pan for this recipe.

Note: If you can't find lady finger bananas (also known as sugar bananas, fig bananas, or date bananas) where you are, you can totally swap in super-ripe Cavendish bananas, though the final result won't be quite as sweet or aromatic.

1 pound lady finger bananas, peeled and sliced into ½-inch pieces (see Note)
¼ cup granulated sugar
2 cups Nước Cốt Dừa Tươi | Fresh Coconut Milk (page 49) or canned coconut milk
2 eggs
¼ teaspoon kosher salt
¼ cup sweetened condensed milk
3 day-old croissants
2 tablespoons unsalted butter, at room temperature
Toasted sesame seeds (see page 19) for garnish

Preheat the oven to 350°F.

Put the sliced banana in a small bowl and sprinkle with 1 tablespoon of the sugar. Gently toss the slices to coat them with sugar, being careful not to accidentally mash them into smaller pieces. Set aside.

Now, make the batter. In a medium mixing bowl, combine 1 cup of the coconut milk, the eggs, and ⅛ teaspoon of the salt. Whisk the ingredients together, and while whisking, slowly drizzle in the sweetened condensed milk. Whisk continuously until thoroughly incorporated.

Slice the croissants into ½-inch chunks and add them to the bowl with the coconut milk mixture. Stir until the croissant pieces begin to dissolve, creating a batter-like consistency. Stash the batter in the fridge to rest for 30 minutes, so the croissants can disintegrate even more; to create an even softer texture, leave the batter in the fridge overnight. After the batter has rested, give it one last stir for good luck. At this point, the pieces should be totally disintegrated. (The key to this recipe is in the cheapo croissants, which should fall apart more easily.)

It's time to layer the bread pudding. Grease the cake pan with the room-temperature butter and dust it with 1 tablespoon of the sugar. Pour a third of the batter into the pan, then top with a single layer of the sugar-coated banana slices. Repeat this process, alternating between the batter and banana slices, with the remaining two-thirds of the batter—sort of like you're making a cake version of lasagna. End with a banana layer on top, since it will look prettiest.

CONTINUED

Bake the bread pudding in the preheated oven for 1 hour, rotating the pan every 20 minutes. After an hour, the pudding should have started to caramelize. A cake tester or wooden skewer plunged into the center of the pudding should come out clean.

Next, caramelize the top. Remove the pudding from the oven and dust the top with another tablespoon of the sugar. Set the oven to a medium broil and position a rack 6 inches from the broiler. Return the bread pudding to the oven for 10 minutes, or until the sugar has fully caramelized and looks glassy. Take the pudding out of the oven and let it cool in the pan set on a cooling rack for 30 minutes.

My mother at the age of 17.

When the pudding has about 10 minutes left to cool, make a coconut milk topping. In a small pot, combine the remaining 1 cup coconut milk, remaining ⅛ teaspoon salt, and remaining 1 tablespoon sugar. Set over low heat and stir constantly to prevent scalding. Heat the mixture until it registers 165°F on a probe thermometer, or when the milk starts to get a little steamy, about 5 minutes. Remove the mixture from the heat.

Once the bread pudding has cooled, run a butter knife around the inside edge of the pan to loosen the pudding. Now, we're gonna do a little flippy magic trick. Place an upside-down plate on top of the pudding, then hold it in place as you invert the pan. Pull the pan away to reveal the pudding. Take a second plate and invert it on top of the pudding, then quickly flip it over again. Now, the caramelized banana layer should be on top.

To serve, first show off the cute pudding to your friends, then cut it into six equal wedges and place each in a shallow bowl. Drizzle some of the coconut milk topping over each slice and finish with a flourish of sesame seeds.

If you don't want to eat the bread pudding immediately, you can cover it in plastic wrap and keep it in the fridge for up to 3 days.

WE ATE WHAT THE GARDEN GAVE US

When I think about the apartment building where I spent my childhood in Oakland, the first thing that comes to mind is the carpeted hallway. The carpets in the building were cheap and musty after soaking in decades of whatever crap folks tracked in from the street, and they were as gross as rubber kitchen mats after a busy brunch service. Since my parents were the building managers, I ended up having to vacuum those carpets from the age of seven. Their grimy smell practically crawled all over your skin, and it was made worse by the fact that my dad nailed our apartment's windows shut as a DIY home security solution, preventing much ventilation.

It's no wonder that I craved the outside. But we lived in the part of town where urban development meant that parks and natural spaces were paved over to make room for freight, freeways, industry, and port operations, exposing us to the worst kinds of pollution. Because of that, the small strip of fenced-in land that surrounded our building was the closest we could get to nature. My mom spent years of back-breaking effort turning it into our version of Eden.

She pulled out all the random crap growing around the property and replaced it with seeds that she brought from Vietnam and roots and clippings received from friends and family, creating a sort of living memory bank of the flavors my family loved. In the damp shadows of bigger trees, diếp cá and spearmint seeds exploded into a vibrant green carpet of herbs that we clipped to pile onto plates of Bún Bò Sả Ớt | Lemongrass Beef, Chile, and Rice Noodle Salad (page 166) and Gỏi Bắp Chuối | Banana Flower Salad (page 158). There were also plastic tubs of bushy lemongrass, with sandpapery blades that flicked at my face as

I harvested them for my dad's meat marinades, and the dense foliage of pots of Thai basil and chile peppers. A few times a year, the stumpy banana trees we inherited would drop their heavy flowers, which meant that banana flower salad would be coming soon. When I was out in the yard, I would squat by the mint and eat it by the handful. On hot days, after the leaves soaked in sunlight for hours, it would taste electrifying and alive.

I know, this sounds like your stereotypical "first taste of a sun-ripened tomato" story, where I end by telling you that's why I only buy my food at farmer's markets. But while the most well-known principles of farm-to-table cuisine—connecting with farmers, eating locally and organically—sound reasonable to me, better grocery shopping shouldn't be the sole endgame. Y'all . . . we can do better than that.

From an early age, I realized that having access to land was essential to my family's survival. It wasn't just the calories we got from what actually grew there, but the dignity of being able to plant and harvest what we ate. Everyone deserves to have space to do that.

The recipes in this chapter are all about my parents' mastery over home-grown food—their proudly Vietnamese version of farm-to-table cuisine. Our memory of taste pulsed through every stalk and flower of the plants we cultivated, surfacing in those small moments of peeling sugar cane, waiting for banana flowers to grow, and rubbing mint between our fingers. We survived in a food desert by growing food that was wholesome, nutritious, and organic. But even more importantly, it was ours.

LƯU TRỘN MUỐI ỚT
POMEGRANATE SEEDS WITH CHILE SALT

Serves 4 as a light snack

2 pomegranates, or 2 cups pomegranate seeds

1 teaspoon Muối Ớt | Chile Salt (page 43)

In the early 2000s, my mom smuggled in some pomegranate seeds from Vietnam to plant at her house in the East Bay. They weren't the seeds of just any pomegranate. They were Thai pomegranates, which have thinner rinds and way sweeter seeds than the Persian ones you'll find at most grocery stores stateside. The smuggled seeds sprouted, then began to grow and flower over the years, and swarms of hummingbirds would zip over to lap up the nectar. In the fall, the tree would produce fist-size fruits that bulged with gleaming, jewel-like seeds, or arils. It's satisfying enough to just suck all the juice out of seeds straight-up, but I've learned that a pinch of homemade chile salt upgrades the fruit from great to mind-blowing.

Opening up a pomegranate might be confusing for first-timers, but it's actually pretty easy to break down. You'll just need a small paring knife. Use the knife to cut into the calyx (the crownlike top) of the fruit at an angle, almost like you would cut around the stem of a strawberry. Eventually, you should be able to dig out the calyx piece. Next, make four shallow cuts into the skin from top to bottom so that you're dividing it into approximate quarters. Use your fingers to split the pomegranate into quarters along the lines you cut.

To remove the seeds, fill a medium bowl of water. Hold each pomegranate quarter rind-side up over the water and use a wooden spoon to smack the rind, helping the seeds fall out. Keep hitting it until it's empty, then repeat with the rest of the fruit. The seeds will sink in the water, while the papery rind bits will float.

Skim the water to remove the rind, then drain the seeds in a colander. You can store the pomegranate seeds in an airtight container in the fridge for up to 5 days. When ready to serve, toss the seeds with the chile salt and enjoy immediately.

GỎI CUỐN CÁ NGỪ
TUNA SUMMER ROLLS

Serves 4

Most gỏi cuốn you'll find at Vietnamese restaurants in the United States are stuffed with a generic combination of crisp greens with pork, poached shrimp, and/or fried tofu. I'm not knocking that classic combination; I'm just saying there's actually a lot of room to improvise with whatever you've got on hand. (If you try to stuff a whole cheeseburger in there, let me know how that goes.)

I see this cá ngừ, or tuna, version of the summer roll as a collaboration between my mom's garden and my dad's lifelong work in the world of fish and seafood. Inspired by his Japanese colleagues' love for tuna and sashimi, dad occasionally brought home ruby-red slabs of tuna and served it to us raw (though my squeamish mom preferred to sear it, just a little). It was a rare treat, and we fit the tuna into our diet the best way we could think of: stuffed into chewy rice paper wrappers with vermicelli noodles, pickles, and crisp lettuce leaves. Instead of seasoning the tuna with soy sauce, like what Japanese folks might do, we dipped the rolls in a coconut-laced fish sauce that gave each bite a splash of bright and citrusy flavor.

The tuna might seem like the star of this dish, but for us, the rolls were always a showcase of my mom's homegrown shiso, her tía tô. Shiso, which really blows up in the garden in the summertime, is bold and intoxicating, with a minty brightness that's a perfect complement to a rich fish like tuna. It has a unique way of lingering on the palate well beyond other flavors, and it shines through the many textures and big flavors of this dish.

Note: Feel free to try this recipe with other types of tuna, like ahi or albacore. Also note that if you're making pickles specifically for this recipe, do so one day in advance.

---

1 pound yellowfin tuna, cut against the grain into ⅛-inch-thick slices

One 12-ounce package rice paper wrappers (see page 23)

4 ounces dried rice vermicelli, cooked (see Note on page 60)

1¾ cups Củ Cải Chua Ngọt | Pickled Carrots and Daikon (page 49), liquid drained

1 green leaf or Little Gem lettuce head, leaves separated

12 cilantro sprigs

½ cup mint leaves

½ cup tía tô (shiso leaves)

1 cup Nước Mắm Dừa | Coconut Fish Sauce (page 41) for serving

---

Arrange the sliced tuna on a cold plate and store in the fridge until you're ready to use it, up to 3 hours. Any longer in the fridge, the tuna will start turning gray. It will still be edible, but the vibe will be kind of grimy. (If you need to store it a little longer, move it to the freezer instead. Just remember to defrost it right before using.)

When you're ready to assemble, set up your rolling station. Prepare a shallow rimmed dish with cold water. Arrange the rice paper wrappers, vermicelli, pickles, lettuce, cilantro, mint, shiso, and tuna slices in your kitchen workspace. Think like a veteran line cook (or sandwich *artiste*) and set everything in a convenient orbit around the cutting board or plate that you'll be making the rolls on. (You can also arrange the components on platters on the table and invite your guests roll their own, which works better for customizing to people's tastes.) Be sure not to set up your rolling station too far in advance, or the rolls will dry out.

To assemble a roll, briefly dip a rice paper wrapper into the water. Lift it out of the water and give it a wiggle to shake off extra water, and set the paper on your work area. You might have to wait a few seconds for it to become pliable, so you can roll without it breaking. Over time, the rice paper will

CONTINUED

become more delicate, making it increasingly difficult to work with. You want to catch a sweet spot where the rice paper is still firm, but not gummy.

Grab ¼ cup rice vermicelli (it's okay to eyeball this) and lay them 1½ inches from the bottom edge of the rice paper wrapper. Top the noodles with 2 or 3 lettuce leaves. Fold the left and right edges of the wrapper inward by ½ inch each, like you're making the roll give itself a hug, then pull up the bottom edge to fully enclose the ingredients in a first layer of rice paper wrapper.

Then, layer the following on top of the initial bundle, as artistically as you'd like: 1 tablespoon of pickles, 2 or 3 cilantro sprigs, 2 or 3 mint leaves, 2 or 3 shiso leaves, and 2 or 3 slices of tuna. Once all the ingredients are piled on, finish the roll by sealing it with the top edge of the paper. Don't stress if the roll ends up looking a little janky. It'll still be delicious. Repeat with the remaining ingredients.

Divide the Coconut Fish Sauce among four small dipping bowls. Serve the sauce alongside the summer rolls, and enjoy immediately.

GỎI GÀ
VIETNAMESE CHICKEN SALAD

Serves 4

It might seem dramatic of me, but I have to say I got hella ticked off when I read a mainstream food publication translate "gỏi gà" as "crunchy Vietnamese chicken salad." To water down and limit this beloved dish to one texture—crunchy? That's like saying a rainbow is red! How can you not pick up on the incredible kaleidoscope of texture sensations in every bite? "Crunchy" is an insult to the sheer hype I feel for this dish. Plus, gỏi gà has infinite variations, so you can change up its texture and flavor. You generally won't find grapes and mayonnaise in ours, but a recipe might have different bases (such as kohlrabi, cabbage, green papaya), garnishes, and dressings to suit the maker's taste.

My version leans hard into the aromas of its ingredients: floral Makrut lime leaves and passion fruit pulp; earthy, fatty peanuts; pepper rau răm; and ginger-spiked chicken. When making gỏi gà with my parents, I'd be sent to the garden to pick the tender, newly sprouted leaves from our Makrut lime tree and the biggest leaves of the rau răm, which grew in the shade of the banana tree. Our passion fruit, or chanh dây, got sweeter with every passing year, and my mom used the sunny pulp to balance out the fish sauce in her salad dressing. Our gỏi gà was littered with carefully grown herbs and fruit; it was sweet, sour, salty, bitter, spicy, and full of umami. It's anything but a basic-ass "crunchy chicken salad." Make it yourself and you'll see.

NƯỚC CHẤM CHANH DÂY (PASSION FRUIT DRESSING)

2 passion fruits

¼ cup fresh lime juice

1 tablespoon chrouk metae or sambal oelek (see page 22)

2 teaspoons minced garlic

2 tablespoons minced shallot

½ cup Sprite

½ cup fish sauce

3 tablespoons granulated sugar

½ cup cold filtered water

First, make the passion fruit dressing. Halve the passion fruits and squeeze the pulp, including the seeds, into a small mixing bowl. Discard the skins. Stir in the lime juice, chrouk metae, garlic, and shallot. Leave the mixture to macerate for 5 minutes. Add in the Sprite, fish sauce, sugar, and water, and stir until the sugar is dissolved. Taste for balance and adjust seasonings as necessary. Set aside. (The dressing can be stored in an airtight container in the fridge for up to 3 days.)

Next, brine the chicken. Combine 4 cups of the water and 2 teaspoons of the salt in a medium pot. Stir to dissolve the salt, then submerge the chicken in the brine and let it sit for 5 minutes. If necessary, use a stack of heavy plates to keep it from bobbing out of the water. After 5 minutes, discard the brine and rinse the chicken under cold water until the water runs clear. Remember to disinfect your hands and the sink after doing this.

Now, poach the chicken. In the same pot, cover the chicken with the remaining 8 cups water, and add in the ginger, fish sauce, and the remaining 1 teaspoon salt. Bring the pot to a simmer over medium-high heat, then turn the heat down to medium so that it bubbles gently. Let the chicken poach for about 15 minutes, until it's cooked through. The chicken is done poaching when a probe thermometer inserted into the thickest part of the meat registers 165°F for 30 seconds straight. Turn off the heat and let the chicken sit in the poaching liquid for an hour.

Pull the chicken out of the poaching liquid and transfer it to a medium bowl. Using your hands or two forks, shred the meat into wispy chunks. Dress it with a quarter of the passion fruit dressing and stash it in the fridge, covered, while you make the salad.

CONTINUED

POACHED CHICKEN

12 cups cold filtered water

1 tablespoon kosher salt

2 pounds boneless chicken thighs

One 1-inch knob fresh ginger, sliced into coins

1 tablespoon fish sauce

SALAD

2 cups shredded green cabbage

2 large carrots, peeled and cut into matchsticks

2 shallots, thinly sliced

½ yellow onion, thinly sliced

10 fresh Makrut lime leaves, thinly sliced

½ cup rice wine vinegar

1 teaspoon kosher salt

1 teaspoon granulated sugar

1 bunch rau răm, leaves picked

¼ cup roasted peanuts

To make the salad, in a large mixing bowl, combine the cabbage, carrots, shallots, onion, and lime leaves. Season the vegetables with the rice vinegar, salt, and sugar, and use your hands or tongs to toss the vegetables with the seasonings, allowing the sugar and salt to dissolve completely. Let the mixture sit for 15 minutes. While the vegetables are resting, soak the rau răm in a separate bowl of cold water for 15 minutes to help perk up the leaves.

After the vegetables have rested, use a colander to strain out any excess liquid. Return the vegetables to the bowl and mix in the marinated shredded chicken, along with the rest of the passion fruit dressing. Toss vigorously to evenly distribute the dressing, and serve topped with the rau răm and peanuts.

GỎI BẮP CHUỐI
BANANA FLOWER SALAD

Serves 4

Miraculously, my mom's garden at our old building in Oakland happened to have a 10-foot-tall banana tree cluster. Not so miraculously, the fruit that it produced was starchy and totally inedible—no banana sundaes for us. But once in a rare while, the tree would drop a flower that looked like a maroon football, and we'd anxiously wait weeks for it to reach its peak. We'd always use it for gỏi bắp chuối, a colorful, vegetable-dense salad. When blanched, the flower petals take on a meaty texture that's similar to cooked artichoke, which is why it's recently gained popularity as a stand-in for fish in vegan recipes.

Note: If you're making pickles specifically for this recipe, you'll need to do so 1 day in advance.

8 cups cold filtered water

1 tablespoon kosher salt

4 lemons

1 banana flower

2 cups shredded cabbage

2 shallots, thinly sliced

½ yellow onion, thinly sliced

2 red bell peppers, seeded and cut into matchsticks

1 cup Củ Cải Chua Ngọt | Pickled Carrots and Daikon (page 49), liquid drained

1½ cups Nước Mắm Tỏi Ớt | Chile Fish Sauce (page 43)

4 Persian cucumbers, cut into matchsticks

8 ounces mung bean sprouts, soaked in cold water for 15 minutes and drained

1 bunch spearmint, leaves picked and soaked in cold water for 15 minutes and drained

¼ cup Củ Hẹ Chiên | Fried Shallots (page 50) or store-bought fried shallots

Banana flower loves to oxidize, so let's keep the petals fresh by setting them up with a nice bath. Fill a large pot with the water and add in the salt and juice from 3 of the lemons (about ½ cup lemon juice). Stir until dissolved. Inspect the banana flower and get rid of any bruised, blemished, or otherwise gnarly petals. Peel off the rest of the petals (including any small buds) and place them in the pot. Set the pot over medium heat and bring the mixture to a low simmer. Cook the petals until they become whiter, semi-translucent, and pierceable with a fork—about 30 seconds. Drain the petals in a colander in the sink and cool them off under cold running water for 5 minutes. Let the petals rest for 15 minutes, then gently squeeze or shake them to remove excess moisture. You can do this step a day in advance and let the petals rest in the fridge overnight, or you can proceed with the recipe now.

Shred the petals by hand into a large bowl and set them aside. In a separate large bowl, combine the cabbage, sliced shallots, onion, and peppers. Squeeze the juice from the last lemon over this mixture and toss to combine.

Add the drained pickles to the cabbage mixture, along with the shredded banana flower petals and Chile Fish Sauce. Mix everything to combine thoroughly. Last, add in the cucumbers, mung bean sprouts, and spearmint, mixing them in gently so you don't break or bruise the delicate sprouts.

Top the salad with the fried shallots and serve immediately.

CANH CÁ NẤU NGỌT
VIETNAMESE FISH HOT POT

Serves 4

1 tablespoon granulated sugar

⅛ teaspoon cracked black pepper

¼ cup fish sauce

1 to 2 pounds whole tilapia or bass, gutted and scaled

1 tablespoon neutral oil (such as vegetable oil)

3 garlic cloves, smashed and peeled

8 cups Nước Luộc Cá | Fish Stock (page 50)

2 cups halved cherry tomatoes

1 stalk Korean celery, peeled and cut into 2- to 3-inch segments, leaves reserved

3 dill stalks

If we were lucky, my family would have some seriously interesting fish for dinner—but we often had dry spells, when my mom would buy dirt-cheap tilapia or basa (a type of catfish) from the Asian grocery store. Look, I'm not saying those fish species are bad—they just didn't excite me. But in my mom's hands, whatever excitement the fish lacked was more than made up for by the vegetables she added to it. This hot pot recipe is just one case in point.

Fertilized for years with fish bones and guts and watered with spoiled milk, the garden's soil was steeped in nutrients. It was a sort of long-game marinade, and it resulted in candylike cherry tomatoes; vibrant, meaty stalks of dill bursting with vigor; and leafy Korean celery, full of sweetness and natural salinity. I know you don't have access to my mom's garden, but here's hoping you get a little window into its flavors with this recipe.

First, make the marinade. Combine the sugar, pepper, and 2 tablespoons of the fish sauce in a medium mixing bowl and stir until the sugar dissolves. Next, score the fish by making several evenly spaced cuts along the flesh at a 45-degree angle, like tiger stripes. Make the same cuts on the other side of the fish, making sure that they more or less align. Transfer the fish to a rimmed tray or baking sheet and place in the fridge while you work on the rest of the recipe.

Prepare the hot pot liquid. Set a medium pot over medium heat for 2 minutes, until hot. Pour in the neutral oil, and once it is shimmering, add in the garlic. Let the garlic toast just a little around the edges—it should barely brown—then add the fish stock. Bring the stock to a gentle simmer (you should see just a few occasional bubbles), then pour in the remaining 2 tablespoons fish sauce. Add in the cherry tomatoes, celery stalk and leaves, and dill. Return the pot to a gentle simmer. I'm serious about gentle! Let it simmer for 10 minutes, keeping an eye on the pot and skimming off any foam that rises to the top.

After 5 minutes, take the fish out of the fridge and and pour the fish sauce marinade over it, using your fingers to lightly rub it into the cuts. Let the fish sit for 5 minutes, then add it to the pot and let it cook for 3 minutes, or until the flesh transitions from translucent to opaque or white. Gently press on the fish with your finger or a utensil. If it springs back and doesn't feel mushy or rubbery, that's a good indication that it is cooked.

When you're ready to serve, set the pot on a trivet on the dinner table or carefully pour the contents of the hot pot into a big serving bowl. Enjoy immediately.

NGHÊU XÀO
STIR-FRIED CLAMS

Serves 4

1 tablespoon neutral oil
(such as vegetable oil)

1 tablespoon minced garlic

1 tablespoon grated ginger

1 serrano pepper or jalapeño, cut on the diagonal into ⅛-inch-thick slices

1 bunch Thai basil, leaves picked

1 cup clam juice or filtered water

1 cup Nước Luộc Gà | Chicken Stock
(page 51) or store-bought stock

1 tablespoon fish sauce

¼ teaspoon MSG

½ teaspoon kosher salt

1 teaspoon granulated sugar

⅛ teaspoon cracked black pepper

4 pounds littleneck clams (see Notes)

1 teaspoon cornstarch (optional)

½ cup cold filtered water (optional)

1 bunch rau răm, leaves picked, for garnish

¼ cup toasted and chopped peanuts
for garnish

Steamed rice (see page 34) for serving
(optional)

Among the many herbs in my mom's garden were pots of Thai basil and rau răm, which thrived in the heat of our East Bay summers. The Thai variety of basil is dominated by the aroma of anise, with subtle notes of licorice and spice. Rau răm, a narrow-leafed herb that you'll often find in Vietnamese salads, is like cilantro seasoned with citrus rind and pepper. Both herbs add a complex perfume to stir fries like this one, which I first had at Bo Da, a Chinese-Vietnamese diner that opened in East San Jose in the '90s.

Notes: While mollusks like clams and mussels are super sustainable and great to eat, you don't want to play fast and loose with storing them, or you'll risk giving yourself the food poisoning experience of a lifetime. Eat them the same day you buy them, and keep them alive right up until it's time to cook. Put them in a colander and cover them with ice and a kitchen towel. Set the colander in the fridge over a bowl to catch any water that drips off.

Give the clams a chance to purge any sand that might be in their systems, which takes about 40 minutes. There are three solid methods for doing this—and all three techniques can work for other mollusks as well. To keep it simple, you could use plain ice water. Or use the Italian method, which requires heavy sprinkles of salt and semolina into the ice water. Or, of course, you can do it the Vietnamese way, swapping the plain ice water for the starchy water that you've used to rinse rice, plus a Thai bird's eye chile for good measure. Regardless of which adventure you choose, soak the clams for 20 minutes. Then, drain the soaking water and put the clams in a colander set over your sink. Cover them with ice to keep them fresh.

Wash out the bowl you used for soaking and refill it with clean cold water. Give the cleaned clams one last soak for 20 minutes; then drain the soaking water and place them back into a colander. Check each clam to make sure they're all still alive: If the clam is slightly open, tap on its shell. If the shell closes, it's okay. If it doesn't react, it's gone to the big clam bed in the sky. Throw it out. And if you're not sure, it's better to throw it out than to risk getting sick.

Set a large frying pan over high heat to prep the broth. Add the neutral oil and allow it to heat through for 2 minutes. Add in the garlic, ginger, half of the sliced serrano pepper, and the Thai basil and sauté for 1 minute. Don't let the mixture brown. Pour in the clam juice and chicken stock and season with the fish sauce, MSG, salt, sugar, and black pepper. Allow the mixture to come to a simmer, then turn down the heat so that the broth doesn't boil. Add the clams to the broth and give them a stir. Cover the pan with a lid and allow the broth to bubble until all the clams have cracked open, 5 to 10 minutes.

If you want the broth to be thicker and more saucelike, make the optional cornstarch slurry. In a small bowl, combine the cornstarch and water and stir until it dissolves. Drizzle the slurry into the broth, stirring vigorously to incorporate, then allow the mixture to return to a simmer. The sauce should become silky and gravy-like in just a few seconds. To serve, transfer the clams to a shallow bowl or large plate and garnish the dish with the remaining serrano pepper slices and the rau răm and peanuts. Serve alongside steamed rice (if using).

BÙN CHẢ GIÒ KHOAI MÔN
TARO SPRING ROLL AND RICE NOODLE SALAD

Serves 6, with 2 rolls per person

Traditionally, chả giò is made to celebrate the Lunar New Year, which comes around in the late winter/early spring. Thus, it's often translated as "spring roll." Viets really love to lean in on the "spring" theme of the dish, pairing it with freshly cut herbs, leafy lettuce, and cold rice vermicelli. For my family, that meant snipping off the tender buds of whatever plants were flourishing in the garden at the time. Scrappy and assertive mint was always a given; if we were lucky, there'd be cilantro and maybe even some diếp cá. If you don't eat pork, a half-and-half mixture of ground beef and turkey works great here.

CHẢ GIÒ

One 1.3-ounce package dried bean thread noodles

2 pounds ground pork

2 cups carrots, peeled and cut into matchsticks

2 cups taro or sweet potato, peeled and cut into matchsticks

2 tablespoons minced garlic

3 tablespoons minced ginger

3 tablespoons fish sauce

¼ cup oyster sauce

1 tablespoon sesame oil

⅛ teaspoon cracked black pepper

1 tablespoon kosher salt

2 tablespoons granulated sugar

One 16-ounce package spring roll wrappers (I recommend Menlo brand)

Neutral oil (such as vegetable oil) for frying

SALAD

8 ounces dried rice vermicelli, cooked (see Note on page 60)

1 cucumber, cut into matchsticks

8 ounces mung bean sprouts

2 cups shredded lettuce (I recommend oak leaf, butter, or iceberg)

1 bunch spearmint, leaves picked

1 bunch diếp cá (fish wort), leaves picked

½ cup Củ Cải Chua Ngọt | Pickled Carrots and Daikon (page 49), liquid drained

1 cup Nước Mắm Tỏi Ớt | Chile Fish Sauce (page 43) for serving

Prep the bean thread noodles. Place the noodles in a medium bowl and cover with cold water. Soak for 1 hour. If they try to float, put a heavy plate or other weight on top to keep them submerged. After soaking, drain the noodles in a colander and use scissors to cut them into 3- to 4-inch pieces.

Prepare the filling mixture. Transfer the cut noodles to a large mixing bowl and add the ground pork, carrots, taro, garlic, ginger, fish sauce, oyster sauce, sesame oil, pepper, salt, and sugar. Use a large spoon or clean hands to toss the ingredients together until thoroughly incorporated—it should take about 5 minutes with your hands and up to 10 minutes with a spoon. Cover the bowl with plastic wrap and stash it in the fridge until you're ready to roll.

Set up your station for rolling. You need a clean surface to roll on, a small bowl of cold water, an opened package of spring roll wrappers, and your filling mixture. To roll, lay a wrapper flat with one corner pointing away from you so it looks like a diamond. Scoop about 2½ tablespoons of filling onto the lower third of the wrapper and shape it into a rough line. Tuck the left and right corners of the wrapper inward by about an inch, then pull the bottom corner up to partially cover the filling. Nestle the bottom corner around the filling so that it's snug, then roll upward until you're 2 to 3 inches away from the top corner. Then, wet your index finger using the bowl of cold water and use it to moisten the flat edges of the wrapper, making them sticky. Finish rolling the wrapper up and press on the end just firmly enough to seal the roll closed. Set the roll on a baking sheet and repeat until you have 12 rolls. (If there's leftover filling, you can sauté it and eat it over rice.)

To prepare to fry the rolls, fill a medium, heavy pot about halfway with neutral oil and set it over medium heat. Meanwhile, line a baking sheet with paper towels. Once the oil reaches 325°F on a probe thermometer, fry the spring rolls in small batches of two or three until they're golden brown on all sides. They should need about 5 minutes per side. Transfer the fried rolls to the paper towel–lined baking sheet to drain any extra grease.

To serve, divide the rice vermicelli among six large, deep bowls. Arrange the cucumber, mung bean sprouts, lettuce, spearmint, and fish wort on each however you want—just make it cute. Top the bowls with the pickles and 2 spring rolls each. For maximum auntie points, use scissors to cut the rolls into thirds. Serve with sides of the Chile Fish Sauce, which folks can pour into the bowls themselves.

BÙN BÒ SẢ ỚT
LEMONGRASS BEEF, CHILE, AND RICE NOODLE SALAD

Serves 4

LEMONGRASS BEEF

1½ pounds tri-tip steak

2 tablespoons minced garlic

1 tablespoon minced shallot

1 tablespoon minced lemongrass

2 tablespoons hoisin sauce

1 tablespoon Maggi seasoning sauce

1 tablespoon fish sauce

1 tablespoon oyster sauce

3 drops sesame oil

2 tablespoons granulated sugar

1 teaspoon kosher salt

⅛ teaspoon cracked black pepper

1 yellow onion, sliced

2 tablespoons neutral oil
(such as vegetable oil)

SALAD

8 ounces dried rice vermicelli, cooked
(see Note on page 60)

1 cucumber, cut into matchsticks

2 cup shredded green leaf or
iceberg lettuce

1 bunch spearmint, leaves picked and
soaked in cold water for 15 minutes

1 bunch diếp cá (fish wort), leaves picked
and soaked in cold water for 15 minutes

1 cup Củ Cải Chua Ngọt | Pickled Carrots
and Daikon (page 49), liquid drained

Nước Mắm Chấm | Everyday Fish Sauce
(page 40) for serving

The kitchen in my family's old apartment was tiny and basically unventilated, with a window that only opened 2 inches. It didn't take much for it to get toasty in there, especially in the summertime. So, for my mom, cooking had to be strategic: When it was hot out, she'd either stick to cold dishes, like salads, or start cooking early enough to beat the sun. I'd sometimes wake up to the aromas of smoky, mouthwatering beef, onions, and sugar caramelizing in a skillet, all mixed in with the brightness of hand-torn herbs and the sharp funk of an open jar of pickles. That's when I knew breakfast was gonna be killer—and that it was gonna be a hot-ass day.

If you can't find tri-tip, you can substitute it with any other stir-fry-friendly steak, such as skirt, flank, or picanha, also known as top sirloin.

Note: If you're making pickles specifically for this recipe, you'll need to do so one day in advance.

First, slice the tri-tip. Place the meat on a cutting board and trim away any fat and gristle. Use a long, sharp knife to cut it against the grain into ⅛-inch-thick slices. A quick reminder: "Against the grain" means making a cut perpendicular to the direction of the muscle fibers. Transfer the slices to a plate and stash in the fridge while you make the marinade.

To make the marinade, stir together the garlic, shallot, lemongrass, hoisin sauce, Maggi seasoning, fish sauce, oyster sauce, sesame oil, sugar, salt, and pepper in a medium mixing bowl. Add in the onion and stir again to incorporate. Now, dump in the sliced steak and use your hands or a spoon to incorporate, making sure to get the marinade all up in the meat. If you can spare the time, let the beef marinate in the fridge overnight—but 30 minutes will work, too.

To cook the steak, set a large skillet or wok over medium-high heat for 3 minutes. Once hot, drizzle in the neutral oil. When the oil shimmers, remove the steak from the marinade, add it to the pan, and turn the heat to high. Stir-fry the steak, tossing frequently, for 5 to 6 minutes, or until the steak is seared on all sides. Transfer the contents of the skillet, juices included, to a bowl and set aside.

To serve, divide the rice vermicelli among four soup bowls, then arrange the cucumber, lettuce, spearmint, and fish wort on top. Tuck the pickles into the bowls, wherever they look nice. Finally, top the noodles with equal portions of steak (about ½ cup each). Feel free to pour on some extra juice from the pan for extra flavor. Serve with Everyday Fish Sauce on the side and enjoy.

SÂM BỔ LƯỢNG
VIETNAMESE HERBAL TONIC DRINK

Serves 4

In Vietnamese cuisine, there's a whole category of desserts called "chè" that are meant to be enjoyed as a kind of snack, especially on hot, muggy days. Chè consists of all kinds of chewy, squishy stuff served over ice, like sticky rice balls, sweet corn, red beans, and pandan jellies. My mom would fill her sâm bổ lượng, an herbal tonic–style chè, with dried seeds and fruits scored on her trips to the Chinese medicine shops in Oakland's Chinatown, supplemented with fresh fruits from her garden. And in the grand tradition of Asian-style "not-too-sweet" desserts, it gets just a small hint of caramelly sweetness in the form of palm sugar.

¼ cup pearl barley

1 cup dried lotus seeds

½ cup sliced dried kombu

½ cup dried jujubes (Chinese red dates)

1 cup dried longan

Filtered water

½ cup palm sugar

GARNISH

¼ cup sliced kumquats

¼ cup fresh goji berries

The first step is to rehydrate all the dried stuff, working in stages. Make sure you keep every ingredient separate from the others, because each one has a different cook time. You'll need five bowls, one for each of the ingredients. Clean the barley and lotus seeds by rinsing them separately under cold running water, then let them soak in their own bowls of cool filtered water for 6 hours at room temperature. After 5 hours, rinse and soak the kombu, jujubes, and longan in three separate bowls, letting them soak for 1 hour. My mom would always cover the bowls with a food screen to keep out any pests, so make sure you do that if your windows are open.

At the end of the soaking period, transfer the longan-soaking liquid to a large bowl and add water to it until you have 4 cups. Set aside. You can drain the rest of the ingredients at this point and discard their soaking water.

Fill a medium pot with 8 cups water. Bring the pot to a simmer over medium-high heat, then add the kombu. Blanch the kombu for 3 minutes, then drain it and set it aside. Refill the same pot with 4 cups fresh water, then bring it to a boil over high heat. Throw in the barley and let it cook for 15 minutes, or until the grains become tender enough to chew. Drain the barley and rinse it under cool running water to stop the cooking and remove some of the extra starch. Set aside.

Cook the lotus seeds. Wipe out the same pot you've been using and pour in the longan liquid. Add in the lotus seeds and bring the pot up to a simmer over medium-high heat. Let the lotus seeds cook for 20 minutes, until they become tender.

Once the lotus seeds are tender, add the blanched kombu, the longan, jujubes, and palm sugar to the pot and return the mixture to a simmer. Once it reaches a simmer, turn off the heat and stir in the cooked barley. Let the mixture cool at room temperature for an hour.

To serve, add 6 to 7 slices of kumquat and a dozen or so goji berries to an 8-ounce glass, then fill the rest of the glass with crushed ice. Stir the sâm bổ lượng with a ladle to distribute the components, then pour it over the ice. Enjoy immediately. The sâm bổ lượng will keep in an airtight container in the fridge for up to a week. If you're storing it in multiple containers, make sure to give the mixture a stir before divvying it up to evenly distribute all the goodies.

7

I RUN
THESE SHORES

Up until now, I've been describing the world that I came from. But now it's time to switch up the scene.

When I graduated from culinary school in my twenties, my world completely changed. I came out freshly cleaned and pressed, with the recipes for béarnaise sauce and croissants pretty much tattooed onto my brain. I worked at restaurants around the Bay Area, moving up and up until I found my way into critically acclaimed, Michelin-starred kitchens, like San Francisco's Acquerello. According to the typical narrative, I was living the hotshot chef dream. After about a decade, I walked away from all of that because, at the end of the day, I wasn't making food that mattered to me, and I wasn't serving the people that mattered to me. That's when Ăn, my pop-up, was born.

With Ăn, I was trying to combine what I learned from professional kitchen spaces with the dishes I enjoyed the most from my childhood. The tasting menu dinners I put on were all about the idea that haute cuisine and Vietnamese food could coexist—that my own culture deserved to be put on a pedestal, too. I paired my mom's homegrown herbs with seaweed that I foraged from the Sonoma coast; I dressed up wontons (page 183) with edible gold flakes. It was a trip to finally see diners dig into dishes that really meant something to me, like the Cá Trích Nhúng Giấm | Vietnamese Fish Shabu Shabu (page 77) that I ate with my maternal grandfather before he passed away.

That's not to say it was a glamorous time, though. I spent a ton of time hauling a fuck-ton of extremely heavy milk crates from location to location, because somebody (me) thought it would be a cool idea to have individual dishes for every one of the nine courses on the menu. Once in a while, I'd drive across the Golden Gate Bridge to a ranch to pick up a whole pig, which I mummified in plastic wrap and kept cool in the backseat with a ton of ice packs. Back home, I butchered it on a steel prep table that I scored from Craigslist and stored the pieces with my other pop-up ingredients in a commercial beverage fridge, also secondhand.

I'll be real with you: I fucked up a lot. From unchewable bánh canh noodles to shattered cornets (page 177) to silken tofu that didn't set, disaster lurked around every corner. With pop-ups, where you're always working in someone else's space, you never know what might go wrong. But that's kind of the exciting part, right? You really learn to let go, and instead of freaking out, you improvise.

Besides the sometimes-weepy tofu, the food at Ăn was controversial from the get-go. I would get people who brought their moms, OGs from north and central Vietnam, and they'd scoff at my very southern Vietnamese and Californian menu: "This isn't real Vietnamese food." It would break my heart, I'm not gonna lie. And then there was the other side, where people would say I was "elevating" Vietnamese food, which I also found so frustrating. "Elevate" always comes off like a value judgement to me. You're telling me I cook better than my mom and aunties because I worked at some Michelin place for a year or two? Telling me I make better bánh cuốn because I put truffles on them? You got me fucked up.

Over time, I realized that the menu would make more sense to people if I actually hung out in the dining room to tell my family's story to my diners. I was really hesitant at first, and I had plenty of excuses to hide in the kitchen as soon as the food hit the tables: I was exhausted from carrying all those damn milk crates; I was "lazy"; I didn't go to school to learn how to speak to crowds. But when I started doing it, that's when people started to really connect with the concept. I shared the stories that I was so eager to hear from my own parents.

As a chef, the way I started to figure out who I was as a person was through food. That's my medium. And so, the food that I was cooking at Ăn reflected my curiosity about my identity and also my self-doubt. Did I belong in the world of fine dining? Or did I just need to look toward home to find myself? To see diners, fellow humans, feel some solace and joy in the dishes that came out of those questions was amazing. I didn't know my food was special—I just wanted to create a space for myself.

Around 2018, the Ăn series wound down as I started to become less interested in the whole fine dining thing. Cooking short ribs in sous vide for four hours and putting a demi sauce on it no longer sounded appealing to me. Dots on a plate? Nah. But food that you eat with your hands? I'm there for all that beautiful mess.

Even though Ăn is very much in my past, the recipes from that time are still so special to me. I love that these dishes show a different side of Vietnamese food that most people in the United States have never had a chance to see. In these recipes, the techniques that I learned from my family—making noodles, squeezing the milk out of soybeans, cooking with scraps and offal—stand side-by-side with methods used in the most high-end, expensive kitchens in the world. I know for a fact that my mom and aunties could hold it down in any Michelin-starred kitchen; and they'd walk out having taught every chef in there a thing or two, just like they taught me.

The recipes in this chapter reflect the way I actually cooked at my pop-up, so a few of them require more specialized equipment than the recipes in the rest of the book. My favorite online retailers for cheffy kitchen tools are JB Prince and Seisuke Knife, but if you have a local restaurant supply store nearby, try that first. You can find some of the more out-there items, like ring molds and soy lecithin, online at WebstaurantStore (www.webstaurantstore.com).

WHERE TO EAT IN OAKLAND

Bánh Mì Ba Lẹ
1909 International Blvd.
Oakland, CA 94606

Oakland's best bánh mì shop is one of the few stateside spots that gets the bread exactly right: cottony and light on the inside, crisp and flaky on the outside.

Co Nam
3936 Telegraph Ave.
Oakland, CA 94609

Bring the homies here for what Viets like to call nhậu—drinking food, like fried quail, garlic noodles (page 186), and spicy baby back ribs.

Monster Phở
360 40th St.
Oakland, CA 94609

I love this phở spot's laid-back vibe and simple, gimmick-free soups.

Phở Ao Sen
1139 E. 12th St.
Oakland, CA 94606

The owners here really take pride in their food, from summer rolls served with crab butter dipping sauce on the side to phở drizzled with Mỡ Hành | Green Onion Sauce (page 47) that's made with bona fide beef fat. So extra.

Phở Gà Hương Quê
1228 7th Ave.
Oakland, CA 94606

This is the prime spot for phở gà, and folks go bananas for the phenomenal Mỡ Hành Gừng | Ginger and Green Onion Sauce (page 47) that's served with every bowl.

Phở King
638 International Blvd.
Oakland, CA 94606

Though it has "phở" in the name, the real highlights at this place are the other star soups of Vietnam: bún bò Huế that will make your soul tingle with happiness and fragrant, delicate bún riêu.

Phở Vy
401 International Blvd.
Oakland, CA 94606

This spot went viral on social media for its birria-style tacos made with Vietnamese beef stew, a genius dish I wish I was forward-thinking enough to come up with myself.

Tay Ho
344 12th St., Suite B
Oakland, CA 94607

At this family-owned restaurant, the mom's silky bánh cuốn, made from fresh rice batter, is a must-order.

Vien Huong
712 Franklin St.
Oakland, CA 94607

Ever since I was a kid, I loved this place's take on Vietnamese-Chinese cuisine, like meatball soups with egg and rice noodles, chewy fried fish cakes (page 69), and spare-rib noodles.

GỎI CUỐN CÁ CORNETS

Serves 4

A go-to small bite at my pop-ups, this is a fine-dining version of the Huyết Cá Tái Chanh | Tuna Bloodline Tartare that my family would make into rolls with nori and rice paper. I would spend hours turning everyday sheets of rice paper into elegant cornets in preparation for the pop-up, all for the satisfaction of seeing my guests flip the fuck out as they chomped down on the things. I'm gonna be real with you, though—this dish only worked, like, 50 percent of the time. If the air in the kitchen was just a little bit too dry or too humid, we were screwed. So if you want to replicate the crunch without all the hassle, skip the rolling step and fry the dry rice paper triangles into crispy chips. For this recipe, you'll need some pretty cheffy equipment: 32 cornet molds, a pastry bag, a spray bottle, and a butane torch. You've been warned.

---

4 sheets 22 cm-square rice paper

½ cup Huyết Cá Tái Chanh | Tuna Bloodline Tartare (page 135)

Uncooked rice for plating

½ cup soft herbs for garnish, such as dill sprigs, micro basil, or chervil

---

Prep the rice paper wrappers by cutting each sheet into eight triangles. In a perfect world, you'll have four to five cornets per person, but extras will come in handy if any of them break.

To make a cornet, fill a spray bottle with cold water and spritz one triangle a few times to just moisten it. When the triangle feels like it can bend without breaking, wrap it around a cornet mold to form a small cone. Press the rice paper onto itself to seal it shut, then invert the mold so that it points upward. Set it aside on a baking sheet. Repeat with the rest of the triangles. When you're finally done—whew!—let the cones dry at room temperature for half an hour. Stash them somewhere that they'll be safe from moisture, like inside an oven with the light on.

Now, toast the cornets. Line up the cones on a heat-safe surface (like the baking sheet), and use a butane torch to toast the rice paper until it gets crispy, puffy, and just a little charred. Pull the finished cones off the cornet molds, being extra, extra careful to not break the rice paper. Place the cones in an airtight container. Repeat with the rest of the cones and set aside.

Prepare the tartare. Dice the fish a little bit finer than instructed in the original tartare recipe so that it has a softer, more scoopable texture. Transfer the mixture to a pastry bag, then cut the tip to make a ¼-inch opening.

To serve, fill four small bowls with uncooked rice to help the cornets stand straight up. Pipe the 20 nicest rice paper cornets with ½ to 1 teaspoon each of the tartare. Stick five cornets into the rice in each bowl so that they stand. Use wooden chopsticks or off-set plating tweezers to garnish each of the cones with a single herb. Serve immediately.

CAVIAR À LA NƯỚC MẮM

Serves 4

12 Capital Reserve oysters
(Puget Sound, WA)

1 cup filtered water

One 1-inch piece dried kombu

1 cup bonito flakes

1 Oro Blanco grapefruit, suprêmed,
then chopped (see Note on page 43)

1 blood orange, suprêmed, then chopped
(see Note on page 43)

1 navel orange, suprêmed, then chopped
(see Note on page 43)

1 pint cherry tomatoes, quartered

2 radishes, thinly sliced

½ cup diced pineapple

¾ cup Nước Mắm Khóm | Pineapple Fish
Sauce (page 42)

1½ tablespoons (16 grams) Osetra caviar

1½ tablespoons (16 grams) Gold Pearl
trout roe

½ teaspoon (3 grams) soy lecithin

1 cup edible flower petals for garnish

Diếp cá (fish wort) for garnish

Oysters, caviar, and Champagne are shorthand for the kind of good life you see in rap videos, and my pop-up played around with the idea of wealth and excess by fusing the flavors I grew up eating with rich people shit. I was still finding my voice as a chef, using irony to work my way through my feelings of insecurity about not being born with a mother-of-pearl spoon in my mouth.

This dish, an elegant chilled course, is a pretty dramatic example of that: meaty, briny oysters paired with tiny glistening globs of Tsar Nicoulai caviar, elegant citrus suprêmes, and dashi whipped into a foam so fluffy, it looks like it's been scooped out of a princess' bubble bath. What grounds the dish in my own story is the pineapple-infused fish sauce, which enhances all the ocean spray notes in the other ingredients.

When working with fresh oysters, most of the work is in keeping them alive, right up until the moment you need them. I'll walk you through the process of using live oysters in their shells, but you can absolutely start with pre-shucked oysters instead. You can also skip the oysters and use this same preparation on other ocean creatures, like bay shrimp, scallops, or mussels. For this recipe, you'll need an immersion blender, a food scale, a steamer, and an oyster knife (or, in a pinch, a flathead screwdriver).

Note: I like to soak oysters like I do mussels, just in case they've got any grit inside of them. For further instructions on how to clean them, see page 163.

Use live oysters the day you purchase them. Right up until you're ready to cook, keep them cold in the fridge by storing them in a colander covered with ice and a kitchen towel. Set the colander over a bowl to catch the water that drips off. Check on the oysters periodically to make sure they're never submerged in water for an extended period, draining off water and replacing the ice as necessary. When you're ready to get started, soak the oysters (see Note).

While the oysters are soaking, make the dashi. Combine the water, kombu, and bonito flakes in a small pot set over high heat. Bring the liquid to a simmer, then take the pot off the heat and let all the umami flavors steep into the water for 10 minutes. Strain the dashi to remove any solids, keeping the liquid in the pot.

Give each oyster a quick once-over, but not too quick. If you eat a dead one, you're in for a very, very bad time. Make sure they're all closed. If you find one that's open, tap it: If it doesn't close, throw it out—it's dead. Set the oysters on a plate that will fit into your steamer and transfer the plate to the steamer. Fill a large pot with 6 inches of water and set the steamer with the oysters on top.

Set the steamer over high heat and bring the water to a nice simmer. Steam the oysters for 8 to 10 minutes, until they all open. Use an oyster knife to fully open them: Insert the knife into the oyster near its hinge, twist it like a key, then gently pry the shell apart. Keep the oyster meat attached to the bottom shell. Arrange the opened oysters each on their half shells into their own individual small bowls.

Garnish each bowl with the citrus suprêmes, cherry tomatoes, radishes, and pineapple. Drizzle the Pineapple Fish Sauce over each oyster and top with dollops of caviar and roe. For an elegant touch, use a mother of pearl spoon to add the caviar.

Now we're going to do some magic with the dashi. Add the soy lecithin to the pot: It works as an emulsifier, which you need to turn this humble broth into a foamy bubble bath. Tilt the pot by about 30 degrees, then use an immersion blender to froth the dashi for 30 seconds, like you're making a smoky umami cappuccino.

Skim off the top layer of dashi foam to gently blanket on top of the oysters. Finally, adorn the dishes with a cute lil' sprinkle of flower petals and fish wort. Serve immediately.

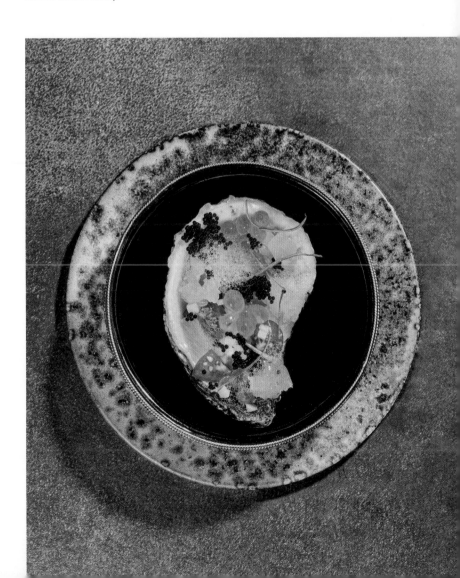

ÂU CƠ TRỨNG
CRAB BEURRE MONTÉ CHAWANMUSHI

Makes 4

This dish is an homage to the mother of the Vietnamese people: Âu Cơ. If you really think about it, the whole story is some pretty wild, Jerry Springer–type stuff. Âu Cơ, an immortal snow fairy, married Lạc Long Quân, a dragon king. One hundred children—the first Vietnamese people—hatched from the egg she laid. Unfortunately, fairy mom and dad got along like ice and fire; they divorced, split custody 50/50, and moved to opposite ends of Vietnam. (Feels like they could have figured that out before having kids, but that's none of my business.) Anyway, the crab and egg in this small bite are symbolic of Âu Cơ and Lạc Long Quân's marriage, though I promise it's not nearly as bitter as their divorce.

Mythology aside, this dish was also my attempt to turn súp măng cua, a velvety crab-and-asparagus soup, into an amuse-bouche that channeled yet another dish: the very technically precise egg amuse invented by the chef Alain Passard at the Michelin-starred L'Arpège in Paris. In my version, I fill an empty eggshell with a light Japanese-style custard, then garnish it with sweet and flaky crabmeat, a velvety butter sauce, and panko breadcrumbs. You'll need a steamer and a pendulum-style specialty egg topper tool to open the eggshells perfectly without cracking them.

CHAWANMUSHI (EGG CUSTARD)

4 eggs

1 cup whole milk

3 tablespoons filtered water

½ teaspoon fish sauce

¼ teaspoon sesame oil

BEURRE MONTÉ

1 tablespoon filtered water

1 stick (4 ounces) unsalted butter, room temperature and cut into chunks

½ teaspoon Knorr hạt nêm or chicken bouillon powder

2 ounces Dungeness crab lump meat

Remove the top lid of an empty plastic egg carton. From the bottom, cut off a 2 egg by 2 egg section. This is what you'll use to hold the eggs steady in the steamer.

To prep the eggshells, use an egg topper to remove the pointier top end of the still-raw eggs, one at a time. Pulling back the spring of the egg topper handle will crack a perfect fracture around a small portion of the eggshell, and you can use a sharp paring knife to finish the job. Pour the egg innards into a bowl, being careful to not burst the yolks, and set aside. You'll use them shortly to make the chawanmushi custard. Toss the eggshell tops into your compost bin.

Rinse the eggshells in a warm bath, being extra careful to not crack them, then let them dry upside down in the egg carton for at least half an hour.

In the meantime, make the chawanmushi. Carefully separate the egg whites and yolks. Put the yolks in a small mixing bowl and add the milk, water, fish sauce, and sesame oil. (Put the egg whites in the fridge and use them for breakfast tomorrow.) Whisk the egg yolk mixture until all the ingredients are more-or-less incorporated.

Flip over the eggshells so that their openings are facing up, then evenly divide the custard between them using a measuring cup with a spout. Don't fill them more than halfway; if you have leftover mix, just add it to tomorrow's breakfast stash.

To steam the custards, fill a pot with 6 inches of water, top it with a bamboo steamer, then place the whole thing on medium-high heat. Once the steamer is emitting a generous amount of steam, place the egg carton with the eggshells inside and steam for 4 to 5 minutes. At 4 minutes, start keeping a

CONTINUED

CRAB BEURRE MONTÉ CHAWANMUSHI,

CONTINUED

BREADCRUMBS

¼ cup panko

1 tablespoon unsalted butter, melted

1 teaspoon extra-virgin olive oil

⅛ teaspoon kosher salt

2 tablespoons grated Parmesan for garnish

close eye on the eggs, and pull them off the heat once the custard is set (it should be just slightly wiggly). Set the custard-filled shells aside while you make the beurre monté.

To make the beurre monté, or emulsified butter sauce, start by bringing the 1 tablespoon water to a gentle simmer in a small pot set over low heat. It seems a little ridiculous to do this with such a small amount of water, but trust me, it works. Gradually add the room-temperature butter to the pot, 1 or 2 cubes at a time. (If you use cold butter, the mixture will get too cold and won't emulsify.) Use a small whisk to combine the butter and water. When all the butter is stirred in, add the hạt nêm to season the sauce. Then, use a spatula or spoon to gently fold in the crabmeat, aiming to keep the chunks as whole as possible. Somehow, when crabmeat gets all shredded, it looks less luxurious and fancy. Keep this mixture on low heat for 5 minutes before serving so that the flavors can meld together.

While the beurre monté rests, make the breadcrumbs. Start by setting a sauté pan over low heat. Meanwhile, in a small mixing bowl, stir together the panko, melted butter, olive oil, and salt. Once the pan is hot, pour the mixture into the pan. Immediately stir or toss the ingredients, stirring continuously so that the panko toasts evenly, about 5 minutes. When the breadcrumbs are golden brown, pour them onto a plate to keep them from burning.

Finally, combine all of the amazing components you just cooked into a gorgeous homage to your divorced great-great-great-great-great-grandparents. Top each of the egg custards with a tablespoon or so of the beurre monté, making sure to get a nice amount of crab into each one. Cover with a sprinkle of the toasted panko and finish with grated Parmesan. Serve immediately.

DUCK LIVER DUMPLINGS

Serves 4 (Makes 20 to 25 dumplings)

I learned to make hoành thánh, the Vietnamese take on Chinese wontons, from my parents. My dad's years of working at a Chinese restaurant made him the Terminator of wonton-making; and a lot of times, we'd have Cantonese-style roast duck and noodles to go along with the meal. There were so many evenings when my family would all sit together at the dinner table, scooping the pork-and-shrimp filling into wrappers and pinching them together while chatting. For my pop-ups, I made the same dumpling recipe, though I punched them up a bit with scratch-made wrappers, rich morsels of duck liver, and edible gold flakes. The raviolo shape of the wontons draws on my training in Italian cuisine, while the sear-and-steam method is a nod to Japanese pub food. To make this recipe, you'll need a pasta machine and three ring molds (2.3 inches, 1.9 inches, and 1.6 inches in diameter).

WRAPPERS

3 cups bread flour, plus more for dusting

1 teaspoon kosher salt

1 cup boiling filtered water

DUMPLINGS

1 pound ground pork

1 pound 16/20 (extra jumbo) shrimp, peeled, deveined, and chopped

1 teaspoon minced garlic

½ teaspoon minced ginger

1 teaspoon cornstarch

½ teaspoon granulated sugar

½ teaspoon kosher salt

⅛ teaspoon cracked black pepper

½ teaspoon fish sauce

⅛ teaspoon sesame oil

¼ pound duck liver, cut into ⅛-inch-thick slices

Start by making the dumpling wrapper dough. Stir together the bread flour and salt in a medium mixing bowl. Trickle in the boiling water, all the while stirring the mixture with a fork or chopsticks. Stop adding water when the dough comes together in a solid mass. Transfer the dough to a clean, lightly floured surface and knead it for 5 to 7 minutes, or until it becomes smooth and elastic. You can adjust the dough by adding more flour or water if it seems too sticky or dry, respectively. Shape the dough into a ball and cover it with a clean kitchen towel or plastic wrap. Let it rest for 30 minutes to allow the gluten to relax, making the dough easier to work with.

While the dough rests, make the filling for the dumplings. In a medium bowl, combine the ground pork, shrimp, garlic, ginger, cornstarch, sugar, salt, pepper, fish sauce, and sesame oil. Gently fold in the duck liver, being careful not to squish the pieces too much as you mix. Place the mixture in the fridge to marinate for a minimum of 15 minutes while you prepare the dumpling wrappers.

After the dough has rested, divide it into four equal portions. (Use a scale if you want to be super anal about it.) Set a pasta machine to its widest setting and pass one of the portions of dough through the machine, guiding it with your hands. Fold the dough in half and pass it through again. Repeat this process several times, using the dial on the pasta machine to gradually reduce the thickness after each pass. Stop once the dough gets to 1.9 millimeters. (You can look up what it'll take to get there in your pasta machine's manual.) Repeat the process with the remaining portions of dough until you have four super-thin sheets. Dust some flour between them to prevent sticking.

Next, cut the dumpling wrappers. Lay one of the thin sheets of dough on a clean, lightly floured surface. Use the 2.3-inch ring mold to plan out the dumplings by gently pressing indentations into the dough, leaving small spaces between the circles.

CONTINUED

DUCK LIVER DUMPLINGS,

CONTINUED

2 cups Nước Luộc Gà | Chicken Stock (page 51) or store-bought stock

Neutral oil (such as vegetable oil) for frying

½ teaspoon chili crisp, such as Lao Gan Ma, for garnish (optional)

Edible gold flakes for garnish (optional)

Once you have mapped them out, fill and seal the dumplings. Set the 1.9-inch ring mold in the center of one of the circles, then spoon 1½ teaspoons of the filling into it. Repeat with the rest of the circles. Moisten the edges of each circle with a finger or pastry brush dipped in water. Place a second sheet of rolled dough on top of the first one. Then, using the 1.6-inch ring mold, press around each heap of filling—without cutting through—just to create a tight seal and remove any air pockets. Finally, use the 2.3-inch ring mold to cut the dumplings free.

Use a spatula to transfer the dumplings to a baking sheet or a tray dusted with flour to prevent sticking. As you go, keep the finished dumplings covered with a dish towel so that they don't dry out and start cracking. You can also dust them with flour or cornstarch to prevent them from sticking to each other. Repeat these steps with the other two sheets of dough and the remainder of the filling. (At this point, you can freeze the dumplings for a maximum of 3 months.)

When you're ready to cook and serve the dumplings, warm the chicken stock in a medium pot over low heat, just to get it warm enough for serving. Then, put a large frying pan over medium heat for 3 minutes. (Choose a frying pan with a lid that fits.) Once the pan is hot, add 1 tablespoon neutral oil. When the oil starts shimmering, gently lay a few of the dumplings in the pan—just enough to keep them from crowding or touching each other. Let the dumplings sear for 2 to 3 minutes, or until you're able to nudge them around the pan with a spatula.

Now, steam the dumplings. Take the pan off the heat, then add in 1 cup water. The steam's gonna come at you in a bit of a jump scare, so watch out. Cover the frying pan and place it over medium-high heat to let the dumplings steam for 5 minutes, or until the water evaporates. Place the finished dumplings on a plate and repeat with the rest.

To serve, portion 5 to 6 dumplings per person into four wide, shallow bowls, then ladle half a cup of the warm chicken stock over each serving. Garnish with chile crisp and edible gold (if using).

MÌ XÀO TỎI NẤM CỤC
TRUFFLED GARLIC NOODLES

Serves 4

In the Bay Area, garlic noodles and Dungeness crab are as indisputable a pairing as bacon and eggs. Credit for the dish usually goes to Thanh Long, a bustling Vietnamese restaurant in San Francisco where the An family has been roasting crabs and stir-frying noodles since 1971. Nowadays, you'll find the noodles pretty much everywhere, from other Vietnamese noodle shops to soul food pop-ups like Chef Smelly's in Oakland. Doused in a powerfully garlicky butter sauce, the noodles get some extra Viet-style umami notes from oyster sauce and fish sauce—or at least, that's my guess. Thanh Long's original recipe is one of the best-kept secrets in the food world, but I think my version, while just a little fancier, is pretty damn good. If you do want to pair these with Dungeness crab, I've written detailed steaming instructions in another recipe (pages 208–209).

---

12 ounces fresh lo mein noodles or dry spaghetti

---

5 garlic cloves, minced

---

3 tablespoons unsalted butter

---

1 teaspoon fish sauce

---

1 tablespoon oyster sauce

---

1 tablespoon hoisin sauce

---

20 grams black Périgord truffles or summer truffles

⅛ teaspoon cracked black pepper

¼ cup sliced green onion, green parts only, for garnish

---

2 tablespoons toasted sesame seeds (see page 19) for garnish

First, make the noodles. Fill a medium pot with filtered water and bring it to a rolling boil over high heat. Add the noodles and cook, stirring, until al dente, 3 to 4 minutes for lo mein or around 8 minutes for spaghetti. Drain the noodles in a colander, reserving ½ cup of the pasta water. Rinse the noodles with cold water to stop them from overcooking and set aside.

Then, start on the sauce. Set a wok or 10-inch frying pan over medium heat. Once hot, add the reserved pasta water and minced garlic. Once half of the water has evaporated, add the butter and stir it in with a vengeance so that it emulsifies. The extra starch in the water, leached off of the noodles, should make this process easy. Next, add the fish sauce, oyster sauce, and hoisin sauce, and keep cooking the mixture until it starts to thicken up, about 2 minutes. Use a Microplane grater to shave just the exterior of the truffles into the sauce, reserving the rest for garnish.

Add the cooked noodles to the wok and toss to coat for 3 minutes. Remove the wok from heat and season with black pepper.

To serve, use tongs to divide the noodles among four pasta bowls. Make sure you scrape all the sauce out, too. Garnish the noodles with the sliced green onion and sesame seeds, and finish them off by grating the rest of the truffles over them.

BÁNH CANH TÔM HÙM
LOBSTER BOBA

Serves 4

Asian American Millennials like to joke about how we're all obsessed with boba, so I made this recipe to make fun of that idea. Little did I know back in the 2010s that boba would still be huge today, especially among the younger generation. This recipe originated with the idea that when most people think of boba, they think of a super-sweet, over-the-top iced tea or coffee loaded up with jelly, brown sugar, salty cheese foam, and squishy tapioca pearls. I thought to myself, what if it was savory? Tapioca pearls are basically round bánh canh noodles, right? So for this dish, I claimed boba in the name of Vietnam and served boba pearls in a lobster stew that was—unapologetically—laced with a shit-ton of fish sauce, peppers, and lemongrass. For this dish, you'll need a spoon, not a straw.

Note: Don't just pick any old lobster when you're at the seafood counter. Smaller lobsters have a sweeter flavor, so this recipe calls for one that weighs about 2½ pounds. Choose a lobster that still has full-length antennae and both claws. If a lobster is missing parts, it's an indication that the lobster has been living in the tank for a long time, which often means a less healthy, weaker lobster. When the fishmonger pulls a healthy lobster out of the tank, it should wriggle around a bunch. Always cook fresh lobster within 24 hours.

1 live Maine lobster, about 2½ pounds

12 cups filtered water

4 tablespoons kosher salt

½ pound bay scallops, rinsed and drained

3 tablespoons neutral oil
(such as vegetable oil)

1 cup finely diced yellow onions

½ cup finely diced carrots

½ cup finely diced celery

½ cup finely diced fennel bulb,
fronds separated and chopped

1 green bell pepper, finely diced

2 red bell peppers, finely diced

2 ounces cognac

1 tablespoon minced lemongrass

2 tablespoons minced garlic

1 teaspoon minced ginger

1 bunch fresh tarragon, leaves chopped

1 bunch dill, fronds chopped

1 bunch parsley, leaves chopped

CONTINUED

To kill a live lobster humanely, stick it in the freezer for 10 to 20 minutes. If you want to make sure it's super double-dead, plunge a knife behind its eyes. To cook the lobster, fill a separate large pot with 12 cups filtered water and bring to a boil over high heat. Meanwhile, prepare an ice bath in a large pot or bowl. Make sure you have enough ice water to fully submerge the lobster. Set the ice bath aside.

Once the water on the stove is boiling, season it with 2 tablespoons of the salt. Add the lobster to the boiling water and cook for exactly 2 minutes. As soon as 2 minutes are up, remove the lobster from the water and immediately submerge it in the ice bath for 5 minutes.

Then, de-shell the lobster. Prepare a paper towel–lined plate to collect the pieces of lobster meat. As you work, reserve the lobster's shell bits and head for use in flavoring the stew.

To start, twist the lobster like you're wringing a towel to separate the tail from the rest of the body. If you've got tough bear paws for hands, press on the tail to crack the shell in half lengthwise. Otherwise, you can wrap the tail in a kitchen towel to protect yourself from the shell's sharp edges before cracking. Peel off the shell and pull the poop vein out from the meat and discard. Slice the tail meat in half lengthwise and put the pieces on the paper towel–lined plate.

Twist off the claws and separate the knuckle segments. Wiggle the thumb-like dactyls off the claws, then use the back of a knife or a specialized cracker to break open the main claw shell. Gently remove the flesh. Using sharp scissors, open up the knuckles and remove the flesh, taking care to keep the pieces as whole as possible. Put the claw meat on the paper

1 bunch Thai basil, leaves chopped

6 cups Nước Luộc Gà | Chicken Stock (page 51) or store-bought stock

2 tablespoons crab paste in soybean oil

1 teaspoon sa tế (see page 22)

2 tablespoons fish sauce

¼ teaspoon Knorr hạt nêm or MSG

1 tablespoon granulated sugar

1 tablespoon tapioca starch

1 cup chopped tomatoes

1 pint cherry tomatoes

½ bunch chives, thinly sliced

1 tablespoon extra-virgin olive oil

Black pepper

½ cup large white tapioca pearls

BEURRE MONTÉ

¼ cup filtered water

8 ounces (2 sticks) unsalted butter, at room temperature and cut into chunks

Kosher salt

GARNISH

1 serrano pepper, sliced

½ bunch chives, sliced into 1-inch batons

Dill fronds

Parsley leaves

towel-lined plate along with the tail and transfer to the fridge. Add the knuckle meat to a medium mixing bowl.

Remove the legs from the lobster's body and use a rolling pin to squeeze the meat out, sort of like toothpaste. Add it to the mixing bowl. Stir the bay scallops into the mixing bowl and stash that in the fridge, too.

To make the soup, set a wide, heavy pot over medium heat, then add in the neutral oil. When the oil starts to shimmer, pour in the reserved lobster shells and head, onion, carrot, celery, fennel bulb, and bell peppers and increase the heat to high. Sauté the mixture for 20 minutes, stirring continuously to prevent scorching. Once the shells turn a brighter shade of red and the onion and fennel start to get toasty at the edges, pull the pan off the heat. Pour in the cognac, then return the pan to the stove over medium heat for 5 minutes. As the liquid bubbles, use a rubber spatula or wooden spoon to scrape up any delicious fond that's stuck to the pan.

After 5 minutes, the liquid should have evaporated, and the aromatics should be starting to stick to the pan again. Now, add the lemongrass, garlic, and ginger to the pot. Let the aromatics sweat for 5 minutes, stirring them constantly, until the garlic and ginger start to stick to the pan. At that point, add in the fennel fronds, tarragon, dill, parsley, and Thai basil. Pour in the chicken stock and bring the broth to a simmer. Add the crab paste and sa tế and stir to incorporate. Return the pot to a simmer, and season the pot with fish sauce, hạt nêm, sugar, and the remaining 2 tablespoons salt. Taste and adjust flavors as necessary.

To thicken the broth, whisk in the tapioca starch a teaspoon at a time. Then allow all those tasty aromatics to simmer until the liquid is thick enough to coat the back of a spoon, about 45 minutes.

Strain the stew through a fine-mesh sieve into a large bowl or pot and discard the solids. Wipe out the stew pot, then return the liquid to it and add in the chopped tomatoes. Return the stew to a simmer over medium heat. Add the bowl of scallops and lobster meat to the pot and fold them in gently with a rubber spatula to avoid breaking up the pieces. Let the mixture simmer, then keep the broth warm over the stove's lowest heat setting while you finish up the remaining components of the recipe.

Prep the cherry tomatoes. Start by bringing a medium pot of salted water to a rolling boil over high heat. Prepare an ice bath in a small bowl and set it by the stove. Using a sharp paring knife, score each cherry tomato with an X, and carefully drop them all into the boiling water. After 30 seconds, remove the tomatoes from the boiling water and transfer them to the ice bath to shock them. The thin skins should start peeling, starting from the spots where you scored them. Remove them and discard. Halve the peeled tomatoes and combine in a small bowl with the sliced chives. Dress them with the extra-virgin olive oil and add salt and pepper to taste. Set aside.

Next, cook the tapioca pearls. If they don't come with instructions, here's what you should do: Fill a 4-quart pot with water and bring it to a hard boil over high heat, then add the pearls. Cook them for 30 minutes, stirring often to prevent sticking, then turn off the heat. Let the pearls continue to plump up in the water for 30 minutes more. Drain the pearls in a colander and rinse them under cold running water to stop the cooking. Set the colander aside.

You think we're done? Ha!

Next, make the beurre monté, which you'll use to infuse the lobster tail and claw meat with extra richness just before you serve the stew. Pour the water into a small pot and bring it to a gentle simmer over low heat. Melt the butter into the water, one or two chunks at a time, and use a small whisk to break it up into smaller bits. Add a pinch of salt and continue whisking until the mixture emulsifies into a nice, creamy sauce. Put the reserved tail and claw meat into the pot with the sauce and use a spoon to baste the pieces with the sauce. Keep the meat in the sauce for 10 minutes—pretty much right up to the moment you're ready to serve. (This is a good time to throw the tapioca pearls into the stew.)

Is the tapioca warm? Has the lobster meat finished poaching?

If so, it's time to serve. Use a ladle to divide the stew among four wide, shallow bowls. Make sure each bowl gets some pearls and an equal share of the lobster meat and scallops, unless you're playing favorites. Top each bowl with a piece of butter-poached lobster and the cherry tomatoes, and garnish with the serrano pepper slices, chive batons, dill fronds, and parsley leaves. Serve immediately.

BÁNH CANH CARBONARA

Serves 4

In Vietnam, you'll mostly find folks slurping up bánh canh noodles in broth, but I think they've got a lot more to offer. So, in this dish, I decided to pair bánh canh with what is true royalty in the Italian pasta kingdom: a rich and salty carbonara sauce. And since this is already a remix of a classic dish, I decided to make all the Italian nonnas cry and put cream in it. Sorry! It really does make the sauce easier.

1 pound bánh canh noodles (see page 70)

4 egg yolks

½ cup heavy cream

Kosher salt

4 ounces guanciale or bacon, cut into small strips

2 cups grated Pecorino Romano, plus more for serving

1 teaspoon fish sauce

⅛ teaspoon cracked black pepper, plus more for serving

Black truffle for garnish (optional)

Cook the bánh canh noodles using filtered water according to the method on page 70. Before you drain the noodles, reserve ¼ cup of the cooking water. Rinse the noodles under cool running water to keep them from overcooking and set aside.

In a small mixing bowl, use a fork to whisk together the egg yolks, heavy cream, and a pinch of salt. Set aside.

Then, get started on the carbonara. Set a large frying pan over medium heat for 2 to 3 minutes. Once hot, add the guanciale along with the reserved water. Crank up the heat to high and allow the water to evaporate; once it does, the guanciale will start to brown. When the guanciale crisps up—after about 5 minutes—remove the pan from the heat and add in the cooked tapioca noodles, the egg yolk mixture, Pecorino Romano, fish sauce, and pepper. Return the pan to the stove over medium-low heat. Stir the hell out of the pasta to get the sauce to emulsify. (If you start to see little curds in the egg sauce, it got too hot! If that happens, you fucked up—you gotta start over.) Turn the heat to low and cook the sauce for a minute longer, or until it's thick enough that it coats the back of a spoon.

Divide the noodles among four pasta bowls. Evenly distribute the cooked guanciale bits. Garnish each bowl with freshly grated Pecorino Romano, pepper, and shaved black truffle (if using). Serve immediately.

XÔI GÀ THẬP CẨM
CHICKEN FAT STICKY RICE

Serves 4

Sticky rice, xôi, comes in all sorts of styles on the streets of urban Vietnam, sold from sidewalk vendors around breakfast time wrapped in banana leaves, lotus leaves, or Styrofoam. The little bundles are as convenient as burritos, and they stay perfectly warm when tucked away in the storage compartment of the average scooter. Sweet xôi ngọt can be topped with waxy steamed corn or cooked with aromatic pandan, while savory xôi mặn—my favorite—is often paired with ingredients like shiitake mushrooms, lạp xưởng (Chinese air-dried sausages), and pork floss. Whenever my mom would make this dish at home, I would stick my face right into the pot so I could absolutely smell everything.

To me, the addition of shredded marinated chicken in xôi gà just pushes that version totally over the top. So, for my pop-up, I did a version of this that resembled Cơm Gà Hải Nam | Hainanese Chicken and Rice (page 74), except I swapped the more understated poached chicken with a luxurious and silky chicken confit. For this recipe, you'll need a 4-inch-deep roasting pan and a rice cooker.

Note: This recipe requires some planning ahead, with some ingredients needing overnight curing and soaking. Plan a few extra hours to soak the rice, too.

CONFIT CHICKEN

4 chicken leg quarters

⅓ cup kosher salt

2 tablespoons cracked black pepper

1 tablespoon granulated sugar

2½ cups neutral oil
(such as vegetable oil)

4 garlic cloves, unpeeled

STICKY RICE

½ cup raw peanuts or black-eyed peas

2 cups long-grain sticky rice

½ cup sliced shiitake mushrooms

¼ cup diced lạp xưởng (Chinese sausage)

¼ cup pork floss

2 tablespoons grated ginger

2 tablespoons minced garlic

1 lemongrass stalk, bruised and cut into 4-inch segments (see page 29)

1 pandan leaf (optional)

There are a couple of things you need to take care of the day before you plan to cook. First, prep the chicken. Season the chicken legs with the salt, pepper, and sugar. Place the seasoned legs in the fridge on a cooling rack set on top of a baking sheet. Cover the chicken legs with plastic wrap and let them cure in the fridge overnight (for at least 12 hours). Take care to ensure that any liquid that drips off the chicken doesn't escape the pan and contaminate other food.

Second, soak the peanuts for the sticky rice. Put the peanuts in a medium bowl and cover with 2 to 3 inches of cold water. Allow them to soak at room temperature overnight (for at least 12 hours).

Early the next day, drain the peanuts in a colander and set them aside. Rinse out the bowl and add in the rice. Cover the rice with 2 to 3 inches of cold water and let it soak for 4 hours. Drain the rice in the colander with the peanuts and set aside. (If you totally spaced on this part, cover the rice with hot water and soak it for an hour.)

When you're ready to confit the chicken, preheat the oven to 325°F. Rinse the cured chicken under cold running water to remove excess seasoning. Use paper towels to pat the chicken legs dry, then set them in a 4-inch-deep roasting pan. Pour in the neutral oil and add the garlic cloves. Make sure the chicken is fully submerged in the oil, adding more oil if necessary. Cover the pan with foil and place it in the oven. Cook the chicken for 2 hours, until the meat is ultra-tender and almost pulled pork–like: You should be able to pierce through the flesh using a chopstick. Remove the pan from the oven and let the chicken cool, still in the oil, at room temperature for an hour.

3 Makrut lime leaves (optional)

¼ teaspoon turmeric powder

2 tablespoons fish sauce

1 cup Nước Luộc Gà | Chicken Stock (page 51) or store-bought stock

½ cup filtered water

4 fresh banana leaves, washed and patted dry

¼ cup sliced green onions, white and green parts, for garnish

Once cooled, use tongs to pull the chicken quarters out of the oil and transfer them to a large bowl. The oil should be super aromatic now; reserve 3 tablespoons of it for later, making sure there aren't any solids in it.

When the chicken is cool enough to handle with your hands, remove and discard the bones and shred the skin and meat. Set aside. You can definitely save the soft, mellow garlic cloves for some other purpose or, you know, just eat them on the spot. You can also reuse the rest of the confit oil to make confit potatoes.

Now, you'll use some of the oil to sauté stuff. Set a large frying pan over medium heat and add the 3 tablespoons reserved confit oil to the pan. Once the oil is shimmering, add the shiitake mushrooms, Chinese sausage, pork floss, ginger, garlic, lemongrass, pandan leaf (if using), and lime leaves (if using) to the pan. Stir-fry the mixture for 2 to 3 minutes, or until the whole mess starts to really perfume the kitchen.

Add the drained peanuts and sticky rice from earlier to the pan, along with the turmeric powder. Stir-fry the mixture again for another 2 to 3 minutes to thoroughly incorporate the turmeric—the whole mixture should be stained yellow. Add the fish sauce and stir-fry for 2 minutes more to evenly distribute it, then take the pan off the hot burner.

If you're a xôi master, now's the part where you wrap the rice mixture into perfect little banana-leaf parcels. But I'm not about that life, so we're gonna go for the rice cooker. Transfer the whole sticky rice mixture from the pan to your rice cooker, along with the chicken stock and water. Flip the "Cook" switch and let the machine do its thing. When the rice finishes cooking, fluff it with a paddle and stir in the shredded confit chicken. Close the rice cooker lid and let the flavors mingle for 15 minutes before serving.

To serve, line four rice bowls with the banana leaves. You can totally cut them into smaller shapes to make them fit nicely. Scoop ½ cup of the confit sticky rice into each bowl, then top with the sliced green onions.

8

UNFAMILIAR
TRADITIONS

So, it's part of chef life that, during the holidays, you have to come up with Holiday Content™ when all the magazines and other publications ask you for it. I've gotta admit that it's been a struggle. I've caught myself lying about what my family supposedly does during the holidays and how we celebrate because, well, I had to make up something, right? To be honest, for a long time I couldn't really relate to people and what the holidays meant to them. The closest I got was with restaurant family staff meals: If we were lucky, we'd get to ball out for special occasions. But that wasn't exactly what people were thinking when they asked me for turkey recipes.

For some immigrant families, Thanksgiving is a time to act out being American: to join in on a big cultural moment and really feel like they belong here. My family was the polar opposite.

For my parents, it was just like any other day, especially since they were usually working. My sister and I spent our holidays at other people's houses, stuffing ourselves with their mashed potatoes, roasted turkeys, and Coca Cola–glazed hams. They were just our neighbors and classmates, but I felt like they were so rich. That's how I gauged someone's wealth: by how they dined during the holidays. It wasn't until my sister and I reached adolescence that we started asking our parents to cook Thanksgiving dinner, and they went to town in their tiny kitchen in an effort to keep us at home. The funny thing is, like the avant-garde chefs that they are, they threw convention out the fucking window and cooked intuitively in the best way they knew how: by being resourceful and making it taste good. The results were some of the best cooking I've ever had in my family's Vietnamese American kitchen.

Holiday meals with my parents weren't bountiful spreads of dozens of side dishes, but they did try to make one extra-special centerpiece. There was my dad's seafood soup (page 207), the broth thick with Dungeness crabmeat, ribbons of beaten egg, and crunchy batons of canned baby corn. At other times, he turned crab into Japanese-style rice bowls (page 208), draping the delicate meat with mustard-colored crab butter and fish sauce. My mom would carefully sculpt the glutinous rice wrappers of her sticky rice dumplings (page 201) for us, making sure to seal the super-savory pork-and-mung bean filling perfectly. At their core, these baller recipes stemmed from my parents asking, "Why are our kids going out to eat bland-ass turkey? We can do better than that!" These occasions were rare, but that just makes the memories even more precious to me.

I finally got to experience holidays the traditional way and not just as a visitor, when I got married to my wife, Jean. I cried at our first Thanksgiving as a couple; I was so overwhelmed. The memories of growing up starving, always eating leftovers or scraps, crashed into me at that table. This was something entirely different. I never had a family Thanksgiving with pies, potatoes, gravy, meatloaf, casserole, ambrosia salad, green bean casserole, and turkey. The rich smells, the warmth, and that syrupy and seductive feeling of true safety reduced me to a puddle of tears. Feeling truly nourished made me feel a gratitude and privilege I had never felt before.

Naturally, Jean and I always make a big deal about the holidays now. We've created new traditions that blend the flavors of our upbringings: hers, Korean, American, and Hawaiian; and mine, a particular Phú Quốc blend of Vietnamese and Khmer. I hope the recipes in this chapter inspire your own feasts. More than that, I hope they inspire you to open your homes and lives to others, the way all the best people in my life did for me.

BÁNH ÍT TRẦN
STICKY RICE DUMPLINGS, TU AND JEAN STYLE

Serves 4 (Makes 10 dumplings)

Chewy, savory, and sour, this dish has all the sensations that my wife Jean and I love. I grew up loving my mom's handmade, special-occasion Bánh Ít Trần, and it's made even better with my wife's electrifying homemade kimchee. The dumplings have a rich, almost fatty taste thanks to a toothy mixture of boiled mung beans and seasoned pork, and the lactic acid in well-fermented kimchee, while not traditional, rounds out their flavor so perfectly. With the simple addition of homemade kimchee, Jean and I were able to adapt this dish into something that really felt like a part of both of us. These make a great appetizer for a dinner party, and you can keep any leftover kimchee on the table to pair with whatever comes next.

Note: Kimchee takes 4 days to make, though most of that time is for fermentation. If you haven't tried making your own kimchee before, I promise that the work is worth it! I spent a lot of time pleading with Jean to share her kimchee secrets for the book, so the following directions are straight from the Jeanius herself. It will make more than you need for the Bánh Ít Trần, but I'm sure you can find many good uses for it. Plus, it lasts years in the fridge! You'll need a 5-liter fermentation crock or specialty kimchee container for that. But if you don't have the space or the time, try looking for a small-batch brand at your local Asian grocer.

KIMCHEE

2 napa cabbages, cores removed and leaves cut into 2-inch chunks

½ cup coarse sea salt

2 Asian pears or Fuji apples, peeled, cored, and cut into small chunks

3 yellow onions, peeled and sliced

10 garlic cloves, peeled

One 1-inch knob fresh ginger, peeled and coarsely chopped

¼ cup fish sauce

1 cup granulated sugar

2 medium carrots, cut into matchsticks

One 3-inch piece daikon, peeled and cut into matchsticks (about 4 ounces)

2 bunches green onions, white and green parts sliced

2 tablespoons gochugaru

Since it needs at least four days to ferment, the first step of this recipe is to make the kimchee. Rinse the napa cabbage in a colander under cold running water to remove any dirt. Let any excess water drain, then add the cabbage to a large mixing bowl. (Keep the colander in the sink for later.) Sprinkle the sea salt evenly over the cabbage and toss the mixture with your hands until it starts to wilt at the edges. Let the cabbage hang out for 2 hours, mixing it every half hour or so. Pour the cabbage back into the colander in the sink and press on it gently to squeeze out more liquid. Set aside.

Pulse the Asian pear, onions, garlic, ginger, fish sauce, and sugar in a food processor until the mixture becomes smooth and pastelike. Set aside.

Combine the salted cabbage, carrots, daikon, and green onions in a large mixing bowl, then mix in the gochugaru. Pour in the pear puree. Gently mix everything together until the ingredients are well-distributed. Store this mixture in a fermentation crock at room temperature for 4 days to ferment. From then, you should store it in the fridge, where it will continue to age and gain a sharper, brighter flavor. It'll stay good for years, as long as you use a sterile utensil to handle it.

Have 4 days passed? Great. Time to get started on the mung bean mixture. This part only needs a couple of hours, I promise. Drain the mung beans and cover them with 2 inches of water in a medium pot. Bring the pot to a gentle simmer over low heat, then let the beans cook until they are tender and just starting to feel crumbly. This should take 1 to 3 hours, so start checking them after 1 hour. Drain and set aside.

CONTINUED

Unfamiliar Traditions

STICKY RICE DUMPLINGS, TU AND JEAN STYLE,
CONTINUED

BÁNH ÍT TRẦN

1 cup split mung beans, rinsed and soaked in water for 4 hours

2 cups glutinous rice flour

1 teaspoon kosher salt

¾ cup filtered water

½ teaspoon sesame oil

1 tablespoon neutral oil (such as vegetable oil)

8 ounces ground pork

1 teaspoon fish sauce

1 teaspoon granulated sugar

½ teaspoon kosher salt

¼ teaspoon Knorr hạt nêm or MSG

⅛ teaspoon cracked black pepper

½ cup Nước Mắm Tỏi Ớt | Chile Fish Sauce (page 43) for serving

½ cup Nước Cốt Dừa Tươi | Fresh Coconut Milk (page 49) for serving

½ cup Mỡ Hành | Green Onion Sauce (page 47) for serving

¼ cup dried shrimp, ground, for serving

Make the dumpling dough. Combine the glutinous rice flour and kosher salt in a large mixing bowl. Drizzle in the water, mixing it in with a fork. Once the mixture comes together, knead the dough, either in the bowl or on a floured surface, until it becomes smooth and supple. That should take 5 minutes. Press a small dimple in the dough with your thumb and pour in the sesame oil. Mix it into the dough by kneading it for 5 minutes more or until the oil seems fully incorporated. Stick the dough in an airtight container and set it aside.

Last prep step—and it's quick—make the pork mixture. Preheat a large frying pan over medium heat, then add in the neutral oil. Once the oil is shimmering, add the ground pork, fish sauce, sugar, salt, hạt nêm, and pepper to the pan. Use a wooden spoon to break up the chunks of meat and stir in the seasonings. Fry the meat until it's just cooked through and no longer pink, about 5 minutes. Set it aside.

Okay, now it's time to put all the pieces together. Using a stand mixer fitted with the paddle attachment or a bowl, big spoon, and your brute strength, mix the boiled mung beans and pork mixture together until they're thoroughly combined. (If you're using the mixer, put it on medium speed for 5 minutes.) Set the mixture aside while you deal with the dumpling dough.

Portion the dough into 10 golf ball–size pieces. Cover them with a dish towel to keep them from drying out while you fill each dumpling. Take one piece of dough and flatten it into a 2½-inch-wide, ⅛-inch-thick circle. Scoop a heaping teaspoon of the mung bean and pork mixture into the center of the dough circle, then fold the edges of the dough over the filling. Roll the folded side gently to press the seams closed. Place the filled dumpling back under the towel. Repeat with the rest of the dough and filling. At this point, you can freeze them until you're ready to cook.

When ready to cook the dumplings, bring a large pot of water to a boil over high heat. Boil the dumplings in batches for 8 minutes.

To serve, divide the dumplings among four shallow bowls and the Chile Fish Sauce among four small dipping bowls. Drizzle the Fresh Coconut Milk and Green Onion Sauce over the dumplings. Garnish with the ground shrimp and serve with small side dishes of kimchee and the Chile Fish Sauce.

GỎI CUỐN HÀN QUỐC
PORK BULGOGI SUMMER ROLLS

Serves 4

At first glance, you might mistake this for one of those dime-a-dozen Asian fusion recipes. Trust me, it's anything but that. If anything, this is more of a Hawaiian-style take on Vietnamese food, dreamed up by Jean, who grew up there. In Hawaii, the borders between cultures tend to be fluid, and the cuisine encompasses the cultures of its immigrants and natives, from Korean to Polynesian to Portuguese. So Jean never hesitates to come up with new combinations inspired by the food and people she loves. This dish, which packages the sweet and savory char-grilled flavor of bulgogi in a traditionally Vietnamese bundle of rice noodles, is one of them.

Note: You'll save yourself a lot of labor in this recipe by buying presliced pork at your local Asian grocer. For this recipe, Jean prefers low-sodium soy sauce to off-set the salinity of the oyster sauce. Also note that if you're making pickles and kimchee specifically for this recipe, you'll need to do so in advance—the pickles need a day, and the kimchee needs at least 4 days.

MARINADE

2 garlic cloves, coarsely chopped

½ yellow onion, coarsely chopped

One 1-inch knob fresh ginger, coarsely chopped

1 Korean pear or Fuji apple, peeled and deseeded

2 tablespoons granulated sugar

1 tablespoon low-sodium soy sauce

1 tablespoon oyster sauce

1 cup sesame oil

2 pounds pork shoulder, sliced very thinly (see Note)

1 tablespoon neutral oil (such as vegetable oil)

2 cups toasted sesame seeds (see page 19; optional)

4 ounces dried rice vermicelli, cooked (see Note on page 60)

1 butter lettuce head, leaves separated

1 bunch perilla leaves or sesame leaves

1 cup Củ Cải Chua Ngọt | Pickled Carrots and Daikon (page 49), liquid drained

¼ cup ssamjang

¼ cup thinly sliced garlic cloves

2 jalapeños, thinly sliced

1 cup kimchee (page 201), liquid drained

One 12-ounce package rice paper wrappers (see page 23)

Start by making a marinade for the pork. Using a food processor, puree the chopped garlic, yellow onion, ginger, pear, and sugar. Transfer the puree to a large mixing bowl, and stir in the soy sauce, oyster sauce, and sesame oil. Using chopsticks or tongs, transfer the sliced pork shoulder to the bowl and gently push it into the marinade without shredding it to pieces. Transfer the contents of the bowl to an airtight container and place in the fridge to marinate for at least 2 hours—though it'll get even better if you let it sit overnight. While the pork marinates, you can prep the rest of the ingredients.

When it's time to cook the bulgogi, the thinness of the pork will be the determining factor in how quickly it cooks, so use your best judgment to get it cooked through without too much charring. In terms of method, there are two ways to choose from, depending on your equipment situation. Either way, before you cook the pork, use a paper towel to wipe off any excess marinade so that the garlic doesn't burn.

If you have a barbecue grill: Preheat the grill to 500°F. Grill the marinated pork slices over indirect heat for 2 or 3 minutes on each side. As the pieces finish cooking, transfer them to a bowl so they retain their juices.

If you'd rather use a frying pan: Set a large frying pan over medium-high heat. Once hot, add in the neutral oil, and once the oil is shimmering, gently add in the marinated pork, enough to just cover the surface of the pan. Don't crowd the pan—you want the pieces to sear. Cook the pork for 2 to 3 minutes on each side, and transfer the cooked pieces to a bowl so they retain their juices. Repeat with the rest of the pork, making sure to wipe out the pan between batches.

Garnish with sesame seeds.

CONTINUED

Unfamiliar Traditions

PORK BULGOGI SUMMER ROLLS,
CONTINUED

Finally, it's time to build the summer rolls. Arrange the pork bulgogi, rice vermicelli, lettuce leaves, perilla leaves, pickles, ssamjang, garlic slices, jalapeño slices, and kimchee on a platter or small plates so everyone can build their own rolls. Fill a wide, shallow dish with cold water so folks can take turns dipping their rice paper wrappers into it.

Here's the method for making rolls: Take a moistened rice paper wrapper and lay it flat on your plate. Add the following ingredients in horizontal rows starting 1½ inches from the bottom edge of the rice paper wrapper: about 2 tablespoons of rice noodles, 2 butter lettuce leaves, and a few perilla leaves. Now fold the left and right edges of the wrapper inward by about ½ inch. Spoon in about 1 tablespoon of the pickles on top of the herbs, then layer on 2 to 3 pieces of pork bulgogi. Dollop ¼ teaspoon ssamjang on the pork and garnish with a few slivers of garlic and jalapeño. Finally, crown it with some kimchee. It's kind of like making bulgogi wraps at the KBBQ spot!

Roll the gỏi cuốn, tucking the sides in as you go, until it is fully sealed. Your first roll might end up like an overstuffed Chipotle burrito, but that's okay—you'll get the hang of it eventually.

SÚP HẢI SẢN THẬP CẨM
SEAFOOD EGG DROP SOUP

Serves 4

2 gallons Nước Luộc Gà | Chicken Stock (page 51) or store-bought stock

1 tablespoon grated ginger

1 tablespoon minced garlic

1 tablespoon oyster sauce

½ teaspoon soy sauce

2 tablespoons fish sauce

½ pound 16/20 (extra jumbo) white Gulf shrimp, peeled, deveined, and minced

½ pound bay scallops, rinsed and drained

¼ pound enoki mushrooms, bottom root removed

¼ pound shiitake mushrooms, stemmed and quartered

¼ cup cornstarch

¼ cup cold filtered water

One 8-ounce can straw mushrooms, rinsed and drained

One 8-ounce can baby corn, rinsed and drained

One 7-ounce can quail eggs, rinsed and drained

5 eggs

2 teaspoons kosher salt

1 teaspoon granulated sugar

One 16-ounce package silken tofu, cut into ½-inch cubes

1 pound Dungeness crabmeat from about 2 crabs (for crab cooking tips, see page 208)

⅛ teaspoon ground white pepper

¼ teaspoon sesame oil

During the holidays, we'd go nuts over this soup, which is a specialty of my dad's. It dresses up canned veggies and quail eggs with silky, sweet hunks of freshly steamed Dungeness crab, scallops, and shrimp. The wisps of crabmeat mingled with golden, noodle-like streamers of beaten egg, and a touch of cornstarch gave the broth a pleasing, almost gravy-like texture. Súp hải sản thập cẩm technically means "mixed seafood soup," but at our house, it really was our way of commemorating the Bay Area's fleeting Dungeness crab season, which coincides with the major winter holidays. To me, this big-ass pot of soup was and is the purest form of holiday cuisine.

Note: You'll find canned quail eggs, baby corn, and straw mushrooms in most Asian markets.

In a large pot, bring the chicken stock to a gentle simmer over medium heat. Stir in the ginger, garlic, oyster sauce, soy sauce, and fish sauce and stir until well combined. Add in the shrimp, scallops, enoki mushrooms, and shiitake mushrooms, and turn up the heat a little bit, just to return the soup to a simmer.

In the meantime, in a small bowl, stir together the cornstarch and water to make a slurry. Drizzle the slurry into the soup, whisking continuously to prevent clumping. Add in the straw mushrooms, baby corn, and quail eggs.

Next, make the egg ribbons. Crack the eggs into a medium bowl and whisk until lightly beaten. Then, stir the soup vigorously to create a vortex. Pour some of the beaten egg mixture into a ladle and drizzle a thin trickle into the vortex. If you did it right, you'll generate long, silky ribbons of egg. Keep doing this until you use up all of the egg mixture.

Allow the soup to return to a simmer, then stir in the salt and sugar. Fold in the tofu and crabmeat, working gently to avoid breaking up the pieces. Return the soup to a low simmer and let it sit undisturbed for 45 minutes, or until the liquid fully emulsifies and the edges start to bubble. Hit the soup with white pepper and sesame oil just before serving.

To serve, use a ladle to divide the soup among four large soup bowls, and enjoy immediately.

COM CUA HẤP
DUNGENESS CRAB DONBURI

Serves 4

On any given Bay Area holiday table, you're more likely to see steamed Dungeness crabs than a big, honkin' turkey. From November 'til April, we go wild over our local crustacean friends, which are known for their succulent flesh and gloriously rich crab "butter," which is actually a gland of the crab that you can eat. In my family, we'd either turn crabs into soup (page 207) or this super-indulgent rice bowl. Freshly steamed crab is piled over jasmine rice and then draped with its own butter. We hit this ultra-rich dish with a dose of citrus—either Nước Mắm Tỏi Ớt | Chile Fish Sauce or Muối Tiêu Chanh | Salt, Pepper, and Lime Dipping Sauce. If you love sashimi-topped rice bowls, I promise you'll be all over this. For this recipe, you'll need a steamer large enough to fit four crabs. Also, using specialty crab crackers and picks (like tiny forks) will make this recipe much easier.

Note: It's best to use live crabs within 6 hours of bringing them home, but you can keep them alive for up to 2 days by keeping them in the fridge wrapped in wet newspaper.

4 live Dungeness crabs, about 2 pounds each

Two 10-ounce cans pale ale beer

2½ cups filtered water

2 cups steamed rice (see page 34) for serving

1 English cucumber, sliced into matchsticks, for garnish

1 bunch spearmint leaves for garnish

1 cup Nước Mắm Tỏi Ớt | Chile Fish Sauce (page 43) or Muối Tiêu Chanh | Salt, Pepper, and Lime Dipping Sauce (page 44) for serving

Steaming live Dungeness crabs might seem intimidating, but it's not super hard. Before you start, leave them in the fridge for at least a half hour to trick them into hibernation. While the crabs are napping, pour the beers and water into the bottom of a large metal steamer pot. Bring the liquid to a boil, then cover the steamer and let it boil for 10 minutes. Meanwhile, prepare a large ice bath.

Place the crabs in the steamer and let them cook at full blast for 12 to 15 minutes. Use tongs to transfer the crabs from the steamer directly to the ice bath. Let them cool in the ice for 15 minutes. (This might also be a good time to steam your rice.)

Next, remove the crabmeat. Now's a good time to put on a reality TV show or something in the background—you might be at it for a bit. Remove the crab's "apron," or the flappy shell piece on its belly, to expose a hole in between its hind legs. Place the thumb of your dominant hand in that hole while using the rest of your hand to cup the crab's legs and body cavity. Use your other hand to pull off the head, being careful not to spill out the greenish-yellow "butter." The butter, or crab fat, is the crustacean's precious innards. Pour the crab butter into a medium bowl and set aside. Use a spoon to scoop out any flesh in the head and put it in a second medium bowl with the rest of the meat you'll be picking. Rinse the body under cold running water.

Snap the crab's body in half, then break the halves into sections between each leg—it's almost like the sections of an orange. Use a crab pick to remove the meat, avoiding the inedible gills, adding it to the medium bowl as you go. Use sharp kitchen shears to split the leg shells and remove the meat, taking care to keep it in nice, big pieces. Use a claw cracker to snap open the claws to get that meat out. Add the leg and claw meat to the bowl and then repeat with the rest of the crabs.

Gently run your fingers through the picked crabmeat, just to double-check for any stray pieces of shell. Reserve the shells and freeze to use in stock (page 50) or discard them.

To serve, divide the rice among four bowls and gently pat it down. Top the rice with the crabmeat and spoon the crab butter over the meat. Garnish with the cucumber and spearmint. Divide the Chile Fish Sauce among four small dipping bowls and serve alongside for seasoning.

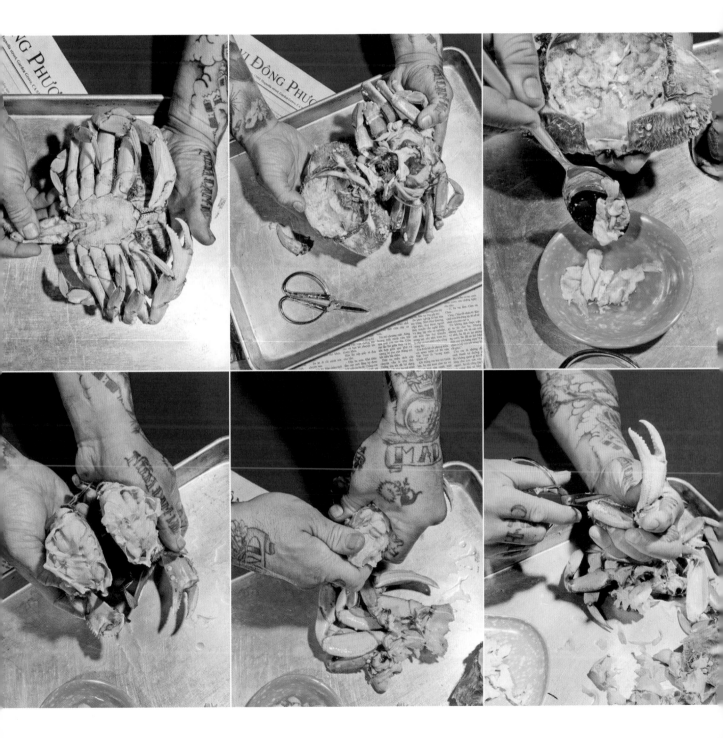

GÀ NƯỚNG KAMPUCHEA
KAMPUCHEA-STYLE BBQ CHICKEN

Serves 4

To keep me and my sister home for Thanksgiving and Christmas, my parents engaged in a holiday season Cold War with blowout dishes of their own, including this ridiculously flavorful chicken my dad learned to make from the Khmer side of his family. Oh, you want some good old rubbery Thanksgiving turkey? How about some juicy, caramelized, lemongrass-rubbed chicken instead? Turkey never even crossed our minds when we knew this bird would be on the table for dinner. The whole process of marinating and cooking this dish takes about 5 hours, but the intense flavor is so worth the effort.

Note: Heritage chickens are extraordinary for long braises and stews. Their bones are ideal for making chicken stock. Both meat and bones are packed with great flavor because their muscles are more developed. However, their meat yields are significantly lower. In contrast, organic chickens are extremely versatile; they are specifically bred to get a better yield.

One 2½-pound heritage chicken

2 tablespoons minced garlic

½ cup minced green onions, white and green parts

2 tablespoons minced lemongrass

½ cup oyster sauce

1 tablespoon Maggi seasoning sauce

½ teaspoon sesame oil

2 tablespoons granulated sugar

Cracked black pepper

Kosher salt

Neutral oil (such as vegetable oil), enough to coat the chicken

Nước Mắm Khóm | Pineapple Fish Sauce (page 42) for serving

For the sake of efficiency—and for even cooking—spatchcock the chicken (you can also have your butcher do this). If you spatchcock the bird yourself, you can save the bones in the freezer to make Nước Luộc Gà | Chicken Stock (page 51) later. To spatchcock the bird, you'll remove the backbone by cutting along both sides of it using a sharp pair of kitchen shears. You should now be able to open up the chicken, sort of like a grisly book. Locate the breastbone and remove it by breaking it off. Carve out the wishbone (like a clavicle), then remove the rib bones. If you're more of a visual learner, there are tons of how-to videos for this on YouTube.

Next, make the marinade by combining the garlic, green onions, lemongrass, oyster sauce, Maggi seasoning, sesame oil, sugar, and ⅛ teaspoon pepper in a small bowl. Set a wire roasting rack on a large, foil-lined baking sheet and lay the chicken on top of it, skin-side down. Generously rub the marinade all over the meat, making sure to get all up in the crevices. Do try to avoid rubbing the marinade on the skin. Let the chicken marinate like this in the fridge for at least 2 hours.

After 2 hours, take the tray out of the fridge—but no, you're not cooking just yet. Flip the chicken over so that the skin is facing up. Wiggle your fingers under the chicken's skin to loosen it, especially around the breast and thighs. Generously season the chicken's skin with salt and pepper, then drizzle neutral oil all over it. Use a brush or paper towel to gently swipe the oil all over the chicken to ensure even browning. Let the chicken rest at room temperature for 2 hours.

Now it's time to roast. Preheat your oven to 450°F. Roast the chicken for about 45 minutes, rotating the pan every 15 minutes, until a probe thermometer inserted into the thickest part of the chicken registers at 165°F for 30 seconds straight. Remove the chicken from the oven and let it rest on a cutting board for 20 minutes.

To serve, separate the drumsticks and thighs, then halve the breast lengthwise. Slice the breast pieces on the diagonal and arrange the pieces on a nice serving platter with Pineapple Fish Sauce on the side.

VỊT NƯỚNG
ROASTED HOISIN-GLAZED DUCK

Serves 4

1 whole duck (I recommend Liberty Farms)

8 cups cold filtered water

4 tablespoons kosher salt

1 tablespoon cracked black pepper

½ teaspoon minced garlic

¼ teaspoon grated ginger

1 tablespoon apple cider vinegar

¼ cup hoisin sauce

1 tablespoon honey
(I recommend raw honey)

1 tablespoon Maggi seasoning sauce

½ teaspoon annatto powder

1 cinnamon stick, ground

¼ teaspoon ground cloves

½ teaspoon ground fennel seeds

5 star anise pods, ground

½ cup Nước Mắm Me | Tamarind Fish Sauce
(page 42) for serving

With a hoisin sauce–based glaze, the duck makes a great showstopper served as-is. But with a few tweaks (detailed below), it can also serve as the base for an incredible duck phở (page 215)—just remember to reserve the trimmings. Otherwise, it's perfect with steamed rice and Rau Muống Xào | Stir-Fried Water Spinach (page 110) or as a filling for bánh mì or summer rolls.

First, brine the duck. Combine the cold water and 2 tablespoons of the salt in a large pot and mix until the salt is mostly dissolved. Keep the duck submerged in the water for 15 to 20 minutes. (You can use a stack of small plates or a heavy can so it doesn't bob out of the liquid.) Once brined, rinse the duck under cold running water and set it on a cutting board. Give it a once-over to remove any excess exposed fat from the carcass. If there are any giblets inside the duck, put them in a gallon-size ziplock bag. That's where your duck trimmings will go in the next step.

Now, spatchcock the bird. Cut out the duck's backbone with a sharp pair of kitchen shears and add it to the bag of duck trimmings. Open up the duck so that it's mostly flat. Remove the breastbone, wishbone, and rib bones and put them in the trimmings bag. Stash the trimmings in the freezer to use for duck stock or for full-on duck phở (page 215).

Lightly press the duck flat, then season it thoroughly on all sides with 1 tablespoon of the salt and pepper. Use a paring knife to make shallow incisions on the skin of the breast in a crosshatched pattern to ensure crispiness. Set a roasting rack on a foil-lined baking sheet and place the duck on top of it, skin-side down. You can stop here and roast the duck the next day; just make sure to take it out of the fridge at least 2 hours before you want to roast it.

While the duck hangs out, make the glaze. Combine the remaining 1 tablespoon salt, garlic, ginger, apple cider vinegar, hoisin sauce, honey, Maggi seasoning, annatto powder, cinnamon, cloves, fennel seeds, and star anise in a small bowl and mix thoroughly. Set the bowl and a basting brush nearby the oven for easy use.

Preheat the oven to 450°F. Roast the duck for 15 minutes, or just until the skin starts to sweat and get tight, then take it out. Brush it on all sides with the glaze. Lower the oven temperature to 350°F, then put the duck back in for another hour, glazing the duck one more time and rotating the pan halfway through. The duck is done when the internal temperature at its thickest part measures 150°F on a probe thermometer. Note: If you are roasting this duck for Phở Vịt Nướng (page 215), pull it out when its internal temperature reaches 130°F (about 45 minutes) and move over to that recipe now.

Once cooked, rest the duck on a cutting board for 20 minutes. Then, remove both leg quarters by cutting along the crevices that divide the legs from the body and pop out the hip joints. Cut between the drumstick and thigh to separate them. Halve the breast by slicing it lengthwise, then cut the breasts on the diagonal into slices. Arrange the pieces on your nicest serving platter and serve with a side of Tamarind Fish Sauce for dipping.

PHỞ VỊT NƯỚNG
ROASTED DUCK PHO

Serves 4

This special holiday version of phở uses well-spiced and beautifully rich Vịt Nướng | Roasted Hoisin-Glazed Duck as its base. It's the extravagant golden child of beef and chicken phở, or perhaps their more glamorous younger sibling. Each bowl of this admittedly very Instagrammable soup gets a big hunk of braised duck leg, plus elegant slices of breast with crispy rendered skin on top.

Note: I like to go all-out and make duck specifically for the purpose of using in this recipe, but you can cheat it by using leftover duck bones in place of the reserved trimmings and a ready-made roasted duck from your favorite Chinese barbecue spot. If you are preparing your own duck, follow the recipe until it is cooked to 130°F. When prompted, move over to this recipe.

1 Vịt Nướng | Roasted Hoisin-Glazed Duck (page 212), cooked to 130°F, trimmings reserved

1 whole yellow onion, unpeeled and cut into 1-inch chunks

1 garlic head, cloves detached, unpeeled

One 1-inch knob fresh ginger, unpeeled, cut into chunks

5 star anise pods

1 cinnamon stick

½ teaspoon fennel seeds

¼ teaspoon whole cloves

7 cups Nước Luộc Gà | Chicken Stock (page 51) or store-bought stock

7 cups filtered water

1 teaspoon kosher salt

2 teaspoons granulated sugar

3 whole shallots, peeled

½ cup stemmed and quartered shiitake mushrooms

¼ cup fish sauce

3 tablespoons oyster sauce

3 tablespoons hoisin sauce

⅛ teaspoon cracked black pepper

14 ounces phở noodles, cooked (page 117)

Preheat the oven to 450°F. Arrange the trimmings on a baking sheet and roast for 30 minutes. Set the pan aside to cool.

While the trimmings are roasting, broil the aromatics. Adjust an oven rack to the top position and set the oven to low broil. Allow the broiler to preheat for 5 minutes. Put the onion, garlic, and ginger in a small oven-safe tray or pan and broil them 6 inches from the heating element for 5 to 7 minutes. (Don't use oil or you'll make the soup greasy.) Shake the pan to rustle the pieces around and expose the uncharred sides, then broil them for 5 to 7 minutes more. Your oven might take more or less time to blacken the aromatics, so keep an eye on them. Once all sides of the aromatics are charred, transfer them to a large stock pot.

Next, toast the spices. Set a small pan over low heat and add the star anise pods, cinnamon stick, fennel seeds, and cloves. Toast them until fragrant, 3 to 4 minutes, shaking the pan constantly to prevent the spices from burning. Transfer the spices to the stock pot with the charred aromatics.

Add the roasted trimmings to the pot and pour in the chicken stock, filtered water, salt, and sugar, then bring the mixture to a boil over medium-high heat. Once boiling, immediately lower the heat to bring the broth to a gentle simmer. It should start smelling really, really rich at this point. Let the broth simmer for the next 20 minutes to soak up that duck bone flavor, keeping an eye on it and skimming off any grime, foam, and fat that come to the surface. Add the shallots and let the broth simmer for 20 minutes more, or until the sharp aroma of the shallot dissipates.

Skim the foam off the broth one last time for good luck, then strain the broth through a fine-mesh sieve into a medium pot. Now this is where this recipe goes off the path from regular phở. Set the medium pot of strained broth over medium-low heat and add in the shiitake mushrooms, fish sauce, oyster sauce, hoisin sauce, and black pepper. Bring the mixture to a low simmer and give it a quick taste for seasoning. You might want to add a little more salt or fish sauce if it's tasting bland.

CONTINUED

Unfamiliar Traditions

ROASTED DUCK PHO, CONTINUED

GARNISH

½ cup sliced green onions, white and green parts

½ cup chopped cilantro

2 serrano peppers, thinly sliced

Hoisin sauce and Sriracha for the table

Next, braise the duck legs. Detach the legs from the duck carcass, then separate the thighs from the drums—there should be 4 pieces total. Plop the pieces into the broth and adjust the heat to bring it back to a low simmer. Let the broth bubble gently for an hour, and while the legs braise, skim off any fat that rises to the surface. After an hour, pull the legs pieces out of the broth—when the flesh is so tender that it falls right off the bone. Make sure the soup remains on an active burner on its lowest setting, just to keep it warm.

Then, cook the duck breasts. You should have two nice pieces of breast with the skin still attached. Place them into a cold cast-iron pan with the skin facing down. Turn the heat to high and cook until you hear the skin start to sizzle, about 2 minutes. Adjust the heat to medium-low and continue to cook, letting the skin crisp up as the fat renders, about 10 to 15 minutes. As the fat accumulates in the pan, carefully pour or spoon it into a heatproof container (save it to use for cooking hash browns or something). Then, flip the duck breasts over and cook on the other side for 1 to 2 minutes, just to warm them through. Transfer the breasts to a cutting board and let them rest for 3 to 5 minutes.

When you're ready to serve the phở, cut each duck breast into eight slices. Divide the noodles among four large soup bowls. In each bowl, fan out 4 slices of duck breast and a piece of duck leg. Use a ladle to divide the stock among the bowls (if you're being scientific, each bowl will get about 10 ounces of soup). Top the phở with the green onions, cilantro, and serrano pepper slices. If you like to dress up your phở, set bottles of hoisin sauce and Sriracha on the table for serving.

WOVEN NOODLES WITH CRISPY PORK BELLY

Serves 4

Bánh hỏi have a strange beauty that makes them an eye-catching side dish at parties and feasts. As delicate as dragonfly wings and shaped like woven mats with "threads" of super-fine rice noodles, bánh hỏi provide a soft and spongy wrap for the crisp-skinned pork belly in this dish. The textures here are a lot like those found in Korean ssam, which you also eat by building the perfect bite out an array of herbs, meat, sauces, and fermented morsels on the table. To me, the casual, communal feel of the eating experience, with plenty of space for socializing between bites, is what makes bánh hỏi a great party dish.

Note: If you're making pickles specifically for this recipe, you'll need to do so one day in advance.

PORK BELLY

One 2-pound pork belly, skin on

1 teaspoon minced lemongrass

2 teaspoons Chef Tu Phở Seasoning or five-spice powder (see page 19)

½ teaspoon garlic powder

½ teaspoon ginger powder

2 teaspoons granulated sugar

1 teaspoon cracked black pepper

1 tablespoon kosher salt

¼ cup rice vinegar

One 17.6-ounce package dried bánh hỏi

½ cup Củ Cải Chua Ngọt | Pickled Carrots and Daikon (page 49), liquid drained

1 bunch mint, tough stems removed

1 bunch perilla, leaves picked

1 butter lettuce or oak lettuce head, leaves separated

¼ cup Mỡ Hành | Green Onion Sauce (page 47)

½ cup Củ Hẹ Chiên | Fried Shallots (page 50) or store-bought fried shallots

½ cup Nước Mắm Tỏi Ớt | Chile Fish Sauce (page 43) or Nước Mắm Me | Tamarind Fish Sauce (page 42) for serving

Preheat the oven to 225°F.

While the oven preheats, render the pork belly. Bring a large pot of water to a simmer over high heat. Gently place the pork belly in the pot and allow it to simmer for 10 minutes. You're just rendering out some of the fat at this point, so it doesn't need to cook all the way through. Remove the pork from the pot and let it rest on a cooling rack for 30 minutes.

Next, make the seasoning for the pork. Combine the lemongrass, phở seasoning, garlic powder, ginger powder, sugar, pepper, and 2 teaspoons of the salt in a small bowl. Mix the ingredients together and set aside.

Prep the pork for roasting. With a fork, pierce the skin side of the pork belly's as much as you can. This will ensure it gets crispy. Flip it over and use a knife to cut through the flesh at 2-inch intervals. Avoid cutting all the way through the skin, though it's probably gonna be too tough for you to do that anyway. (Don't take that as a challenge, please.) Season the flesh (but not the skin) with the seasoning mix you just made. Cover the flesh of the pork with foil, but leave the skin exposed for crisping. Place the pork belly skin-side up in a roasting pan and season the skin with 2 tablespoons of the rice vinegar and ½ teaspoon of the salt.

Roast the pork at 225°F for an hour, or until the flesh turns from pink to a whiter color. Increase the oven temperature to 400°F, then remove the pork from the oven and season the skin again with the remaining 2 tablespoons rice vinegar and ½ teaspoon salt. When the oven reaches 400°F, put the pork back in and let it roast for 50 minutes, or until the skin starts to bubble up and turn amber.

While the pork cooks, prepare the noodles. First, line a serving dish with oiled parchment paper or wax paper, and prepare additional oiled parchment paper to use later. Set aside. Bring a large pot of water to a rolling boil over high heat. Put the bánh hỏi in a large bowl—not in the pot—and pour the boiling water from the pot over the noodles to cover them. Don't stir the noodles, or they'll fall apart. Let the noodles soak in the hot water until they are tender but still slightly firm, which should take 1 to 2 minutes. Drain the noodles in a colander, then gently rinse with very cold water to stop the cooking process

CONTINUED

and help them cool. Shake off any excess moisture, then transfer the noodles to the prepared serving dish, placing oiled parchment paper between each layer to prevent sticking, and set aside.

Remove the pork belly from the oven and allow it to rest for 20 minutes before cutting. Slice it into ½-inch pieces.

Finally, set everything up for serving. Arrange the pork belly, pickles, mint, perilla, and lettuce on one side of a nice big party platter. Prepare the bánh hỏi by rolling each piece into a cigar-like bundle and lining them up all on the other side of the platter. Spoon the Green Onion Sauce and Fried Shallots over the noodles. Divide the Chile Fish Sauce among four small dipping bowls.

I'm not gonna pretend there's one perfect way to enjoy this dish—to each their own—but here's how I like to build my rolls: one lettuce leaf, one flat piece of bánh hỏi, a few slices of pork, herbs, then pickles. Don't forget to dip!

BŌ QUAY KAMPUCHEA

KAMPUCHEA-STYLE PRIME RIB

Serves 10

From his mom, the link to the Khmer side of his family, my dad learned to use a heavy hand with lemongrass. So, to me, that citrusy bite is the key to Kampuchea-style barbecue and a core flavor memory of all our family gatherings. In a parallel world where we were rich—like Kardashian- or House of Ho–rich—we probably would have eaten this lemongrass-rubbed prime rib for the holidays, laid on top of truffled garlic noodles (page 186) and served with big bottles of Hennessey.

You'll want the roast French trimmed, so ideally ask your butcher to do that before you bring it home. But if you forgot to do that, or if for some reason your butcher doesn't like you, I got you. Directions are below. Note that this recipe requires an overnight marinating period.

---

5 to 6 pounds 3-bone beef prime rib roast

---

2 tablespoons minced garlic

½ cup sliced green onions,
white and green parts

---

2 tablespoons minced lemongrass

---

1 cup hoisin sauce

---

1 tablespoon Maggi seasoning sauce

½ cup oyster sauce

½ teaspoon sesame oil

---

2 tablespoons granulated sugar

⅛ teaspoon cracked black pepper

---

3 tablespoons neutral oil
(such as vegetable oil)

To French trim the roast, you're basically cutting away some of the sinewy meat from the ribs to expose a section of the bones. First, place the roast on a cutting board, fat cap facing up. Use a chef's knife to make an incision across one of the end bones three inches from the edge of the roast. Flip the roast over and make a parallel incision to match the first one. Flip the roast over again and cut through the flesh to connect the incisions. Use your knife to gently peel the flesh off the bone, starting at the incision near the main loin section and pushing it away along the bone, toward the edge of the roast. Repeat with the remaining bones. Use your fingers to peel off any flesh or silver skin lingering on the bones.

Next, make the marinade. Combine the garlic, green onions, lemongrass, hoisin sauce, Maggi seasoning, oyster sauce, sesame oil, sugar, and pepper in a small bowl and mix thoroughly to blend.

Set a roasting rack on a large foil-lined baking sheet. Lay the roast on top of the pan, fat cap facing down. Slather the marinade all over the roast, making sure to get it into all the nooks and crannies. Refrigerate the roast, uncovered, for 12 to 24 hours to allow it to marinate.

The next day, take the marinated roast out of the fridge an hour before cooking. Preheat the oven to 350°F. Use a fork or butter knife to scrape any excess marinade off of the roast.

Sear the roast. Set a cast-iron pan or Dutch oven over high heat, then pour in the neutral oil. Once the oil is shimmering, sear the roast on each side until golden brown, 3 to 5 minutes per side. After searing, return the roast to the rack and let it rest there for 30 minutes.

Roast the prime rib in the oven, rotating the pan every 30 minutes, for about 1½ hours or until the temperature at its thickest section reads 125°F on a probe thermometer. When finished cooking, let the roast rest on a cutting board for at least 20 minutes before carving. Serve immediately after carving.

CHÈ TRÔI NƯỚC
STICKY RICE DUMPLINGS IN SYRUP

Serves 4

Just like a gift-wrapped present, you really never know what might be inside of sticky rice dumpling—but you know it'll be something good. In this version, which has the same dough wrapper as my mom's sticky rice dumplings (page 201), a sweet red bean filling, coconut milk sauce, and ginger syrup put it squarely into dessert territory. Use this recipe as a kick-off point for other filling ideas that might pop into your head. The pleasure of a glutinous, chewy dough obeys no culinary boundaries.

DUMPLINGS

½ cup canned adzuki beans

2 cups glutinous rice flour

½ teaspoon kosher salt

¾ cup filtered water

3 drops sesame oil

GINGER SYRUP

One ½-inch piece fresh ginger, unpeeled and sliced into coins

1 cup brown sugar

3 cups filtered water

COCONUT MILK SAUCE

1 cup Nước Cốt Dừa Tươi | Fresh Coconut Milk (page 49) or canned coconut milk

1 tablespoon granulated sugar

⅛ teaspoon kosher salt

1 tablespoon cornstarch

¼ cup filtered water

GARNISH

1 tablespoon toasted sesame seeds (see page 19) for garnish

To start, mash the adzuki beans for the filling. Use the pulse setting on a food processor to purée the beans until they become a smooth mixture. Scoop the mixture out of the food processor into a small bowl and set it aside.

Next, make the dumpling dough. Combine the glutinous rice flour and salt in a large mixing bowl. Drizzle in the water, mixing it in with a fork. Once the mixture comes together, knead the dough, either in the bowl or on a floured surface, until it becomes smooth and supple. Kneading should take 5 minutes. Use your thumb to press a small indent in the dough and pour in the sesame oil. Mix it into the dough by kneading it for 5 minutes more, or until all of the oil is absorbed. Stick the dough in an airtight container until you're ready to assemble the dumplings.

When you're ready to make the dumplings, portion the dough into 10 golf ball–size pieces. Keep the dough balls covered with a dish towel to keep them from drying out while you make the dumplings. Take one portion of dough and flatten it into a 2½-inch-wide, ⅛-inch-thick circle. Scoop a heaping teaspoon of the red bean paste into the center of the dough circle, then fold the edges of the dough over the filling.

Roll the folded side gently to press the seams of the dumplings closed. Repeat with the rest of the dough and filling. Keep the dumplings under the towel while you make the ginger syrup and coconut sauce.

To make the syrup, combine the ginger, brown sugar, and water in a medium saucepan over medium heat. Bring the mixture to a simmer, stirring to dissolve the sugar. Once the pot simmers, take it off the heat. Strain the mixture by pouring it through a fine-mesh sieve into a bowl and discard the solids. Pour the syrup back into the pot and place it on the stove on the lowest heat setting, just to keep it warm.

Now, boil the dumplings. Bring a large pot of water to a boil over high heat, then boil the dumplings in batches for eight minutes. Using a slotted spoon, transfer them to the pot of ginger syrup. Hopefully, they'll all float. If they sink to the bottom of the pot, return them to the boiling water to cook for a minute or two longer. Make sure the ginger syrup doesn't reach a boil. It shouldn't bubble at all or the dumplings will cook into a sad mush. Take the pot off the heat and let it hang out until you are ready to serve.

Make the coconut sauce. Pour the coconut milk into a small saucepan, then add the sugar and salt. Feel free to adjust the sugar and salt levels to your taste. Place the saucepan on the stove and bring the coconut milk to a gentle simmer over low heat to prevent scalding. In a separate bowl, make a cornstarch slurry by whisking together the cornstarch and water. Gradually whisk the cornstarch slurry into the coconut milk while it simmers, a tablespoon at a time. Stop once the sauce is thick enough to coat the back of a spoon, and remove the saucepan from the heat. Strain the sauce by pouring it through a fine-mesh sieve to remove any lumps.

To serve, portion the dumplings into four dessert bowls. Pour 2 tablespoons of the ginger syrup into each bowl, then pour 1 tablespoon of the coconut sauce over the tops of the dumplings. Garnish with the toasted sesame seeds and enjoy immediately.

ACKNOWLEDGMENTS

TU DAVID PHU

I want to express my heartfelt gratitude to my mother for all she taught me about cooking and food. Her passion for cooking was rooted in her dedication to providing nourishing meals for our family. It has been an inspiration to me throughout my life. Thank you, Mom. You are the reason I am able to share my love of food with the world, and I am forever grateful for all that you have given me.

I sincerely thank my wife for her unwavering support and encouragement during the creation of this cookbook. Her enthusiasm for my cooking and her love of food have been a constant source of inspiration to me. My wife has always been my biggest fan and my harshest critic, pushing me to strive for excellence in every dish I create. Her feedback, guidance, and unwavering support have been invaluable throughout the writing and testing of the recipes in this cookbook.

A special thanks goes out to my pop-up team, which was made up of friends, colleagues, and supporters who worked tirelessly to help execute my vision for Ăn, my 2015–2018 award-winning pop-up series. Their dedication and support is the reason why I'm here today, to write this book.

I also want to extend my gratitude to my paternal (Phu) and maternal (Le) families. In particular, my maternal uncle Cậu Năm and auntie Mợ Năm, and my paternal auntie Cô Tám and her daughter Mỹ Tiên, deserve special mention. They have always welcomed me and reminded me that I have a second home on Phú Quốc Island. This book was inspired by our family stories and memories. Their love and support have been instrumental in shaping my culinary journey, and I'm deeply thankful for their presence in my life.

I want to offer a special thank you to my paternal auntie, our family matriarch, Cô Hai, who has now passed on. Thank you for the time spent cooking your delicious Bánh Canh Chả Cá and nourishing our village on Phú Quốc Island. You and your food were loved. Your spirit lives in me. I know you would be so proud to see who I am today and the chef that I've become. We miss and love you.

Lastly, I would like to thank my publisher, editor, creative director, coauthor, designer, and photography team for their guidance, patience, and expertise in bringing this book to life. It has been an honor to work with such a talented and dedicated team.

Thank you to everyone who contributed to this book in ways big and small. I hope these recipes bring joy and nourishment to your table for years to come.

This cookbook was made possible thanks to the support of Son Fish Sauce, Water2Table, and Four Star Seafood.

SOLEIL DÂNVỸ HO

Thank you to my husband, Chris, my ride-or-die for sixteen years and counting.

To my mother, Francie, who always reminds me to notice all the things I can't see. And to my sister, Briana, for hanging in there with me.

To my aunt Thuy for teaching me to love books, and to my many aunts, uncles, and cousins for showing me the endless ways to make a home.

To my agent, Rica Allannic, and the teams at 4 Color Books and Ten Speed Press for being extremely good at what they do.

To my editors at the *San Francisco Chronicle*—Serena, Janelle, Michael, and Matt—who were totally chill with me splitting my brain in two for this project.

To Clement, Katherine, and James, for all the coffee and kaya buns.

To Eler, for their nightly TikTok deluges.

To San Francisco.

And to my grandparents, Tường Bá Nguyễn and Hoa Huỳnh, for making the journey.

ABOUT THE CONTRIBUTORS

TU DAVID PHU is a Vietnamese American, *San Francisco Chronicle* Rising Star Chef, a *Top Chef* alumnus, an author, and an Emmy-nominated filmmaker from Oakland who cut his culinary teeth in some of the nation's top restaurants. In 2024, he became the executive chef and managing partner at District One in Las Vegas. Tu has cooked across various cultures, from the American culinary greats to classical European traditions. But it is what he calls "the memory of taste" that pulled him back to his roots: the practices, ingredients, techniques, and flavors of Vietnamese cuisines. He is passionate about sharing the riches and lessons of his birthright through food.

SOLEIL HO is a Vietnamese American writer, podcaster, and burnt-out chef. They served as the *San Francisco Chronicle*'s restaurant critic for four years, and their food and culture writing has also appeared in *The New Yorker*, Bitch Media, *GQ*, and the 2019 and 2021 editions of *The Best American Food Writing*. In 2022, they won the James Beard Foundation's Craig Claiborne Distinguished Restaurant Review Award. They live in San Francisco with fifty cherished houseplants and a human man.

JENI AFUSO is a photographer and artist based in Los Angeles. As an LA native with years living in Japan and travels to over forty countries, Jeni's work is known for evoking a sense of calmness, joy, and life, drawing from her experiences abroad and cultural influences. Her editorial photography graces publications like *Vogue*, *New York Times*, *Bon Appétit*, and *Travel + Leisure*, earning recognition from Photo District News, International Association of Culinary Professionals, and the James Beard Foundation. Jeni currently lives in Los Angeles with her partner and wild child (cat) Kiyoko.

DYLAN JAMES HO is a commercial and editorial photographer and food writer based in Los Angeles, focusing on travel, food, cocktail, portraiture, interior and lifestyle photography. Formerly an advertising art director and digital designer, he has been working professionally in the hospitality industry for the last fifteen years. His work has been recognized by the James Beard Foundation in both photography and writing, Photo District News (PDN), and the International Association of Culinary Professionals (IACP).

INDEX

A

Acquerello (San Francisco), 172
adzuki beans, in Sticky Rice Dumplings in Syrup, 222
Ăn, 172–73
aping, about, 106
apple cider vinegar, about, 22
Arabiyya (Assil), 130
Asian Seafood Improvement Collaborative, 9
Asian-style peeler knives, about, 32
Assil, Reem, 130
Âu Cơ Trứng (Crab Beurre Monté Chawanmushi), 181
authenticity, 130

B

baby corn, in Seafood Egg Drop Soup, 207
bacon, in Bánh Canh Carbonara, 193
Banana Bread Pudding, Mom's, 143
Banana Flower Salad, 158
banana leaves
    about, 29
    in Chicken Fat Sticky Rice, 194
bánh canh, about, 26
Bánh Canh Carbonara, 193
Bánh Canh Chả Cá (Fish Cake and Tapioca Noodle Soup), 69
Bánh Canh Tôm Hùm (Lobster Boba), 189
Bánh Chuối Nướng (Mom's Banana Bread Pudding), 143
Bánh Hỏi Heo Quay (Woven Noodles with Crispy Pork Belly), 217
Bánh Ít Trần (Sticky Rice Dumplings, Tu and Jean Style), 201
Bánh Phở (Phở Noodles), 117
Bánh Tôm (Prawn Fritters), 114
bánh tráng (rice paper wrappers)
    about, 23
    Gỏi Cuốn Cá Cornets, 177
    in Herring Salad, 60
    Pork Bulgogi Summer Rolls, 203
    Taro Spring Roll and Rice Noodle Salad, 165
    Tuna Summer Rolls, 152
    in Vietnamese Fish Shabu Shabu, 77
basil. See Thai basil
BBQ Chicken, Kampuchea-Style, 210
bean sprouts. See mung beans
beef
    Kampuchea-Style Prime Rib, 220
    Lemongrass Beef, Chile, and Rice Noodle Salad, 166
    Southern-Style Beef Phở, 122
    Thinly Sliced Steak, 125
Beurre Monté Chawanmushi, Crab, 181

bird's eye chiles
    about, 15, 30
    Chile Fish Sauce, 43
    Chile Salt, 43
bitter melons, in Stir-Fried Bitter Melon and Eggs, 132
black-eyed peas
    in Chicken Fat Sticky Rice, 194
    in xôi chè đậu trắng, 127
black pepper, Vietnamese
    about, 20–21
    Salt, Pepper, and Lime Dipping Sauce, 44
bonito, in Caviar à la Nước Mắm, 178
Bò Quay Kampuchea (Kampuchea-Style Prime Rib), 220
Bò Tái (Thinly Sliced Steak), 125
Bread Pudding, Mom's Banana, 143
Broken Rice, 34
    about, 23
    in Caramelized Pan-Fried Pork Chops, 139
    in Fish and Seafood Porridge, 94
    Scorched Rice with Ginger and Green Onion Sauce, 109
budae jjigae, 106
Bulgogi Summer Rolls, Pork, 203
bún, dried. See rice vermicelli
Bún Bò Sả Ớt (Lemongrass Beef, Chile, and Rice Noodle Salad), 166
Bún Chả Giò Khoai Môn (Taro Spring Roll and Rice Noodle Salad), 165
Bụng Cá Hồi Sốt Cà Chua (Tomato-Braised Salmon Belly), 96
Bún Kèn (Curry Coconut Noodles), 67
Bún Nhâm Hà Tiên (Coconut and Fish Sauce Rice Noodle Salad), 24, 65

C

cabbage
    in Banana Flower Salad, 158
    in Coconut and Fish Sauce Rice Noodle Salad, 65
    in Curry Coconut Noodles, 67
    in Sticky Rice Dumplings, Tu and Jean Style, 201
    in Vietnamese Chicken Salad, 155
Cá Bơn Chiên Muối Sả Ớt (Fried Sand Dabs with Lemongrass and Chile Salt), 99
Cá Khô (Fish Jerky), 15, 134
Cá Kho Tộ (Clay Pot Catfish), 113
cane sugar, organic, about, 19
Canh Cá Nấu Ngót (Vietnamese Fish Hot Pot), 161
Canh Chua Đầu Cá Hồi (Hot Pot-Style Salmon Head Sour Soup), 89
Cánh Gà Kho Gừng (Ginger-Braised Chicken), 136

Caramelized Pan-Fried Pork Chops, 139
Caramelized Pan-Fried Pork Chops and Macaroni, 140
Carbonara, Bánh Canh, 193
carrots
    pickled. See Pickled Carrots and Daikon
    in Sticky Rice Dumplings, Tu and Jean Style, 201
    in Taro Spring Roll and Rice Noodle Salad, 165
    in Vietnamese Chicken Salad, 155
Catfish, Clay Pot, 113
Cá Trích Nhúng Giấm (Vietnamese Fish Shabu Shabu), 77
Caviar à la Nước Mắm, 178
Cá Vược Nướng Giấy Bạc (Foil-Baked Whole Sea Bass), 101
Cháo Cá (Fish and Seafood Porridge), 94
Chawanmushi, Crab Beurre Monté, 181
chè, about, 169
Chè Trôi Nước (Sticky Rice Dumplings in Syrup), 222
chicken
    Chicken Fat Sticky Rice, 194
    Ginger-Braised Chicken, 136
    Hainanese Chicken and Rice, 74
    Kampuchea-Style BBQ Chicken, 210
    Southern-Style Chicken Phở, 118
    Vietnamese Chicken Salad, 155
Chicken Fat Sticky Rice, 194
Chicken Stock, 51
    in Duck Liver Dumplings, 183
    in Hainanese Chicken and Rice, 74
    in Lobster Boba, 189
    in Roasted Duck Phở, 215
    in Seafood Egg Drop Soup, 207
    in Southern-Style Chicken Phở, 118
Chile Fish Sauce, 43
    in Banana Flower Salad, 158
    in Coconut and Fish Sauce Rice Noodle Salad, 65
    in Green Mango and Dried Squid Salad, 62
Chile Salt, 43
    Fried Sand Dabs with Lemongrass and, 99
    Pomegranate Seeds with, 151
chrouk metae, about, 22
circular cutting boards, about, 32
clams
    in Fish and Seafood Porridge, 94
    Stir-Fried Clams, 163
Clay Pot Catfish, 113
clay pots, about, 113
climate change, 8
Coconut and Fish Sauce Rice Noodle Salad, 65

Coconut Caramel Sauce, 36
    in Clay Pot Catfish, 113
    in Ginger-Braised Chicken, 136
coconut cream, in Curry Coconut
    Noodles, 67
Coconut Fish Sauce, 41
coconut milk
    about, 24
    Coconut and Fish Sauce Rice Noodle
      Salad, 65
    Curry Coconut Noodles, 67
    in Mom's Banana Bread Pudding, 143
    recipe, Fresh Coconut Milk, 49
    in Sticky Rice Dumplings, Tu and Jean
      Style, 201
    in Sticky Rice Dumplings in Syrup, 222
    in Thai-Style Sticky Rice with Mango, 126
coconut shredders, about, 32
coconut soda. See also Coco Rico
    about, 24
coconut vinegar
    about, 22
    in Vietnamese Fish Shabu Shabu, 77
Coco Rico, 24, 36
    in Chile Fish Sauce, 43
coffee grinders, about, 32
Cơm Chay Mỡ Hành Gừng (Scorched
    Rice with Ginger and Green Onion
    Sauce), 109
Cơm Cua Hấp (Dungeness Crab
    Donburi), 208
Cơm Gà Hải Nam (Hainanese Chicken and
    Rice), 74
Cơm Tấm (Broken Rice), 34
    about, 23
    in Caramelized Pan-Fried Pork Chops, 139
    in Fish and Seafood Porridge, 94
    Scorched Rice with Ginger and Green
      Onion Sauce, 109
condiments. See also specific condiments
    about, 21–22
Con Sò Ướp Chao (Grilled Scallop with
    Fermented Tofu), 63
Cornets, Gỏi Cuốn Cá, 177
corn silk, dried, about, 27
crab (crabmeat)
    Crab Beurre Monté Chawanmushi, 181
    Dungeness Crab Donburi, 208
    in Seafood Egg Drop Soup, 207
Crab Beurre Monté Chawanmushi, 181
Crispy Skin Pan-Roasted Salmon Fillets, 93
Củ Cải Chua Ngọt (Pickled Carrots and
    Daikon), 49
    in Banana Flower Salad, 158
    in Lemongrass Beef, Chile, and Rice
      Noodle Salad, 166
    in Pork Bulgogi Summer Rolls, 203
    in Taro Spring Roll and Rice Noodle
      Salad, 165
    in Tuna Summer Rolls, 152
    in Woven Noodles with Crispy Pork
      Belly, 217
cucumbers
    in Banana Flower Salad, 158
    in Herring Salad, 60
    in Lemongrass Beef, Chile, and Rice
      Noodle Salad, 166

    in Taro Spring Roll and Rice Noodle
      Salad, 165
    in Vietnamese Fish Shabu Shabu, 77
Củ Hẹ Chiên (Fried Shallots), 50
Curry Coconut Noodles, 67

D

daikon
    in Fish Cake and Tapioca Noodle Soup, 69
    pickled. See Pickled Carrots and Daikon
    in Sticky Rice Dumplings, Tu and Jean
      Style, 201
Dán Me (Tamarind Paste), 35
    in Hot Pot-Style Salmon Head Sour
      Soup, 89
    in Tamarind Fish Sauce, 42
    in Tuna Bloodline Tartare, 135
Dán Sả (Lemongrass Paste), 36
dehydrators, about, 32
desserts
    Mom's Banana Bread Pudding, 143
    Sticky Rice Dumplings in Syrup, 222
    Thai-Style Sticky Rice with Mango, 126
    Vietnamese Herbal Tonic Drink, 169
diếp cá (fish wort), 30
    in Curry Coconut Noodles, 67
    in Lemongrass Beef, Chile, and Rice
      Noodle Salad, 166
    in Taro Spring Roll and Rice Noodle
      Salad, 165
Đồ Chua. See Pickled Carrots and Daikon
duck
    Duck Liver Dumplings, 183
    Roasted Duck Phở, 215
    Roasted Hoisin-Glazed Duck, 212
Duck Liver Dumplings, 183
dumplings
    Duck Liver Dumplings, 183
    Sticky Rice Dumplings, Tu and Jean
      Style, 201
    Sticky Rice Dumplings in Syrup, 222
Dungeness Crab Donburi, 208

E

Eating Viet Nam (Holliday), 118
eggs
    in Crab Beurre Monté Chawanmushi, 181
    Seafood Egg Drop Soup, 207
    Stir-Fried Bitter Melon and Eggs, 132
18 Reasons, vii
Everyday Fish Sauce, 40

F

farm-to-table dining, 7, 130, 148
fennel, in Lobster Boba, 189
fish and seafood
    about, 82, 85, 130
    prep tips, 85–88
    Caviar à la Nước Mắm, 178
    Clay Pot Catfish, 113
    Crab Beurre Monté Chawanmushi, 181
    Crispy Skin Pan-Roasted Salmon
      Fillets, 93
    Curry Coconut Noodles, 67
    Dungeness Crab Donburi, 208
    Fish and Seafood Porridge, 94
    Fish Cake and Tapioca Noodle Soup, 69

    Foil-Baked Whole Sea Bass, 101
    Fried Salmon Frames, 92
    Fried Sand Dabs with Lemongrass and
      Chile Salt, 99
    Grilled Scallop with Fermented Tofu, 63
    Herring Roe on Kelp, 98
    Herring Salad, 60
    Hot Pot-Style Salmon Head Sour Soup, 89
    Lobster Boba, 189
    Prawn Fritters, 114
    Seafood Egg Drop Soup, 207
    Stir-Fried Clams, 163
    Tamarind Black Tiger Prawns, 72
    Tomato-Braised Salmon Belly, 96
    Tuna Bloodline Tartare, 135
    Tuna Summer Rolls, 152
    Vietnamese Fish Hot Pot, 161
    Vietnamese Fish Shabu Shabu, 77
Fish and Seafood Porridge, 94
Fish Cake and Tapioca Noodle Soup, 69
fish jerky, dried
    about, 27
    recipe, Fish Jerky, 15, 134
Fishless Dipping Sauce, 40
fish sauce
    Phú Quốc island, about, 22, 39, 56
    about, 3, 21, 39
    Chile Fish Sauce, 43
    Everyday Fish Sauce, 40
    Fish Sauce Caramel, 37
    Ginger Fish Sauce, 41
    Pineapple Fish Sauce, 42
    Tamarind Fish Sauce, 42
Fish Sauce Caramel, 37
    in Fish Jerky, 134
Fish Stock, 50
    in Curry Coconut Noodles, 67
    in Fish and Seafood Porridge, 94
    in Fish Cake and Tapioca Noodle Soup, 69
    in Hot Pot-Style Salmon Head Sour
      Soup, 89
    in Vietnamese Fish Hot Pot, 161
fish wort. See diếp cá
five-spice powder
    about, 19
    Caramelized Pan-Fried Pork Chops, 139
    Woven Noodles with Crispy Pork
      Belly, 217
flours. See also glutinous rice flour
    about, 25
Foil-Baked Whole Sea Bass, 101
food waste, 5, 7–8, 106
Four Star Seafood, 88
Fresh Coconut Milk, 49
Fried Salmon Frames, 92
Fried Sand Dabs with Lemongrass and Chile
    Salt, 99
Fritters, Prawn, 114

G

Gà Nướng Kampuchea (Kampuchea-Style
    BBQ Chicken), 210
Gạo Thơm Hoa Nhài (Jasmine Rice), 34
    in Hainanese Chicken and Rice, 74
garden, 148
    ingredients, 29–30
garlic, fried, about, 21

Garlic Noodles, Truffled, 186
ginger
    about, 29
    Ginger and Green Onion Sauce, 47
    Ginger-Braised Chicken, 136
    Ginger Fish Sauce, 41
    peeling tip, 29
    Scorched Rice with Ginger and Green
        Onion Sauce, 109
    in Sticky Rice Dumplings in Syrup, 222
Ginger and Green Onion Sauce, 47
    Scorched Rice with, 109
Ginger-Braised Chicken, 136
Ginger Fish Sauce, 41
ginseng, about, 27
glutinous rice
    about, 25
    Thai-Style Sticky Rice with Mango, 126
glutinous rice flour
    about, 25
    in Sticky Rice Dumplings, Tu and Jean
        Style, 201
    in Sticky Rice Dumplings in Syrup, 222
gochugaru, about, 19
Gỏi Bắp Chuối (Banana Flower Salad), 158
Gỏi Cá Trích (Herring Salad), 60
Gỏi Cuốn Cá Cornets, 177
Gỏi Cuốn Cá Ngừ (Tuna Summer Rolls), 152
Gỏi Cuốn Hàn Quốc (Pork Bulgogi Summer
    Rolls), 203
Gỏi Gà (Vietnamese Chicken Salad), 155
Gỏi Xoài Xanh Khô Mực (Green Mango and
    Dried Squid Salad), 62
goji berries
    about, 27
    in Vietnamese Herbal Tonic Drink, 169
grapefruit, in Caviar à la Nước Mắm, 178
Green Mango and Dried Squid Salad, 62
green onions
    about, 29
    Ginger and Green Onion Sauce, 47
    Green Onion Sauce, 47
    Scorched Rice with Ginger and Green
        Onion Sauce, 109
Green Onion Sauce, 47
    Ginger and, 47
    Scorched Rice with Ginger and, 109
Grilled Scallop with Fermented Tofu, 63
guanciale, in Bánh Canh Carbonara, 193

H
Hainanese Chicken and Rice, 74
halibut, in Curry Coconut Noodles, 67
Hà Tiên, 65
Herbal Tonic Drink, Vietnamese, 169
herbs. See also specific herbs
    about, 30
herring
    about, 60, 88
    Herring Roe on Kelp, 98
    Herring Salad, 60
    selection and prep tips, 88
    in Vietnamese Fish Shabu Shabu, 77
Herring Roe on Kelp, 98
Herring Salad, 60
hoành thánh, 183
Ho Chi Minh Trail, 110, 113

hoisin sauce
    about, 21
    Roasted Hoisin-Glazed Duck, 212
holiday meals, 198
Holliday, Graham, 118
Hot Pot
    -Style Salmon Head Sour Soup, 89
    Vietnamese Fish, 161
    Vietnamese Fish Shabu Shabu, 77
Huyết Cá Tái Chanh (Tuna Bloodline
    Tartare), 135

J
Jasmine Rice, 34
    in Hainanese Chicken and Rice, 74
JB Prince, 173
jerky. See fish jerky, dried
jicama, in Fish Cake and Tapioca Noodle
    Soup, 69
jujubes
    about, 27
    Vietnamese Herbal Tonic Drink, 169

K
Kampuchea-Style BBQ Chicken, 210
Kampuchea-Style Prime Rib, 220
Khmer pepper, about, 20–21
Khmer Rouge, 2, 106
Khổ Qua Xào (Stir-Fried Bitter Melon and
    Eggs), 132
kimchee
    Pork Bulgogi Summer Rolls, 203
    Sticky Rice Dumplings, Tu and Jean
        Style, 201
kitchen tools, 32
    sources, 173
Knorr brand's hạt nêm, about, 19
Koda Farms, 23, 25
kombu
    about, 24
    in Caviar à la Nước Mắm, 178
    in Vietnamese Herbal Tonic Drink, 169
kumquats
    about, 30
    Vietnamese Herbal Tonic Drink, 169

L
lạp xưởng (Chinese sausage), in Chicken Fat
    Sticky Rice, 194
lemongrass
    about, 29, 36
    Fried Sand Dabs with Lemongrass and
        Chile Salt, 99
    Lemongrass Beef, Chile, and Rice Noodle
        Salad, 166
    Lemongrass Paste, 36
Lemongrass Beef, Chile, and Rice Noodle
    Salad, 166
Lemongrass Paste, 36
Lisbon lemons, about, 30
Lobster Boba, 189
longan, in Vietnamese Herbal Tonic Drink, 169
Lunar New Year, 25, 30, 165
Lườn Cá Hồi Áp Chảo (Crispy Skin Pan-
    Roasted Salmon Fillets), 93
Lựu Trộn Muối Ớt (Pomegranate Seeds with
    Chile Salt), 151

M
Maggi seasoning sauce, about, 21–22, 40
Makrut lime leaves, about, 29
mangos
    about, 126
    Green Mango and Dried Squid Salad, 62
    Thai-Style Sticky Rice with Mango, 126
medicinal ingredients, about, 27
"merroir," 39
Miền Tây, 15, 24, 30
mint, 30. See also spearmint
    in Coconut and Fish Sauce Rice Noodle
        Salad, 65
    in Curry Coconut Noodles, 67
    in Green Mango and Dried Squid Salad, 62
    in Herring Salad, 60
    in Tuna Summer Rolls, 152
    in Vietnamese Fish Shabu Shabu, 77
    in Woven Noodles with Crispy Pork
        Belly, 217
Mì Xào Tỏi Nấm Cục (Truffled Garlic
    Noodles), 186
Mochiko, 25
Mỡ Hành (Green Onion Sauce), 47
    Ginger and, 47
    Scorched Rice with Ginger and, 109
Mỡ Hành Gừng (Ginger and Green Onion
    Sauce), 47
    Cơm Cháy Mỡ Hành Gừng, 109
Mom's Banana Bread Pudding, 143
monosodium glutamate (MSG), about, 19
mortars and pestles, about, 32
mung beans
    about, 25–26
    in Banana Flower Salad, 158
    in Sticky Rice Dumplings, Tu and Jean
        Style, 201
    in Taro Spring Roll and Rice Noodle
        Salad, 165
Muối Ớt (Chile Salt), 43
    Fried Sand Dabs with Lemongrass and, 99
    Pomegranate Seeds with, 151
Muối Tiêu Chanh (Salt, Pepper, and Lime
    Dipping Sauce), 44
mushrooms. See also shiitake mushrooms
    in Seafood Egg Drop Soup, 207
    shiitake, dried, about, 27

N
Nghêu Xào (Stir-Fried Clams), 163
nhậu (drinking snacks), 44
noodles. See also specific noodles
    about, 26
    Truffled Garlic Noodles, 186
    Woven Noodles with Crispy Pork
        Belly, 217
nori
    in Herring Roe on Kelp, 98
    in Tuna Bloodline Tartare, 135
Nui Sườn Chiên (Caramelized Pan-Fried Pork
    Chops and Macaroni), 140
Nước Chấm Chanh Dây (Passion Fruit
    Dressing), 155
Nước Chấm Chay (Fishless Dipping
    Sauce), 40
Nước Cốt Dừa Tươi (Fresh Coconut
    Milk), 49

Nước Luộc Cá (Fish Stock), 50
  in Curry Coconut Noodles, 67
  in Fish and Seafood Porridge, 94
  in Fish Cake and Tapioca Noodle Soup, 69
  in Hot Pot-Style Salmon Head Sour
    Soup, 89
  in Vietnamese Fish Hot Pot, 161
Nước Luộc Ga (Chicken Stock), 51
  in Duck Liver Dumplings, 183
  in Hainanese Chicken and Rice, 74
  in Lobster Boba, 189
  in Roasted Duck Phở, 215
  in Seafood Egg Drop Soup, 207
  in Southern-Style Chicken Phở, 118
Nước Mắm, about, 39, 40
Nước Mắm, Caviar à la, 178
Nước Mắm Chấm (Everyday Fish Sauce), 40
Nước Mắm Dừa (Coconut Fish Sauce), 41
Nước Mắm Gừng (Ginger Fish Sauce), 41
Nước Mắm Khóm (Pineapple Fish Sauce), 42
  in Caviar à la Nước Mắm, 178
Nước Mắm Me (Tamarind Fish Sauce), 42
Nước Mắm Sánh Kẹo (Fish Sauce
    Caramel), 37
  in Fish Jerky, 134
Nước Mắm Toi Ot (Chile Fish Sauce), 43
  in Banana Flower Salad, 158
  in Coconut and Fish Sauce Rice Noodle
    Salad, 65
  in Green Mango and Dried Squid Salad, 62
Nước Màu Dừa (Coconut Caramel Sauce), 36
  in Clay Pot Catfish, 113
  in Ginger-Braised Chicken, 136
Nước Sốt Me (Tamarind Sauce), 35
  in Tamarind Black Tiger Prawns, 72

O
Oakland, 148
  where to eat, 174
Ohlone people, 9
okra, in Hot Pot-Style Salmon Head Sour
    Soup, 89
oranges, in Caviar à la Nước Mắm, 178
oysters, in Caviar à la Nước Mắm, 178
oyster sauce
  about, 22
  in Caramelized Pan-Fried Pork Chops, 139
  in Kampuchea-Style Prime Rib, 220
  in Taro Spring Roll and Rice Noodle
    Salad, 165

P
palm sugar
  about, 19
  in Herring Salad, 60
  in Tamarind Fish Sauce, 42
Pan-Fried Pork Chops, Caramelized, 139
Pan-Fried Pork Chops and Macaroni,
    Caramelized, 140
Pan-Roasted Salmon Fillets, Crispy Skin, 93
pantry ingredients, 15–27
  author's story, 15–16
  canned and dried goods, 23–26
  condiments, 21–22
  preserves, 27
  recipes for, 33–51
  spices, 19–21

passion fruit
  about, 30
  Passion Fruit Dressing, 155
pasta
  about, 26
  Bánh Canh Carbonara, 193
  Caramelized Pan-Fried Pork Chops and
    Macaroni, 140
  Pecorino Romano, in Bánh Canh
    Carbonara, 193
perilla, 30
  in Coconut and Fish Sauce Rice Noodle
    Salad, 65
  in Pork Bulgogi Summer Rolls, 203
  in Roasted Duck Phở, 215
  in Woven Noodles with Crispy Pork
    Belly, 217
phở, origins of, 122
Phở Bò Miền Nam (Southern-Style Beef
    Phở), 122
Phở Gà Miền Nam (Southern-Style Chicken
    Phở), 118
Phở Noodles, 117
Phở Vịt Nướng (Roasted Duck Phở), 215
Phú Quốc Island, 1, 2, 5, 15, 43, 47, 56,
    82, 98
  fish sauce, about, 22, 39, 56
  recipes, 60–77
  where to eat on, 58
Pickled Carrots and Daikon, 49
  in Banana Flower Salad, 158
  in Lemongrass Beef, Chile, and Rice
    Noodle Salad, 166
  in Pork Bulgogi Summer Rolls, 203
  in Taro Spring Roll and Rice Noodle
    Salad, 165
  in Tuna Summer Rolls, 152
  in Woven Noodles with Crispy Pork
    Belly, 217
pineapple
  in Caviar à la Nước Mắm, 178
  Hot Pot-Style Salmon Head Sour Soup, 89
  in Tuna Bloodline Tartare, 135
  in Vietnamese Fish Shabu Shabu, 77
Pineapple Fish Sauce, 42
  in Caviar à la Nước Mắm, 178
pineapple juice, about, 26
pomegranates, about, 30, 151
Pomegranate Seeds with Chile Salt, 151
pork
  Caramelized Pan-Fried Pork Chops, 139
  Caramelized Pan-Fried Pork Chops and
    Macaroni, 140
  in Duck Liver Dumplings, 183
  in Fish Cake and Tapioca Noodle Soup, 69
  Pork Bulgogi Summer Rolls, 203
  Sticky Rice Dumplings, Tu and Jean
    Style, 201
  in Taro Spring Roll and Rice Noodle
    Salad, 165
  Woven Noodles with Crispy Pork Belly, 217
Pork Bulgogi Summer Rolls, 203
Porridge, Fish and Seafood, 94
Postelsia, 8, 9
poultry. See chicken; duck
Prawn Fritters, 114

prawns
  Prawn Fritters, 114
  Tamarind Black Tiger Prawns, 72
preserves, about, 27

Q
quail eggs, in Seafood Egg Drop Soup, 207

R
Rau Muống Xào (Stir-Fried Water
    Spinach), 110
rau răm
  about, 30
  in Green Mango and Dried Squid Salad, 62
  in Stir-Fried Clams, 163
  in Vietnamese Chicken Salad, 155
rice
  about, 23, 34
  Cơm Tấm (Broken Rice). See Broken Rice
  cooking tips, 34
  glutinous. See glutinous rice
  Hainanese Chicken and Rice, 74
  Jasmine Rice, 34
  Xôi (Sticky Rice). See Sticky Rice
rice paper wrappers. See bánh tráng
rice vermicelli
  about, 26
  in Coconut and Fish Sauce Rice Noodle
    Salad, 65
  cooking tips, 60
  in Curry Coconut Noodles, 67
  in Herring Salad, 60
  in Lemongrass Beef, Chile, and Rice
    Noodle Salad, 166
  in Pork Bulgogi Summer Rolls, 203
  in Taro Spring Roll and Rice Noodle
    Salad, 165
  in Tuna Summer Rolls, 152
  in Vietnamese Fish Shabu Shabu, 77
rice vinegar
  about, 22
  in Pickled Carrots and Daikon, 49
Roasted Duck Phở, 215
Roasted Hoisin-Glazed Duck, 212
rolls. See summer rolls

S
salads
  Banana Flower Salad, 158
  Coconut and Fish Sauce Rice Noodle
    Salad, 65
  Green Mango and Dried Squid Salad, 62
  Herring Salad, 60
  Lemongrass Beef, Chile, and Rice Noodle
    Salad, 166
  Taro Spring Roll and Rice Noodle
    Salad, 165
  Vietnamese Chicken Salad, 155
salmon
  Crispy Skin Pan-Roasted Salmon
    Fillets, 93
  Fried Salmon Frames, 92
  Hot Pot-Style Salmon Head Sour Soup, 89
  prep tips, 85–87
  Tomato-Braised Salmon Belly, 96
Salt, Pepper, and Lime Dipping Sauce, 44

sambal oelek
   about, 22
   in Southern-Style Beef Phở, 122
Sâm Bổ Lượng (Vietnamese Herbal Tonic Drink), 169
Samuelson, Hoang, 114
Sand Dabs, Fried, with Lemongrass and Chile Salt, 99
sa té, about, 22
scallops
   Grilled Scallop with Fermented Tofu, 63
   in Lobster Boba, 189
   in Seafood Egg Drop Soup, 207
   selection tips, 63
Scorched Rice with Ginger and Green Onion Sauce, 109
sea bass
   in Fish and Seafood Porridge, 94
   Foil-Baked Whole Sea Bass, 101
   in Vietnamese Fish Hot Pot, 161
seafood. See fish and seafood
Seafood Egg Drop Soup, 207
seaweed, dried. See also kombu
   about, 24
sesame oil, about, 19–20
sesame seeds
   about, 19–20
   in Pork Bulgogi Summer Rolls, 203
Shabu Shabu, Vietnamese Fish, 77
shallots, fried
   about, 21
   recipe, 50
shiitake mushrooms
   in Chicken Fat Sticky Rice, 194
   dried, about, 27
   in Roasted Duck Phở, 215
   in Seafood Egg Drop Soup, 207
shrimp
   in Duck Liver Dumplings, 183
   Prawn Fritters, 114
   in Seafood Egg Drop Soup, 207
   in Tamarind Black Tiger Prawns, 72
shrimp, dried
   about, 24–25
   in Coconut and Fish Sauce Rice Noodle Salad, 65
   in Stir-Fried Water Spinach, 110
Sóc Trăng, 9
Son Fish Sauce, 39
soups
   Fish and Seafood Porridge, 94
   Fish Cake and Tapioca Noodle Soup, 69
   Hot Pot-Style Salmon Head Sour Soup, 89
   Roasted Duck Phở, 215
   Seafood Egg Drop Soup, 207
   Southern-Style Beef Phở, 122
   Southern-Style Chicken Phở, 118
Southern-Style Beef Phở, 122
Southern-Style Chicken Phở, 118
spearmint, 30. See also mint
   in Banana Flower Salad, 158
   in Lemongrass Beef, Chile, and Rice Noodle Salad, 166
   in Taro Spring Roll and Rice Noodle Salad, 165

specialty tools, 32
spices. See also specific spices
   about, 15, 19–21
squid, dried
   about, 27
   Green Mango and Dried Squid Salad, 62
squid, in Fish and Seafood Porridge, 94
Sriracha, about, 22
star anise, about, 20
steamers (metal or bamboo), about, 32
Sticky Rice, 35
   Chicken Fat, 194
   Dumplings, Tu and Jean Style, 201
   Dumplings in Syrup, 222
   Thai-Style, with Mango, 126
Stir-Fried Bitter Melon and Eggs, 132
Stir-Fried Clams, 163
Stir-Fried Water Spinach, 110
stocks
   chicken. See Chicken Stock
   fish. See Fish Stock
summer rolls
   Pork Bulgogi Summer Rolls, 203
   Taro Spring Roll and Rice Noodle Salad, 165
   Tuna Summer Rolls, 152
   in Vietnamese Fish Shabu Shabu, 77
Sườn Chiên (Caramelized Pan-Fried Pork Chops), 139
Súp Hải Sản Thập Cẩm (Seafood Egg Drop Soup), 207
suprême citrus, tips, 43
sustainability, 7–9
sweet potatoes
   in Prawn Fritters, 114
   in Taro Spring Roll and Rice Noodle Salad, 165

T
Tamarind Black Tiger Prawns, 72
Tamarind Fish Sauce, 42
Tamarind Paste, 35
   in Hot Pot-Style Salmon Head Sour Soup, 89
   in Tamarind Fish Sauce, 42
   in Tuna Bloodline Tartare, 135
tamarind pulp, about, 20
Tamarind Sauce, 35
   in Tamarind Black Tiger Prawns, 72
Tapioca Noodle Soup, Fish Cake and, 69
tarantulas, 106
Taro Spring Roll and Rice Noodle Salad, 165
Tartare, Tuna Bloodline, 135
Thai basil
   about, 30, 163
   in Curry Coconut Noodles, 67
   in Lobster Boba, 189
   in Stir-Fried Clams, 163
   in Tamarind Black Tiger Prawns, 72
Thai-Style Sticky Rice with Mango, 126
Thanh Long (San Francisco), 186
Thanksgiving, 198
Thinly Sliced Steak, 125
tía tô (shiso), in Tuna Summer Rolls, 152
Tiger Saté, 22

tofu, 172
   Grilled Scallop with Fermented Tofu, 63
   in Seafood Egg Drop Soup, 207
Tomato-Braised Salmon Belly, 96
tomatoes, cherry
   in Caviar à la Nước Mắm, 178
   in Lobster Boba, 189
   Tomato-Braised Salmon Belly, 96
   in Vietnamese Fish Hot Pot, 161
Tôm Rang Me Chua Ngọt (Tamarind Black Tiger Prawns), 72
Tran, Danny, 39
Truffled Garlic Noodles, 186
Trứng Cá Trích Tảo Bẹ (Herring Roe on Kelp), 98
tuna
   Tuna Bloodline Tartare, 135
   Tuna Summer Rolls, 152
Tuna Bloodline Tartare, 135
   in Gỏi Cuốn Cá Cornets, 177
Tuna Summer Rolls, 152
turmeric
   about, 20
   in Curry Coconut Noodles, 67

V
vermicelli. See rice vermicelli
Việt Cộng, 106, 110, 118, 126
Vietnamese Fish Hot Pot, 161
Vietnamese Fish Shabu Shabu, 77
Vietnamese Herbal Tonic Drink, 169
Vietnam War, 2, 106, 110
vinegar, about, 22
Vịt Nướng (Roasted Hoisin-Glazed Duck), 212

W
Water Spinach, Stir-Fried, 110
white pepper, Vietnamese, about, 21
white supremacy, 4
WildAid, 9
Woven Noodles with Crispy Pork Belly, 217

X
Xôi (Sticky Rice), 35
   Chicken Fat, 194
   Dumplings, Tu and Jean Style, 201
   Dumplings in Syrup, 222
   Thai-Style, with Mango, 126
Xôi Chè Đậu Trắng, 127
Xôi Gà Thập Cẩm (Chicken Fat Sticky Rice), 194
Xôi Xoài Thái (Thai-Style Sticky Rice with Mango), 126
Xương Cá Hồi Chiên Giòn (Fred Salmon Frames), 92

Y
yellow onions, about, 30

Published in the United States by 4 Color Books, an imprint of the
Crown Publishing Group, a division of Penguin Random House LLC,
New York.
4ColorBooks.com

4 Color Books and the 4 Color Books colophon are registered
trademarks of Penguin Random House LLC.

Typefaces: Republish Foundry's Barber, Mark Simonson Studio's
Etna, and Milieu Grotesque's Maison Neue

Library of Congress Cataloging-in-Publication Data

Names: Phu, Tu David, 1985- author. | Ho, Soleil, author. Title:
The memory of taste: Vietnamese American recipes from Phú
Quốc, Oakland, and the spaces between / Tu David Phu and Soleil
Ho. Identifiers: LCCN 2023031729 (print) | LCCN 2023031730
(ebook) | ISBN 9781984861900 (hardcover) | ISBN 9781984861917
(ebook) Subjects: LCSH: Cooking, Vietnamese. | LCGFT: Cookbooks.
Classification: LCC TX724.5.V5 P547 2024 (print) | LCC TX724.5.V5
(ebook) | DDC 641.59597–dc23/eng/20230714

LC record available at https://lccn.loc.gov/2023031729
LC ebook record available at https://lccn.loc.gov/2023031730

Hardcover ISBN: 978-1-9848-6190-0
eBook ISBN: 978-1-9848-6191-7

Printed in China

Editor-in-Chief: Bryant Terry | Creative Director: Amanda Yee
Acquiring Editor: Kelly Snowden | Project Editor: Claire Yee
Editorial Assistant: Gabby Ureña Matos
Managing Editor: Kristin Sargianis | Production Editor: Serena Wang
Cover and Interior Designer: Ohn Ho | Executive Art Director: Betsy
Stromberg | Production Designers: Mari Gill and Faith Hague
Production Manager and Prepress Color Manager: Jane Chinn
Prop Stylist: Jeni Afuso
Copyeditor: Allie Kiekhofer | Proofreader: Kate Bolen
Indexer: Stephen Callahan
Publicist: Kristin Casemore | Marketer: Andrea Portanova

10 9 8 7 6 5 4 3 2 1

First Edition